INTERRELIGIOUS DIALOGUE: FACING THE NEXT FRONTIER

Edited By
Richard W. Rousseau, S.J.

VOLUME ONE

MODERN THEOLOGICAL THEMES:
SELECTIONS FROM THE LITERATURE

RIDGE ROW PRESS

University of Scranton Press
Chicago Distribution Center
11030 S. Langley
Chicago IL 60628

CONTENTS

INTRODUCTION

OVERVIEW OF THE ESSAYS

Cliche though it might be, "global village" now describes our world. People and places and cultures which for our forefathers might as well have been on the moon are now only a few hours away by jet and have become our neighbors. Intercultural and interreligious questions have become urgent issues. As far as Hinduism, Buddhism, Confucianism, Shinto etc. are concerned, we are in a new universe of discourse. As Vern Failletaz says, in the first essay in this collection, we are facing the next frontier, one that takes us beyond intra-Christian dialogue and even intra-western conversation to an interreligious dialogue with the East.

According to Failletaz, such interreligious dialogue has many advantages: it will help us to confront our fears about God's saving ways, see more clearly how God works in human experience and understand more thoroughly how communities of faith interact generally with human culture. In so doing, we will clarify our own identities, bear mutual witness to profound human and divine values and appreciate more fully God's loving power in the world.

Leonard Swidler, the distinguished editor of The Journal of Ecumenical Studies, in a second essay, provides an aerial map of this new territory whose frontier we have crossed by suggesting a number of valuable rules, culled from practical experience, for carrying on such interreligious dialogue.

The author of the third essay is Bishop Lesslie Newbigin, well known for his many contributions to the

Indian and world religious scene through his participation in the formation of the Church of South India and his active contributions to the World Council of Churches. He proposes several models of interreligious dialogue including their theological presuppositions. He stresses the importance of asking the right questions in this area and sets out clearly the various theories which he considers to be inadequate: 1. other religions are wholly false; 2. other religions are the work of devils; 3. other religions are a preparation for Christ and are fulfilled by the Gospel; 4. other religions contain a number of fine values which are brought to a peak of excellence by contact with Christianity; 5. other religions are on the periphery of a circle whose center is the Christian God and his Church; 6. and finally, other religions are the way through which God's saving grace reaches those not yet touched by the Gospel.

Bishop Newbigin then proposes his own model of interreligious dialogue. According to him, its purpose is a faithful obedience to the Christian imperative of love which rules out conversion of the other as its prime principle. What we must do is listen to the other and share mutually our religious experiences, trusting that this exchange will lead both partners to a greater fidelity to their own ideals, with the outcome of this risky business left in the hands of God.

S. Wesley Ariarajah, writing from the perspective of his own Indo-Christian experience and his work on the staff of the World Council of Churches, speaks, in the fourth essay, on the development of a new theology of dialogue. He feels that this new theology of dialogue is necessary because: 1. we have recently become more aware that God's saving activity focusses on all of human life and not just on its "religious" side; 2. current styles of dialogue have so frequently led to impasses that changes are required; 3. this kind of dialogue is needed by third world Christian churches to help them work out a fully authentic relationship to their contextual cultures.

Such newly conceived dialogue must be flexible and this flexibility must include the use of "stories." The Christian partner tries to understand the other's "story" as an interpretation of the common human predicament. And then the Christian presents his "story" in answer to the same human predicament. This mutual exchange of "stories" should be comprehensible, manageable, respectful of each other's ideals, and mutually beneficial. This may mean that the Christian will have to develop some new understanding of the Scriptures, but this is part of the effort that every good dialogue requires.

A perennnial question that arises in this connection is "What is the relationship between dialogue and mission?" Anton Stalder, in a fifth essay, specifies this question further by adding, "Does dialogue complement, modify or replace mission ?" For his answer he goes to the official statements of both the World Council of Churches in its various Assemblies and Consultations as well as to the various Roman Catholic Documents and structures related to Vatican II. Stadler concludes from this analysis that though both Protestant and Catholic developments represent advances over earlier positions, they still do not come fully to grips with the "dialogue-mission" question. The W.C.C. seems more interested in dialogue than in mission and the R.C.C. seems more interested in mission than in dialogue, with neither fully addressing the tension between the two. Stadler's suggestion to get out of this impasse is for all the parties to examine more carefully the biblical theme of covenant.

Since this covenantal area, both Old and New, is where the people of Yahweh related religiously to him and to their pagan neighbors, Stadler sees it as a place where universalistic motifs were developed. The pursuit of these universalistic motifs and their application to the contemporary cultural and religious scene would, he feels, at long last begin to address directly the "mission-dialogue" problem. As an example where this kind of initiative has been fruitful, he cites the accomplishments of the ongoing Jewish-Christian dialogue.

A further explanation of the boundaries and bases of interfaith dialogue is offerred by Monika Hellwig in a sixth essay. She writes from her wide experience with what she considers to be the most urgent of the dialogues, namely the Christian-Jewish- Muslim one. She sees a number of common points of departure in that dialogue, namely: 1. the vision of the One God; 2. the conviction that history has a goal; 3.

the agreement to pursue social justice; 4. the vocation of persons to the community of salvation; 5. and finally, a common ground of biblical texts and spiritual heroes.

Hellwig then examines how a number of current interpretations of basic Christian convictions have an influence on this dialogue: 1. the conviction of revelation and redemption in Jesus Christ has accumulated so many historical interpretations and evaluations that it is difficult to deal with in a dialogue situation; 2. the concrete role played by the Church in Christianity has so many different historical ramifications that its analysis can cause a certain amount of confusion; 3. the trinitiarian understanding of God among Christians, including the claim of divinity on behalf of Jesus Christ, has been understood and conceptualized so variously over the centuries, that this very richness poses a dialogue problem. If difficulties of this kind are openly recognized and attempts to deal with them are made, then the dialogue will be helped. And as an example of the direction in which a successful dialogue of this kind ought to go, Hellwig points to the biblical notion of covenant, especially the Abrahamic and Noachic ones.

One of the important names in this theoretical discussion of interreligious dialogue is that of Hendrik Kraemer. Antonio Gualteri, in a seventh essay, examines and criticizes Kraemer's approach by focussing on the validity of his theological assumptions. Among those assumptions, as he sees them, are the following: 1. non-Christian religions are human achievements or part of a human quest for an understanding of existence; 2. these human achievements have a dialectical character, that is, they include both obedience and disobedience to God's plans; 3. "empirical Christianity," a "human" form of Christianity, is related to these non-Christian religions, while "true Christianity" and its revelational element, remain apart. Gualteri concludes that Kraemer's so called dialectical judgement on non-Christian religions (despite later attempts to soften its impact), is not really dialectical at all, but rejectionist. Because of these inner contradictions within Kraemer's theology of religion, he feels that we should reconsider its application to the question of interreligious dialogue.

Quite another aspect of this question is that of the relationship of traditional Christology to the theology of world religions. Lucien Richard, in an eighth essay, offers an extended overview from this perspective of recent Christological literature. It is clear from his study that the theologies of Christology and religious pluralism are capable of integration but that Christology itself will not remain uninfluenced in the process.

He examines in turn the Christologies of a number of current authors including George Rupp, John Cobb, Schubert Ogden, Wolfhart Pannenberg, John Hick, Don Cupitt, John A.T. Robinson, Charles Davis, Raymond Pannikar and Karl Rahner. Richard concludes that Christologies today: 1. are very much influenced by religious pluralism; 2. are exploring a variety of anthropological implications and perspectives; 3. see the Logos as having universalistic dimensions; and 4. are comparing the existential experience of Christ with the basic existential religious experiences of other religions.

John Hick is one of the best known recent writers on this question of the relationship between Christianity and other world religions. His proposal for a Copernican revolution in Theology is so well known and widely admired that it is not included in this collection. Not everyone agrees with Hick, however, and J. J. Lipner, in a ninth essay, offers a dissent to Hick that is of considerable interest not only because of its calm and reasonable style but also because his analysis of the question, especially of what he calls the absolutist position, is incisive and illuminating.

Lipner speaks of two extremes, the absolutist and the relativist and then proposes what he claims is a median position. For him the absolutist is the one for whom to engage in any kind of interreligious dialogue is to try to convince the other person of the deficiencies of his non-Christian views, and therefore essentially missionary in aim. Lipner agrees with Hick's critique of this position as ultimately incompatible with the Christian God of love. As for the other extreme, the relativist, this is where he places Hick, even though he evinces considerable sympathy for his position. He does so because he believes that Hick's use of the term "God" is ambiguous. It is ambiguous because he seems to be using it in a Christian sense while at the same time protesting against a kind of Ptolemaic-Christian understanding of God and revelation. Lipner also objects to Hick's development of how one is born with a "Ptolemaic" viewpoint that then needs to be overcome, by suggesting that this presupposes the pre-existence of some kind of noumenal entity.

Lipner, then, after this extended critique, proposes his median position. This consists mainly of stating briefly, without much supporting positive argumentation, that God's revealing act in the Christ-event is not necessarily to be understood as exclusivist but may affect human consciousness in other religions.

Among the important contributions that Karl Rahner has made to the theological scene, his theory of the "anonymous Christian" has been particularly influential. Robert Schreiter, in a tenth essay, proposes a detailed analysis of Rahner's theory, which, quite apart from its careful examination of Rahner's thought, provides a valuable outline of all the major theological issues that have to be dealt with in theorizing about interreligious dialogue.

These are some of the theories or issues as seen by Schreiter: 1. the universal salvific will of God; 2. Christ and redemption theology; 3. the relation between the universal salvific will of God on the one hand, and both Christianity and the Church on the other; 4. salvation and the person of Jesus; 5. the relation of the Incarnation and human culture to each other and to the interreligious dialogue.

After a critique of "anonymous Christianity" as inadequate, Schreiter proposes his own views as to how to proceed in this area. He suggests a renewed version of Logos Christology which would draw its inspiration from the attitudes and theories of the very earliest Christian communities. The reason why he turns to them is that he feels that they were in a frontier dialogue situation with the religions of their day as well as with the Greco-Roman culture in which they were immersed and that we can learn from their example.

After the earlier analyses of the theories of Hendrik Kraemer, John Hick and Karl Rahner on interreligious dialogue, Paul Knitter, in an eleventh and final essay, examines the thought of Hans Kung. Though sympathetic to Kung in general and to his approach to this particular subject, Knitter nevertheless criticizes Kung sharply for his treatment of the "uniqueness" of Christianity.

Knitter gives three main reasons for this opposition: 1. Such claims of absolute uniqueness as made by Kung for Christianity are not necesary for either Christian identity or its ongoing life. In support of this argument, he examines in turn the hermeneutical aspects of the question, Jewish apocalyptic contributions to the idea of uniqueness, certain mythical patterns, the nature of survival language and the distinction between classicist and modern cultures. 2. Such claims to uniqueness are not conducive to interreligious dialogue. He claims that some of Kung's preliminary assumptions and his blurred view of the reality of other religions lead him into a position which would make genuine dialogue difficult with representatives of other religions. 3. Claims to uniqueness of this kind are in difficulty when judged in the light of theological and historical-critical methodology. Involved in this third point are versions of David Tracy's model of revisionist theology and elements of the classic debate about the Christ of history and the Christ of faith. Finally, he examines with a critical eye Kung's underlying theology of the Incarnation as heavily influencing his theories in this area.

AREAS OF CONSENSUS

What then are some of the areas of consensus and disagreement as they emerge from this series of essays on interreligious dialogue ? There is first of all an overwhelming consensus that in this latter part of the twentieth century we have entered a new era of interreligious relationships. The shrinking of our globe has forced everyone, Christians included, to reexamine and reevaluate older attitudes towards other world religions. It is this consensus that lies behind the phrase in the title of this book "The Next Frontier."

A second consensus focusses on the various theories of interreligious relationship. There is the widespread feeling

vii

that these theories can be grouped into two opposing camps. In one camp lies a group of theories that allow one to judge all other religions of the world as inferior to one's own, absolutely speaking, even if that superiority is only slight. The primary reason for conversation with a member of a differing religion under this model would be an act of kindness that helps that person make up for the deficiencies in his or her religion. A general name for this cluster of positions, one suggested by Stadler in his essay, is "Mission." In the other camp lie a group of theories that claim that it is possible to maintain one's own religious identity and integrity while genuinely respecting the validity and integrity of those in other religions. The primary purpose of conversation with a member of a differing religion, in this case, would be a sharing of religious experiences and witnesses, trusting that wherever all this might lead, it will turn out to be mutually beneficial. A general name for this group of theories, the other half of Stadler's dichotomy, is "Dialogue." One way then of summarizing this debate over interreligious relationships would be to characterize it as the "Mission-Dialogue Problem."

A third consensus that emerges from these discussions is a sense of caution or uneasiness on both the "Mission" and "Dialogue" side. Among those who favor "Mission" there is an increasing disavowal of the strict exclusivistic or absolutist positions of earlier, more culturally isolated centuries, (other religions are the work of the devil, kind of thing) and a greater sensitivity to the need for a more nuanced understanding of living, contemporary relationships among religions. Some would see Rahner's theory of the "anonymous Christian" as the latest and most refined attempt of this kind. On the "Dialogue" side, however, there is also a certain uneasiness. This is less theoretically or historically oriented than that of the "Mission" side. It would seem to spring from the natural caution that accompanies the exploration of unknown territory. Christians know only so much about even Judaism and Islam, and they know even less about Hinduism, Buddhism and other Eastern religions. "Dialogue" is thus very much a venture into the unknown. There is also the understandable caution that arises out of the uncertainty as to how this process will affect one religiously. True religious dialogue involves the risk of change, and presumably, in true dialogue that change will be genuine, authentic and reinforcing. But the risk and the tentativeness remain.

THE UNFINISHED AGENDA

If these represent areas of considerable consensus, what are the areas of future concern, the unfinished agenda ahead ? Among the questions suggested by the essays in this book are the following: how do Christians properly exchange their religious experiences and their "story" for the religious experiences and "stories" of other religions ? Are there ways of doing this that will facilitate its succcess ? Are there ways that will lead to disaster ? How may the methodology of the religious "story" be worked out successfully ? What are the norms ? How does one recognize an authentic insight into the common human predicament ? Where is the boundary line between a religious insight into that predicament and a secular one ? Or is that a useful distinction ? How much does culture influence this process and how do we deal with the variables ? Are the universalistic motifs in the biblical notion of covenant useful guides for us in these discussions ? If so, how does one sort them out properly in the first place and then apply them judiciously in the second ? Are the Abrahamic and Noachic covenants especially apt for this purpose ? How useful is the distinction between "empirical" Christianity and "true" Christianity ? Should this distinction be pursued further or abandoned ? Have theologians concerned with this question sufficiently investigated modern anthropological theories as serious contributions to the understanding of cultural, interreligious relationships ? Is there a need for an in-depth study, which would include help from linguistic analysts, of such key terms as "true," "unique" and "exclusive"? Is insufficient attention being paid to the Christological dimension of the problem of interreligious dialogue ? Is it possible to conceive of such a thing as a contemporary Christology that, while building upon the past, would be strongly influenced by the need to correlate God's salvific will and Christ himself with the reality of millions of human beings seriously practicing their faith in other world religions ? Does the answer to many of the Christological questions lie in the direction of a

ix

contemporary Logos Christology which would build upon the universalistic implications of that Logos in both Scripture and the traditions of the earliest Christian communities ? Should more pointed and specific studies of Classic-Modern and East-West cultures be undertaken so as to shed more light on interreligious relationships ? In what way can the use of the historical-critical method of inquiry be useful or even necessary to this enterprise and in what way can it be misused ?

These are only some of the questions on interreligious dialogue raised by the essays in this volume. As they indicate, there is much unfinished business on the road ahead.

Richard W. Rousseau, S.J. , University of Scranton

Note: For reasons of accuracy, each author's form of critical apparatus has been preserved with only minor changes.

THE NEXT FRONTIER

UNDERSTANDING OTHER

COMMUNITIES OF FAITH

Vern Failletaz

Since World War II our denomination, like other Christian communities has made meaningful strides in breaking out of the isolationism that protected immigrant communities. The American Lutheran Church has moved from a distrust of American cultures to a strong sense of mission and a genuine sense of security about its witness to the Christian gospel in America. We have participated in the ecumenical movement and shared in the work of the World Council of Churches. The last decade has seen productive conversations with the Roman Catholic bishops, and new co-operation with Roman Catholic parishes and priests in almost

Vern Failletaz is a member of the Religious Studies Department at St Olaf's College in Northfield, Minnesota. He specializes in Biblical Studies and the History of Religion. He has a B. A. from the University of California at Berkeley, a B. Th. from Lutheran Theological Seminary in St Paul and a PhD from the University of Chicago in Biblical Studies. He recently spent a sabbatical year at the Harvard Center for World Religions working in the area of Islam.

This selection is from Dialog; A Journal of Theology, Vol. 17, 1978, pp. 170-173. Reprinted by permission of the publisher and the author.

every comunity. At the international level we have particicipated in attempts to disavow antisemitism and to make the world safe for Jews. We are about the process of eliminating stereotypes from curriculum and from community interactions, though we have some distance to go.

The years since the second world war have seen us broaden our understanding of the gospel. Forgiveness and freedom in Christ open the doors for faith and individual commitment; they give us as well a gospel to be witnessed to in actions that liberate all men and women from social oppressions. We have new concerns for the Native Americans, the Blacks, the Mexican Americans. With the ordination of women to ministry and the calling of women pastors we have begun to affirm that the gospel implies new opportunities and new social tasks for women. We no longer live in ghettos. We are no longer an isolationist community of faith. We have begun to share accountability for our nation as a whole. We have begun to exercise a prophetic ministry in American culture.

We now face another frontier. We have come of age within American culture and have discovered our responsibility for justice. Our horizon now includes a new awareness of the other cultures of the world. However large the problems of our country loom in the foreground, our horizon includes the whole human species. The evening news reports on Africa, the Middle East, and India before it reports on Washington. At least half of the news from Washington concerns our relations with other nations. No longer do contacts with the traditional Western countries dominate. Relations with African, Arab, Indian, Vietnamese, Japanese, Chinese push our consciousness. We relate to those whose traditions and languages differ substantially from ours. We relate to peoples who participate in Muslim, Hindu, Buddhist, and Jewish communities of faith. About these communities we know very little.

Most of us have grown up wearing protective glasses so that we do not see the character of other religions clearly. Some wear rose-tinted glasses. All religions look rosy. All communities contribute to the sum of religiousness. All communities speak with the same clarity about God and humanity. This perspective is innocent. Men and women of

2

faith attach themselves to different symbols of the ultimate and attach themselves deeply to these symbols. People of faith have deep heritages of understanding and grace in which they find fulfillment. Jews, Hindus, Buddhists do not regard themselves as crypto-Buddhists or crypto-Muslims. The degree to which these traditions ground themselves in a single ultimate reality needs to be explored without pre-judgments. Each of these traditions has its own moments of grandeur and its own moments of shame. Rosy tolerance is paternalistic, defensive and innocent. Some of us will have to take off our rose-tinted glasses.

More of us wear dark glasses. We have learned to look on other religions as competitors, sometimes even as anti-Christian. We have compared other persons' problems with our achievements, the best Christian with the worst Hindu. We have confused cultural sophistication and religious depth and have assumed that faith was corrupt because nations do not have as much literacy, technology, or democracy as Americans have. Yet traditions such as Hinduism and Buddhism have an age and dignity comparable to Christianity. Islam achieved a splendid cultural development before Christians achieved a medieval synthesis; Islam successfully evangelized Christian Africa and now ministers to as many or more of the world's folk than Christianity. All of these traditions have popular forms that flower among illiterates, but they also have brilliant philosophical traditions comparable to the flowering of Christian theology in the West. They have rich systems of prayer and worship. They motivate their devotees to social responsibility and cultural creativity. However much we believe that Christ may bring them to fuller humanness, we can no longer look down on their present achievements and profound experiences of the ultimate. To keep on our dark glasses any longer will not simply be an act of ignorance, but an act of defensiveness. True witness proceeds from the richness of Christ, not fear of human truth.

Any effective conversation with other communities of faith must be based on our understanding of their history, integrity, and our respect for their achievements. We must cross another frontier. We must set out to understand other communities of faith and to understand them fairly and sympathetically. We have good reasons to do this. So many,

3

that I believe there is a moral imperative about their frontier similar to those others we have crossed. Consider a few of these reasons.

1. Understanding other religious communities will help us confront our own fears. A deep strain of anxiety laces our faith in God and in Christ. The mere presence of those who do not believe the gospel makes us question our own commitments, our own convictions about how God uses us. The presence of whole communities of persons with deep faith like our own, faith not directed toward Christ, arouses questions about our own theology and faith. Witness that roots in anxiety will communicate anxiety, not faith. The gospel is not coercive. God loves persons into freedom. Authentic witness reflects dependence upon the gospel, genuine trust in God, not fear. Authentic witness communicates love, not fear; confidence, not a sense of inadequacy. Fear arises from ignorance, in part, an ignorance of our neighbors in other communities. By understanding other communities, their woes, their blessings we will dispel our ignorance and learn to know them as fellow human persons. Then we will be free to confront the part of our fear that stems from our ignorance of the love of God in Christ.

2. Understanding other religious communities will help us understand more fully the way God works in human experience. As Lutherans we have tended to the heresy of exclusive emphasis on the second article of faith. Without the first and third articles the second turns into a romantic spiritualism. Christ becomes a private religious experience and not a statement about the fundamental being of God and a source for continuing revelation in the spirit. The Apostolic faith clearly interprets Christ as a statement about God who created, sustains the world, and acts in all human experience. The Apostolic Canon witnesses that God's actions with Israel form the basis of the revelation in Christ. Human experience in the first place, and the experience of another religious community in the second place, reveal God first dimly and then clearly. God's word of Christ addresses human experience; it addresses humans already in some kind of conversation with being. It is essential to understand what God says in creation, in history, in significant religious experience, if we are to understand clearly what God says in

Christ. Within human experience most significant are the structures of religious experience of the great traditional faiths. From them as from history we can learn of the work of God we know as general revelation. We may learn more than this, but religions are certainly as revealing as power, death, and the fundamental limits of our life.

3. A comparative understanding of other religious communities will help us understand the processes by which communities of faith interact with the ongoing process of human culture. As Christians we need to understand how we are shaped by general human culture. We need to sort out what is for good and what must be resisted. As Christians we desire to contribute the gospel which we believe will free human culture for more creative, more moral, more humane life. To be self-critical and to minister prophetic criticism of human culture and to announce gospel creatively to culture, we need to know the patterns and shapes of interaction of religious structures when we compare our own traditions with those of similar age and experience, Muslim, Jewish, Buddhist, Hindu. Comparison will reveal something of the general processes of culture and so alert us to our dangers and our opportunities. Understanding other communities takes much time and work. Comparison takes even more, but the results of such careful analysis can be both revealing and helpful. Such understanding might take a century. We had best get on with the job.

4. Understanding the struggles of other religious communities helps us to understand our own religious situation. We all face a similar threat. Religious communities in developed and developing countries all face a secularity devoid of symbols of depth. Limit situations remain the same as ever: death, war, sin, guilt, suffering. Yet modern humans often lose their capacity for symbol and ritual and remain inarticulate in the face of these threats. Dumb we are and often deaf as well to any words of God, because we no longer hear symbols. We have color TV and stereo sound, but inner ears hardly resonated to the thunder of revelation. When we learn something of the present experiences of persons of other faiths, we will understand the structures of meaninglessness of our life much better.

5. Understanding of other religious communities can be a small contribution toward international interdependence and

world order. This reason does not come first or near first in the list because we must attend to intrinsic reasons before extrinsic reasons lest we distort the center of our faith and vision. The extensiveness and devastating character of the wars and weapons of this century have taken peace and order out of the category of an expediency and made it a necessity. We will survive as a species only if we find ways for creative interdependence among nations. Isolation is no longer a possibility in such a highly developed economic and political system. Whatever happens in any part of the globe not only appears on the TV screen in America, but affects American interests as well. The price of bread in the supermarket links itself with the number who die of starvation in India. There is no escape from this deadly interdependence. It can work for good or ill. The urgency of peace and the goodness of the goal make it a moral imperative for Christian persons to work for world peace. Yet this turns out not to be an extrinsic reason at all. God's will for human life is justice and peace. The paradise vision pictures a world community of people from all nations and peoples in a unity of praise. Christians have the obligation to symbolize God's future for humanity by acts that witness to God's will, acts that tend toward peace and international interdependence. In so many places, strife between religions gets used to mask the struggles of class and power. Persons of faith need to state their faiths in a prophetic manner that witnesses to the vision of human community intrinsic to religious traditions. Our understanding of other communities will help us in this task.

6. Understanding other faiths will help us understand ourselves and our unique identities more clearly. I will never forget the first ecumenical student conference I attended. I had not planned to be Lutheran, nor was I trying to represent a Lutheran perspective. Yet in the midst of a discussion I suddenly discovered that I sounded Lutheran, in fact, I actually was a Lutheran whose experience centered on faith and grace. In a community of differences we see our own uniqueness more clearly. Most of us feel our uniqueness in our faith in deity, yet Jews, Muslims, some Buddhists and Hindus believe in diety. It is our vision of the shape of deity and revelation that divide us. We make much of Christianity as a religion of love, but other communities have similar notions. It's the function of love in our faith that

sets us apart. Yet I suspect even these perceptions are still theoretical perceptions of how we perceive our uniqueness. Our sense of identity needs the enrichment of how persons of different persuasions perceive us. Understanding other faiths will help us understand ourselves.

7. Understanding other faiths will lay the foundation for an era of mutual witness. Except in a few areas of the globe the paternalistic approach to evangelical witness is dead. We can no longer act as lords and masters, as persons who are bringing truth to inferior folk. The arrogance of American power means that any paternalistic mission work will finally be rejected as American imperialism. Only those approaches which show full respect to those we serve will bear lasting fruit. Respect means listening as well as speaking. We must be prepared to receive a witness and take it to heart, in order to have the right to give a witness to the truth of gospel. Only dialog is non-coercive. And we do have things to learn. We neglect much in our faith. There is much more to know about Christ then we now know. Listening can help us to understand and it will enable us to witness fully and openly to Christ and let the power of Christ effect its own changes.

8. Understanding other communities of faith will give us new insights into God's goodness and the power of Christ. It is clear and unchanging for Christians that God has spoken to us in Christ. Though we have theorized long, we do not know clearly how God has spoken to other communities of faith, until we understand them in more depth. In general there have been two approaches to Christology. One has been to find more depth of clues to Christ in general human experience, to seek for the clarity of other revelations as revelations of God under the first article. Some early Christians took another route. John, confronted with the universal meaning of Jesus Christ, affirmed that the creative speech of God which revealed itself in Jesus was in fact present and active in the creation of nature and human history. Though we seldom reflect on this distinction, he clearly suggests that the logos acts before Christ and in general experience, but later acts more fully in Christ. Paul too, or his disciples, in Colossians and Ephesians again affirms the Christ before Christ, the Son who antedates Jesus. Justin the Apologist thought the logos had inspired

7

Plato. There is clear Christian precedent for thinking that the power of God which became historically visible in Jesus was operative prior to and after the birth of Jesus. Early Christians knew that goodness came from God. Christ is the sign of this goodness. Where goodness exists, Christ must have been there. Both the approach from the first article and that from the second have problems. There may be other approaches as well. Christians have different resemblances with Jews and Muslims than with Hindus and Buddhists. Christians incorporated Jewish Scripture as Christian revelation. Perhaps there are special harmonies between us that differ from one community to another. I do not know the way through these difficult questions. Yet I know the power of God in Christ, so I expect that my understanding of other communities will enlarge my vision of God's power and goodness and will sooner or later enlarge my understanding of the mysteries in Christ.

We have crossed many frontiers in the last three decades. We now face another. There are many good reasons for crossing this frontier with courage and some hope. These reasons persuade me there is a call to us to take up this task of understanding other communities. As we undertake this task we will learn much about others and even about ourselves. We may even one day find many of our present reasons trite, but they will have served a useful task, if they give us the courage to cross the next frontier.

GROUND RULES FOR

2

INTERRELIGIOUS DIALOGUE

Leonard Swidler

By dialogue is meant a conversation on a common subject between two or more persons with differing views. The primary goal of dialogue is for each participant to learn from the other. Stated negatively, dialogue is not debate. Each partner must listen to the other as openly and sympathetically as he or she can in an attempt to understand the other's position as precisely and, as it were, from within, as possible. Such an attitude automatically includes the assumption that at any point we might find the partner's position so persuasive that, if we would act with integrity, we would have to change our own position accordingly. That means that there is a risk in dialogue; we might have to change, and change can be disturbing. But of course that is the point of dialogue--change and growth. We enter into dialogue so that we can learn, change and grow, not so we can force change on the other, as one hopes to do in debate--a hope which is realized in inverse proportion to the frequency and ferocity with which debate is entered into. On the other hand, because in dialogue each partner comes

---

Leonard Swidler, B. A., St. Norbert's College, M. A. Marquette Univ., S.T.L., Tubingen, Ph.D. Univ. of Wisconsin. He is Professor of Catholic Thought and Ecumenism in the Religion Department at Temple University, Philadelphia, and editor of the Journal of Ecumenical Studies. His publications include The Ecumenical Vanguard, Freedom in the Church and Bishops and People.

Journal of Ecumenical Studies, Vol XV, Summer, 1978, n. 3, pp. 413-415. Reprinted by permission of the publisher.

9

with the intention of learning and changing him or herself, one's partner in fact will also change. Thus the alleged goal of debate, and much more, is accomplished far more effectively in dialogue.

We are here speaking of a specific kind of dialogue, an interreligious dialogue. To have such it is not sufficient that the dialogue partners discuss a religious subject. Rather, they must come to the dialogue as persons somehow significantly identified with a religious community. If I were neither a Jew, a Christian, nor a Muslim, for example, I could not participate as a "partner" in a Jewish - Christian - Muslim interreligious dialogue, though I might listen in, ask some questions for information, and make some helpful comments.

Because of this "corporate" nature of interreligious dialogue, and since the primary goal of dialogue is that each partner learn and change him or herself, it is also necessary that interreligious dialogue be a two-sided project. Each participant must not only enter into dialogue with her partner across the faith line--the Christian with the Muslim, for example--but also with her correligionists, with her fellow Christians, to share with them the fruits of the interreligious dialogue. Only thus can the whole community eventually learn and change, moving towards an ever more perceptive insight into reality.

The following are some basic ground rules of inter-religious dialogue that must be observed if dialogue is actually to take place. These are not theoretical rules, but ones that have been learnt from hard experience.

First, each participant must come to the dialogue with complete honesty and sincerity. No false fronts have any place in dialogue.

Secondly, each participant must assume a similar complete honesty and sincerity in the other partner. Not only will the absence of sincerity prevent true dialogue from happening, so also will the absence of the assumption of the partner's sincerity. In brief: no trust, no dialogue.

Thirdly, each participant must define herself. Only the Jew, for example, can define from the inside what it means to be a Jew. The rest can only describe what it looks like from the outside. Moreover, because dialogue is a dynamic medium, as each participant learns she will change and hence continually deepen, expand, and modify her self-definition as a Jew--being careful to remain in constant dialogue with her fellow Jews. Thus it is mandatory that each dialogue partner herself define what it means to be an authentic member of her own tradition.

Fourthly, each participant must come to the dialogue with no hard-and-fast assumptions as to where the points of disagreement are. Rather, each partner should not only listen to the other partner with openness and sympathy, but also attempt to agree with the dialogue partner as far as is possible while still maintaining integrity with his own tradition; where he absolutely can agree no further without violating his own integrity, precisely there is the real point of disagreement-- which most often turns out to be different from the point of disagreement that was falsely assumed ahead of time.

Lastly, although interreligious dialogue must occur with some kind of "corporate" dimension to it, that is, the participants must be involved as members of a religious community--e.g., qua Buddhists, Hindus, or Muslims--it is also fundamentally true that it is only persons who can enter into dialogue. But a dialogue among persons can be built only on personal trust. Hence it is wise not to tackle the most difficult problems in the beginning, but rather to approach first those issues most likely to provide some common ground, thereby establishing the basis of human trust. Then gradually, as this personal trust deepens and expands, the more thorny matters can be undertaken. Thus, as in learning we move from the known to the unknown, so in dialogue we proceed from commonly held matters--which given our mutual ignorance resulting from centuries of hostility, will take us quite some time to discover fully--we proceed to discuss matters of disagreement.

In conclusion it should be noted that there are at least three phases in interreligious dialogue. In the first phase we unlearn misinformation about each other and begin to

11

know each other as we truly are. In phase two we begin to discern values in the partner's tradition and wish to appropriate them into our own tradition. For example, in the Catholic-Protestant dialogue Catholics have learned to stress the Bible, and Protestants have learned to appreciate the sacramental approach to Christian life, both values traditionally associated with the other's religious community. If we are serious, persistent, and sensitive enough in the dialogue, we may at times enter into phase three. Here we together begin to explore new areas of reality, of meaning, of truth, of which neither of us had even been aware before. We are brought face to face with this new, unknown-to-us, dimension of Reality only because of questions insights, probings produced in the dialogue. We may thus dare to say that patiently pursued dialogue can become an instrument of new revelation.

THE BASIS, PURPOSE

3

AND MANNER OF

INTER-FAITH DIALOGUE

Lesslie Newbigin

All intellectual activity implies some presuppositions. Thoughts can only be formulated in words and these words have been formed by the previous thought of the community whose language they are. Even the most radical scepticism can only be formulated in terms of presuppositions which are --for the moment--unquestioned. (See Michael Polanyi: Personal Knowledge, Chapt. 9, "The Critique of Doubt," pp. 269-298).

Lesslie Newbigin served in Madras, India as a minister of the Church of Scotland. In 1947 he was consecrated Bishop in the Church of South India, formed by the union of Anglican, Methodist and Reformed Churches in India. He served from 1947 to 1959 as Bishop of Madurai and as a member of the Central Committee of the World Council of Churches. In 1959, as General Secretary of the International Missionary Council, he helped to arrange the merger of that body into the World Council of Churches. He was recalled as Bishop of Madurai in 1965 and retired in 1975.

This selection is a draft originally prepared at the request of the Lutheran Church in America, Division for World Mission and Evangelism and appeared in The Scottish Journal of Theology, Vol. 30, pp. 253-270. A revised version has appeared in The Open Secret, published by Eerdmans in 1959. Reprinted by permission of the publisher and author.

In dialogue between representatives of different faiths the participants are called upon to submit their most fundamental presuppositions, the very grammar and syntax of their thought, to critical questioning. It is therefore essential at the outset to lay bare the presuppositions of the undertaking. No one enters into a conversation without presuppositions, and it is essential that these should be brought into the open. No one can bring a totally open mind to a dialogue except an imbecile who has not yet learned to use a human language.

1. Modern interest among Western Christians in the comparative study of religion is a product of the eighteenth century Englightenment. Looking back upon this period it is easy to identify the presuppositions which lay behind the study. All religions, including Christianity, were required to make good their claims at the bar of reason, and reason was understood in terms of the tradition of thought which stemmed from Descartes. Lineal descendants of this type of thinking are the various theories of religion as illusion-- theories which John Oman has classified under a threefold scheme: theories of a Hegelian type which see religion as a primitive, anthropomorphic science; theories of the Schleiermacher type which see religion as a product of human psychology; and theories of a Kantian type which see religion as the result of the moral pressure of the community upon the individual. /1/ Theories of this kind are the logical development of the presupposition--implicit in many studies in comparative religion--that there are criteria drawn from outside of the religious experience itself by which the religious experience can be evaluated.

2. A much more ancient model of interreligious dialogue takes as its basic presupposition that there is a common core of reality within all the varieties of religious experience. The classic statement of this position is the famous voice from the Rig Veda, "The real is one, though sages name it variously." In the long history of Indian religion this faith has been pressed to its farthest limit. Its most eloquent modern exponent has been Dr. S. Radhakrishnan. /2/ More often it is present as an un-expressed and unexamined axiom. When W. Cantwell Smith (The Meaning and End of Religion), recommends that we should cease talking about different "religions" and speak

14

rather of the religiousness which is the human response to the one transcendent reality, and when John Hick (in <u>God and the Universe of Faith</u>) calls for a "Copernican revolution" in our thought about religions so that we can see God as the one centre around which all the religions revolve, it is accepted as axiomatic that there is one reality behind or within all the forms of religion. Most frequently this has been identified with the mystical experience.

3.   A third model for interreligious dialogue is based on the practical need for political and social unity. One might find the classic example of this in the work of the Emperor Akbar (1556-1605), who encouraged representatives of different faiths to engage in dialogue and experimented with a universal religion designed to knot into one all the people of his empire. India since 1947 has again witnessed the strong pressure of the mood for national unity upon the thinking of responsible people in the various religious communities. This pressure can be understood in a superficial way which simply subordinates a concern for truth in religion to a concern for political unity. But it can also be understood in a more fundamental way. Outstanding Christian thinkers such as Paul Devanandan and M. M. Thomas saw that both the renaissance of Hinduism and the growth of a concern for nation-building were part of the consequences of the impact of Christ upon Indian society. /3/ They therefore called their fellow-Christians to the work of inter-faith dialogue in the context of the quest for national unity with the conviction that this was part of the continuing work of Christ in Indian society. The basis of their call to dialogue was in their Christian faith. It is a different matter when the basis of dialogue is simply the demand for national (or global) unity, without any deeper understanding of the reality on which the unity can be grounded.   When dialogue is conducted in this way, religious truth is being subordinated to something else.

4.   A Christian who participates in dialogue with people of other faiths will do so on the basis of his faith. The presuppositions which shape his thinking will be those which he draws from the Gospel. This must be quite explicit. He cannot agree that the position of final authority can be taken by anything other than the Gospel--either by a philosophical system, or by mystical experience, or by the

requirements of national and global unity. Confessing Christ--incarnate, crucified and risen--as the true light and the true life, he cannot accept any other alleged authority as having right of way over this. He cannot regard the revelation given in Jesus as one of a type, or as requiring to be interpreted by means of categories based on other ways of understanding the totality of experience. Jesus is for the believer the source from whom his understanding of the totality of experience is drawn and therefore the criterion by which other ways of understanding are judged.

In this respect the Christian will be in the same position as his partners in dialogue. The Hindu, the Muslim, the Buddhist and the Marxist each has his distinctive interpretation of other religions, including Christianity; and for each of them his own faith provides the basis of his understanding of the totality of experience, and therefore the criterion by which other ways of understanding--including that of the Christian --are judged.

The integrity and fruitfulness of the inter-faith dialogue depends in the first place upon the extent to which the different participants take seriously the full reality of their own faiths as sources for the understanding of the totality of experience.

II.

If this is the basis upon which the Christian participates in the dialogue, what understanding of other faiths does this imply ? Many different answers have been given and are given to this question. Many volumes would be needed to state and examine them. The following is only a series of headings for the purpose of orientation:

I. Other religions and ideologies are wholly false and the Christian has nothing to learn from them. On this three things may be said:

(a) The sensitive Christian mind, enlightened by Christ, cannot fail to recognize and to rejoice in the abundant spiritual fruits to be seen in the lives of men and women of other faiths. Here we must simply appeal to the witness of Christians in all ages who have lived in friendship with those of other faiths.

(b)   In almost all cases where the bible has been translated into the languages of the non-Christian peoples of the world, the New Testament word Theos has been rendered by the name given by the non-Christian peoples to the one whom they worshipped as the supreme being. It is under this name, therefore, that the Christians who now use these languages worship the God and Father of Jesus Christ. The very few exceptions, where translators have sought to evade the issue by simply transliterating the Greek or Hebrew word, only serve to prove the point; for the converts have simply explained the foreign word in the text of their Bibles by using the indigenous name for God. (I owe this piece of information to a conversation with Dr. Eugene Nida.) The name of the God revealed in Jesus Christ can only be known by using those names for God which have been developed within the non-Christian systems of belief and worship. It is therefore impossible to claim that there is a total discontinuity between the two.

(c)   St. John tells us that Jesus is the light that lightens every man. This text does not say anything about other religions, but it makes it impossible for the Christians to say that these outside the Church are totally devoid of the truth.

2.   The non-Christian religions are the work of devils and their similarities to Christianity are the results of demonic cunning.

This view is stated by Justin in his Apology, and is linked by him with the assertion that the Logos speaking through Socrates and others sought to lead men to the light and away from the work of demons--the logos who was made man in Jesus Christ. A sharp distinction is here drawn between pagan religion (the work of demons) and pagan philosophy (in which the Logos was shedding his light). There are two points which should be made regarding this view.

(a)   It would be wise to recognize an element of truth here: the sphere of religion is the battle field par excellence of the demonic. New converts often surprise missionaries by the horror and fear with which they reject the forms of their old religion--forms which to the secularised Westerner are interesting pieces of folklore and to the third generation successors of the first converts may come to be prized as part of national culture. Religion-- including the Christian religion--can be the sphere in which evil exhibits a power against which human reason and conscience are powerless. For religion is the sphere in which a man surrenders himself to something greater than himself.

(b) Even the strange idea that the similarities to Christianity in the non-Christian religions are evidences of demonic cunning points to an important truth. It is precisely at points of highest ethical and spiritual achievement that the religious find themselves threatened by, and therefore ranged against, the Gospel. It was the guardians of God's revelation who crucified the Son of God. It is the noblest among the Hindus who most emphatically reject the Gospel. It is those who say, "We see," who seek to blot out the light (John 9:41).

3. Other religions are a preparation for Christ: the Gospel fulfills them. /4/

This way of understanding the matter was strong in Protestant missionary circles in the early years of this century and is fully expressed in the volume of the Edinburgh Conference of 1910 on "The Missionary Message." The non-Christian religions can be seen as preparation for the Gospel either as the "revelation of deep wants in the human spirit" (loc. cit., p. 246) which the Gospel satisfies, or as partial insights which are corrected and completed by the Gospel. Obviously such a view can be discussed only on the basis of an intimate and detailed knowledge of mankind's religions. There is, indeed, a vast missionary literature, mainly written in the first half of this century, which studies the religions from this point of view. (One could wish that modern Roman Catholic writers who are now advocating something like the Preparation-Fulfillment view would study the earlier arguments). Briefly one has to say that this view had to be abandoned because--in R. Otto's phrase-the different religions turn on different axes. The questions that Hinduism asks and answers are not the questions with which the Gospel is primarily concerned. One does not truly understand any of the religions by seeing it as a preparation for Christianity. Rather, each religion on its own terms and along the line of its own central axis.

4. A distinct but related view of the matter--the one dominant at the Jerusalem Conference of 1928-seeks for "values" in the religions and claims that while many values are indeed to be found in them, it is only in Christianity that all values are found in their proper balance and relationship.

The final statement of the council lists such spiritual values as "the sense of the Majesty of God in Islam, "the deep sympathy for the world's sorrow in Buddhism, the "desire for contact with ultimate reality" in Hinduism, "the belief in a moral order of the universe" in Confucianism, and "disinterested pursuit of truth and of human welfare" in secular civilizations as "a part of the one Truth" (Jerusalem Report I, p. 491). And yet, as the same statement goes on to say, Christ is not merely the continuation of human traditions: coming to him involves the surrender of the most precious traditions. The "values" of the religions do not together add up to him who alone is the Truth.

5. A different picture of the relation between Christianity and the other religions is given in the Papal Encyclical Ecclesiam Suam (1964). /5/ Here the world religions are seen as concentric circles having the Roman Catholic Church at the centre, and other Cristians, Jews, Muslims, other theists, other religionists and atheists at progressively greater distances. In respect of this proposal one must repeat that the religions cannot be rightly understood by looking at them in terms of their distance from Christianity. They must be understood--so to speak--from within, on their own terms. And one must hold that this model particularly fails to do justice to the paradoxical fact-- central to the whole issue--that it is precisely those who are (in one sense) closest to the truth who are (in another sense) the bitterest opponents of the Gospel. Shall we say, that the Priest and the Levite--guardians of God's true revelation--are nearer to the centre than the semi-pagan Samaritan ?

6. Recent Roman Catholic writing affirms that that non-Christian religions are the means through which God's saving will reaches those who have not yet been reached by the Gospel.

Karl Rahner (Theological Investigations, vol. 5, pp. 115-134) argues as follows: God purposes the salvation of all men. Therefore he communicates himself by grace to all men, "and these influences can be presumed to be accepted in spite of the sinful state of men". Since a saving religion must necessarily be social, it follows that non christian religions have a positive salvific significance. In this respect they are parallel to the Judaism of the Old Testament, which--though it was a mixture of truth and error--was, until the coming of Christ, "the lawful religion willed by God for them." The adherent of a non-Christian religion is thus to be regarded as an anonymous Christian. But a Christian who is explicitly so "has a much greater chance of salvation than someone who is merely an anonymous Christian."

This scheme is vulnerable at many points. The devout adherent of another religion will rightly say that to call him an anonymous Christian is to fail to take his faith seriously. The argument from the universal saving purpose of God to the salvific efficiency of non-Christian religions, assumes, without proving, that it is religion among all the activities of the human spirit which is the sphere of God's saving action. The unique relation of the Old Testament to Jesus Christ is not adequately recognized.

Its most serious weakness, however, is one which is shared in some degree by the other views we have examined : it assumes that our position as Christians entitles us to know and declare what is god's final judgment upon other people. On the question of the ultimate salvation of those who have never heard the gospel, most contemporary Protestant writers are content to say that it is a matter to be left to the wise mercy of God. Some contemporary Roman Catholics (Hans Kung, for example), rebuke the attitude as a failure to do one's theological duty. On the basis of Luke 13:23f one might reply that those who claim to know in advance the limits of God's saving action are going beyond their authority. The basis of our meeting with people of other faiths cannot be in this kind of claim to know their ultimate standing before God. All such claims go beyond what is authorized. The basis of our meeting can only be the much more humble acknowledgement that we have been chosen by one greater than ourselves to be witnesses to him. It is in this direction that we have to look for the basis of dialogue.

III.

1. The starting point for my meeting with those of other faiths is that I have been laid hold of by Jesus Christ to be his witness. This is an act of his pure grace, prior to my knowledge of it, which I can only confess and acknowledge in thankfulness and praise to him.

2. This acknowledgment and confession means that I acknowledge and confess in Jesus Christ, in his life and teaching, his death and passion, his resurrection and exaltation, the decisive turning point of human history, the centre from which alone the meaning of my own personal life, and the meaning of the public life of mankind, is disclosed. It means that I acknowledge and confess Jesus as the Saviour of the world; the meaning and effect of what he is and has done cannot apply to anything less than the totality of all that is. It is from this centre that I try to understand and participate in the common human history of which I am a part.

3. With this as my clue I expect to find and do find everywhere in the life of mankind signs of the kindness and justice of God which are manifested in Jesus. These signs are to be found throughout the life of mankind, not only-- not even primarily--in his religion. The same clue enables me to recognize the fact that precisely these signs of God's goodness can be and are used as means by God. Patterns of piety, of belief and of conduct drawn from the experience of god's grace then become the basis for a claim against God. The classic model of this is the role of the religious leaders of Judaism in the passion and death of Jesus. The same thing is repeated again and again both in the history of religions and in the history of the Christian Church. Thus the Cross of the risen Jesus, which is the centre of the Christian Gospel, stands throughout history over against all the claims of religion including the claims of the Christian religion--to be the means of salvation. To put the love and power in Jesus entitles and requires me to believe that god purposes the salvation of all men, but it does not entitle me to believe that this purpose is to be accomplished in any way

21

which   ignores or bypasses the historic event by which it was in fact revealed and effected.

4. The accomplishment of this saving purpose is to be by way of and through a real history--a history whose centre is destined by the events which took place "under Pontius Pilate." The end envisaged is the reconciliation of all things in heaven and earth in Christ (Col. 1:20), the "summing up of all things in Christ" (Eph. 1:1), the liberation of the entire creation from its bondage (Rom. 8:19-21). The salvation which is promised in Christ, and of which his bodily resurrection is the first fruit, is not to be conceived simply as the fulfilment of the personal spiritual history of each individual human being. To speak in this way is to depart both from Scripture and from a true understanding of what it is to be a person. We are fully persons only with and through others, and in Christ we know that our personal history is so rooted in Christ that there can be no final salvation for each of us until he has "seen of the travail of his soul" and is satisfied (Isa. 53:11j). The New Testament itself suggests at many points the need for the patience which this requires (e.g. Heb. 2:39-40, Rev. 6:9-11).

5. Because this salvation is a real consummation of universal history, and not simply the separate consummations of individual personal lives conceived as abstracted from the public life of which they are a part, it follows that an essential part of the history of salvation is the history of the bringing into obedience to Christ of the rich multiplicity of ethical, cultural spiritual treasures which God has lavished upon mankind. The way in which this is to be understood is shown in the well known verses from the fourth Gospel:

"I have yet many things to say to you, but you cannot bear them now. When the Spirit of truth comes, he will guide you into all the truth; for he will not speak on his own authority, but whatever he hears he will speak, and he will declare to you the things that are to come. He will glorify me for he will take what is mine and declare it to you. All that the Father has is mine; therefore I said that he will take what is mine and declare it to you." (John 16:12-51)

We can spell out what is said here in a threefold form.

(a) What can be given to and grasped by this group of first-century Jews is limited by the time and place and circumstances of their lives. It is true knowledge of the only true God and in that sense it is the full revelation of god (John 17:3,6). But it is not yet the fulness of all that is to be manifested.

(b) It will be the work of the Holy Spirit to lead this little community, limited as it now is within the narrow confines of a single time and place and culture, into "the truth as a whole" and specifically into an understanding of "the things that are to come"--the world history that is still to be enacted.

(c) This does not mean, however, that they will be lead beyond or away from Jesus. Jesus is the Word made flesh, the Word by which all that is came to be and is sustained in being. Consequently all the gifts which the Father has lavished on mankind belong in fact to Jesus, and it will be the work of the Spirit to restore them to their true owner. All these gifts will be truly received and understood when the Holy Spirit uses them and declares their true meaning and use to the Church.

We have here the outline of the way in which we are to understand the witness of the Church in relation to all the gifts which God has bestowed upon mankind. It does not suggest that the Church goes into the world as the body with nothing to receive and everything to give, quite the contrary. The Church has yet much to learn. This passage suggests a trinitarian model which will guide our thinking as we proceed. The Father is the giver of all things. They all belong rightly to the Son. It will the the work of the Spirit to guide the Church through the course of history into the truth as a whole by taking all God's manifold gifts given to all mankind and declaring their true meaning to the Church as that which belongs to the Son.

As we look back upon the story of the Church and trace its encounter first with the rich culture of the Hellenic world and then with one after another of the cultures of mankind, we can see, with many distractions and perversions and misunderstandings, the beginnings of the fulfilment of this promise.

23

6. The Church, therefore, as it is in via, faces the world not as the exclusive possessor of salvation, not as the fulness of what others have in part, not as the answer to the questions they ask, and not as the open revelation of what they are anonymously. The Church faces the world rather as arrabon of that salvation, as sign, first-fruit, token, witness of that salvation which God purposes for the whole. It can do so only because it lives by the word and sacraments of the Gospel by which it is again and again brought to judgment at the foot of the Cross. And the bearer of that judgment may well be, often is, a man or woman of another faith (cf. Luke 11:31f). The Church is in the world as the place where Jesus--in whom all the fulness of the godhead dwells--is present, but it is not itself that fulness. It is the place where the filling is taking place (Eph. 1:3). It must therefore live always in dialogue with the world--bearing its witness to Christ but always in such a way that it is open to receive the riches of God which belong properly to Christ but have to be brought to him. This dialogue, this life of continuous exchange with the world, means that the Church itself is changing. It must change if "all that the Father has" is to be given to it as Christ's owm possession (John 16:14f). It does change. Very obviously the Church of the Hellenic world in the fourth century was different from the Church which met in the upper room in Jerusalem. It will continue to change as it meets ever new cultures and lives in faithful dialogue with them.

7. One may sum up--or at least indicate the direction of--this part of the paper by means of an image. We have looked at and rejected a series of models which could be so expressed. We will suggest (following Walter Freytag) the simple symbol of a descending and rising staircase (with a flat landing in between on which rises the Cross) as serving to indicate the true basis for dialogue between Christians and those of other faiths. /6/

The staircases represent the many ways by which man learns to rise up towards the fulfilment of God's purpose. They include all the ethical and religious achievements which so richly adorn the cultures of mankind. But in the middle of them is placed a symbol which represents something of a different kind--a historic deed, in which God exposed himself in a total vulnerability to all man's purposes, and in that meeting exposed mankind as the beloved of God who is--even in his highest religion--the enemy of god. The picture expresses the central paradox of the human situation, that God comes to meet us at the bottom of our stairways, not at the top; that our (real and genuine) ascent towards God's will for us takes us farther away from the place where he actually meets us. "I came to call not the righteous, but sinners." Our meeting therefore, with those of other faiths, takes place at the bottom of the stairway, not at the top. For "Christianity' as it develops in history, takes on the form of one of these stairways. The Christian also has to come down to the bottom of his stairway to meet the man of another faith. There has to be a kenosis, a self-emptying The Christian does not meet his partner in dialogue as one who possesses the truth and the Holiness of God, but as one who bears witness to a truth and Holiness which are god's judgment on him, and who is ready to hear that judgment spoken through the lips and life of his partner of another faith.

IV.

On the basis which has been laid down one can speak briefly of the purpose with which the Christian enters into dialogue with people of other faiths. This purpose can only be obedient witness to Jesus Christ. Any other purpose, any goal which subordinates the honour of Jesus Christ to some purpose derived from another source, is impossible for the Christian. To accept such another purpose would involve a denial of the total lordship of Jesus Christ. A Christian cannot try to evade the accusation that, for him, dialogue is part of his obedient witness to Jesus Christ.

But this does not mean that the purpose of dialogue is to persuade the non-Christian partner to accept the Christianity of the Christian partner. Its purpose is not that Christianity should acquire one more recruit. On the contrary obedient witness to Christ means that whenever we come with another person (Christian or not) into the Presence of the Cross, we are prepared to receive judgment and correction to find that our Christianity hides within its appearance of obedience the reality of disobedience. Each meeting with a non-Christian partner in dialogue therefore puts my own Christianity at risk.

The classic biblical example of this is the meeting of Peter with the Gentile Cornelius at Caesarea. We often speak of this as the conversion of Cornelius, but it was equally the conversion of Peter. In that encounter the Holy Spirit shattered Peter's own deeply cherished image of himself as an obedient member of the household of god. ("No Lord; for I have never eaten anything that is common of unclean.") It is true that Cornelius was converted, but it is also true that "Christianity" was changed. One decisive step was taken on the long road from the incarnation of the Word of God as a Jew of the first century Palestine to the summing up of all things in him.

The purpose of dialogue for the Christian is obedient witness to Jesus Christ who is not the property of the Church but the Lord of the Church and of all men, and who is glorified as the living Holy Spirit takes all that the Father has given to man--all men of every creed and culture--and declares it to the Church as that which belongs to Christ as Lord. In this encounter the Church is changed and the world is changed and Christ is glorified.

V.

What is to be said, on the basis of the preceding discussion, of the manner of inter-faith dialogue? We have already suggested that it is the doctrine of the Trinity which provides us with the true grammar of dialogue and we shall proceed accordingly.

1. We participate in dialogue with men of other faiths believing that we and they share a common nature as those who have been created by the one God who is the Father of all, that we live by his kindness, that we are both responsible to him and that he purposes the same blessing for us all. We meet as children of one Father, whether or not our partners have accepted their sonship.

This has at least three implications:

(a) We are eager to receive from our partners what God has given them, to hear what God has shown them. In Karl Barth's words, we must have ears to hear the voice of the Good Shepherd in the world at large.

26

Eagerness to listen, to learn, to receive even what is new and strange will be the mark of one who knows the word of Jesus: "All that the Father has is mine." In our meeting with men of other faiths we are learning to share in our common patrimony as human beings made by the one God in his own image.

(b) We meet in a shared context of things, of non-personal entities. The importance of this becomes clear if one recalls the division which arises when dialogue is conceived as the encounter of pure naked spirits. For those who regard the mystical experience of undifferentiated unity with pure Being the core of religion, it will be natural to conceive dialogue as being directed towards a meeting of persons at a level "deeper" than that which can be conceptualized. But, while fully acknowledging that there may be in such a personal meeting more than either of the partners can put into words, it must be insisted that truly personal relationships develop in the context of impersonal realities. We do not become more fully persons by trying to abstract ourselves from the world of things. The Christian in dialogue with men of other faiths rejoices to share with his partners the one common world which is the gift to both of the one God.

(c) Moreover, in the dialogue we meet at a particular place in time in the ongoing history of the world, a history which we believe to be under the providence and rule of God. We do not meet as academics studying dead traditions from the past, but as men and women of faith struggling to meet the demands and opportunities of this moment in the life of our city, our nation, our world. To recognize this will prevent us from simply shooting at each other from old fortresses. We shall meet in the open country where all of us, of whatever faith, are being called upon to bring our faith to the test of decision and action in new and often unprecedented situations. It is this open encounter in the field of contemporary decision that true dialogue takes place. This dialogue may and often should, lead into common action on many matters of public life.

2. We participate in the dialogue as members in the body of Christ--that body which is sent into the world by the Father to continue the mission of Jesus. This has three consequences for the manner of the dialogue.

(a) It means that we are vulnerable. We are exposed to temptation. We have no defences of our own. We do not possess the truth in an unassailable form. A real meeting with a partner of another faith must mean being so open to him that his way of looking at the world becomes a real possibility for me. One has not really heard the message of one of the great religions that have moved millions of people for centuries if one has not been really moved by it, if one has not felt in one's soul the power of it. Jesus was exposed to all the power of men's religious and ideological passion, to the point where he could cry, "My God, my God, why did you forsake me ?" and yet remain wholly bound to his Father and commit his spirit into his Father's hands. The true disciple will be exposed without defence in his dialogue with men of other faiths and yet will remain bound to Jesus.

(b) One may put this point in the form of the image mentioned above. The Christian has to come down to the bottom of his stairway to meet his partner. Much of his "Christianity" may have to be left behind in this meeting. Much of the intellectual construction, the piety, the practice in which his discipleship of Christ has been expressed may have to be called in question. The meeting place is at the Cross, at the place where he bears witness to Jesus as the Judge and Saviour both of the Chhistian and of his partner.

(c) The implication of this is that the Christian who engages in dialogue must be firmly rooted in the life of the Church--its liturgy, teachings, sacraments and fellowship. The world of the religions is the world of the demonic. It is only by being deeply rooted in Christ that one can enter in complete self-emptying and with complete exposure into this world in order to bear faithful witness to Christ.

3. We participate in the dialogue believing and expecting that the Holy Spirit can and will use this dialogue to do his own sovereign work to glorify Jesus by converting to him both the partners in the dialogue.

(a) The Christian partner must recognize that the result of the dialogue may be a profound change in himself. We have referred to the story of the meeting of Peter and Cornelius, which is the story of radical conversion both for the apostle and for the pagan Roman soldier. Klaus

28

Klostermeier writes as follows of his experience of dialogue with Hindus: "Never did I feel more inadequate, shattered and helpless before God....all of a sudden the need for a metanoia in depth became irrepressibly urgent." /7/

The Holy Spirit who convicts the world of sin, of righteousness and of judgment, may use the non-Christian partner in dialogue to convince the Church. Dialogue means exposure to the shattering and upbuilding power of God the Spirit.

(b) The Christian will also believe and expect that the Holy Spirit can use the dialogue as the occasion for the conversion of his partner, to faith in Jesus. To exclude this belief and expectation is to reduce dialogue to something much less than its proper importance. What we have said about the "conversion of Peter" in the encounter at Caesarea must not be used to overshadow the conversion of Cornelius, without which there would have been no conversion of Peter. A distinguished Hindu writer on religious and philosophical questions, Dr. R. Sundarara Rajan of Madras, has recently commented on the current developments in the field of Hindu-Christian dialogue. He points out that the emphasis upon a self-critical attitude, the demand that each party should try to see things from within the mind of the other, and the disavowal of any attempt by either side to question the faith of the others, can easily mean that dialogue is simply an exercise in the mutual confirmation of different beliefs with all the really critical questions excluded. "If it is impossible to lose one's faith as a result of an encounter with another faith, then I feel that the dialogue has been made safe from all possible risks." /8/ A dialogue which is safe from all possible risks is no true dialogue. The Christian will go into dialogue believing that the sovereign power of the Spirit can use the occasion for the radical conversion of his partner as well as of himself.

(c) When we speak of the Holy Spirit we are speaking of the one who glorifies Christ by taking all the gifts of God and sowing them to the Church as the treasury of Christ (John 16:14f). The work of the Spirit is the confession of Christ (I John 4:2f; I Cor. 12:3). The Spirit is not in the possession of the Church but is Lord over the Church, guiding the Church from its limited, partial and distorted understanding of and embodiment of the truth into the fulness of the truth in Jesus who is the one in whom all things consist (Col. 1:7). Not every spirit is the Holy Spirit. Not every form of vitality is his work. There is need for the gift of discernment. Peter at Caesarea, and later the congregation in Jerusalem, had need of this discernment to recognize that this strange and (at first) shocking reversal of deeply held religious beliefs was the work of the Holy Spirit and not of the antichrist (Acts 11:1-18).

There is no substitute for the gift of discernment, no set of rules or institutional provisions by which we can be relieved of the responsibility for discernment. Dialogue cannot be "made safe from all possible risks." The Christian who enters into dialogue with people of other faiths and ideologies is accepting the risk. But to put my Christianity at risk is precisely the way by which I can confess Jesus Christ as Lord over all worlds and Lord over my faith. It is only as the Church accepts the risk that the promise is fulfilled that the Holy Spirit will take all the treasures of Christ, scattered by the Father's bounty over all the peoples and cultures of mankind, and declare them as the possession of Jesus to the Church.

The mystery of God's reign can only be made safe against all risk by being buried in the ground. It can only earn its proper profits if those to whom it is entrusted are willing to risk it in the commerce of mankind.

NOTES

/1/   John Oman, The Natural and the Supernatural (1931) pp. 29-46.

/2/   E.g., S. Radhakrisnan, Eastern Religion and Western Thought, (1939).

/3/   E.g., Devanandan and M. M. Thomas (eds.), Christian Participation in Nation Building (1960); M.M. Thomas, The Acknowledged Christ of the Indian Renaissance, (1971).

/4/   Perhaps the best known example is J. N. Farquhar, The Crown of Hinduism, (1913).

/5/   Loc. cit., Chapter III, "The Dialogue".

/6/   W. Freytag, The Gospel and the Religions (1958), p. 21.

/7/   In Inter-religious Dialogue, ed. H. Jai Singh (Bangalore, 1967).

/8/   "Negations: an article on dialogue among religions", by R. Sundarara Rajan, Religion and Society (Bangalore), XXI (4), p. 74.

TOWARDS A THEOLOGY

4

OF DIALOGUE

S. Wesley Ariarajah

Theology can be defined in many ways, but for our purposes it can tentatively be defined as "systematic discourse concerning God and his ways". It arises in the first instance on the basis of specific religious experience, which takes place in a particular context. Here the phrases "specified religious experience" and "particular context" are important. All theology must arise out of a specific religious experience; it must be related to a given context. For Christian theology, the point of departure is the experience of Jesus Christ, faith in him and commitment to his message.

The Rev. S. Wesley Ariarajah has a B. D. from United Theological College, Madras, a B. Sc. from Madras Christian College, South India, a Th. M. from Princeton Theological Seminary, New Jersey, and an M. Phil. from King's College, London. His field of concentration has been the History of Religions with a focus on Hinduism. Active as a Minister of the Methodist Church in Sri Lanka and as a lecturer in the History of Religions at the Theological College of Lanka, he has been active in ecumenical affairs and in January 1981 became a staff member of the W. C. C. sub-unit with particular responsibility for Hindu and Buddhist relations. He now lives and works in Geneva, Switzerland.

This paper was originally presented at a consultation on Asian and African contributions to contemporary theology held at the Ecumenical Institute in Bossey, Switzerland in June 1976. This revised version appeared in The Ecumenical Review, Vol 29, 3-11. June 1977. Reprinted with permission of the publisher.

The shape of theology, however, will depend on the particular context within which Christ is experienced and the nature of the commitment such context demands. This is why Christian theology in Asia, Africa and Latin America can never be the same. Even though the point of departure for all is the one Lord, Jesus Christ, the vastly varying contexts in which we live make it almost impossible for us to say the same things about him. Commitment to him can never mean the same thing in different cultural situations or in different centuries.

For the same reason theology, rightly understood, is also done in the context of the life of the believing community. It cannot be separated from the life and witness of the community. It is in struggling to understand the significance of Jesus Christ in a given context, in searching for the meaning of faith and the nature of the commitment it demands, that theology is done. One need not labor the point because the New Testament and the history of the early Church are outstanding examples of both the nature of the theological task and the way of doing it. One cannot read the Acts of the Apostles without being struck by the tremendous amount of searching and groping into the significance of the Gospel that it contains.

There are many reasons why we need to turn "towards a theology of dialogue." May I suggest three among them as points of departure for the thoughts that are to follow:

Firstly, there is a growing recognition of something that has always been grudgingly admitted but kept at bay in theological work, namely that all human life--not just an artificially isolated segment called the "religious life"--and that all human beings--not just Christians--are part of God's activity in this world and share a common future. Christian theology has, in varying degrees, either refused to face this issue or given it marginal treatment. This can no longer be done. Today all human life and all human beings are the center of theological reflection. Nothing that deals almost exclusively with Christians, with only marginal treatment of the rest, can be accepted. This new attitude and agenda for theology require new tools and new methods of working. /1/

Second, steps towards a theology of dialogue have become essential because of the apparent impasse to which dialogue has come. In the past many have entered into living dialogues with people of other faiths and ideologies and much has happened, both to the people who entered into dialogue and to their concepts. Very little of this new experience can be expressed within the framework of traditional theology. There is much new wine that cannot be put into old wineskins without the wineskins bursting and the wine being wasted. New wine needs new bottles.

Third, and most important, the Christians of Asia, Africa and Latin America have now come to realize the meaning of what has been described as the "'Teutonic captivity' of Christian theology, seldom offering a chance to break out of the western and historical cultural framework to which the Word of God in the Bible has been made captive". /2/ The intellectual framework provided by Greek philosophy, institutions and laws as fashioned by the Roman Empire, Germanic temperament and the major heart of the Christian religion that the churches in Asia and Africa are in virtual intellectual and institutional bondage. Happily, from the stage of blaming all and sundry for our bondage, we have now come to the stage of breaking loose so that we can struggle with our own experience of Christ in our own context. Asian and African theology has yet to emerge, and it can only do so as we enter into deeper and fuller dialogue with our context in the same way as the early Church. What, then, is our theological basis for dialogue and what aspects of our faith in Jesus compel us to enter into dialogue? It is to these questions that we need to turn now.

Towards a new attitude to religion and Theology

A theology of dialogue must have, in the first instance, a new understanding of the nature of religion and theology. One of our sins in the past has been to absolutize the Christian religion and theology, implying that the other religions were false, or at any rate "not true." Two hundred years ago Fielding's Parson Thwackum could say: "When I mention religion I mean the Christian religion; and not only the Christian religion but the Protestant religion; and not only the Protestant religion but the Church of England." /3/ Today, although none of us would be naive enough to say so,

34

a close examination of our attitudes, theological affirmations and evangelistic methods would confirm that not many churches in Asia and Africa have moved from a similar position. We must emphasize that what we call a religion, whatever religion it may be, is a human phenomenon, all too human for any of them to make exclusive claims over others. The biggest confusion in the mind of an average churchgoer in Asia today is reflected in his refusal to distinguish between the Church and the Kingdom and between religion and faith. Of course the Christian faith as its distinctive character in that it is about Jesus Christ and that it announces the in-breaking of the rule of god over all life, but this gives no additional validity to what can be historically traced as the Christian religion. Religion is the manifestation of the faith of a people in history at a particular time and place, and by virtue of necessity, it expresses itself in thought forms, symbols and rites that are prevalent in the culture, religion and culture each exerting mutual influence over the other. There can be nothing sacrosanct, thererore, about its form, mode or life. /4/

This is also true of theology. Rightly understood, all theology is "story-telling." It is the framework within which one seeks to give expression to one's experience and faith. All religions seek to tell their religious experience within the framework of a "story" of the nature of the world, of man, of God and destiny of life, a necessary framework to hold different aspects of its experience. The danger and temptation are to hold that one "story" is more valid than the others. For example, the Hindu may speak of his religious experience within a "story" which includes a particular view of history, the law of Karma and rebirth and an understanding of an essential unity of man and God. The Buddhist may express his experience with an analysis of the nature of man and the universe that does not necesarily correspond to the Hindu view. The Judeo-Christian on the other hand may speak of his experience within the context of the "creation-fall-redemption" story. The point is to realize that all stories have no enduring value in themselves, except to give a framework within which the community celebrates its faith and experience.

Reasons for importance

Why, one might ask, is this understanding of religion and theology important for a theology of dialogue ? There are many answers:

First, the greatest obstacle to genuine theological thinking is the inordinate fear of syncretism. This arises only when one tends to absolutize a religion, a doctrine or a theological system as the ultimate truth. When it is understood as a human phenomenon it is possible to break away from bondage to dogmatism into the freedom of the Spirit.

Second, in a dialogue one has to take one's partner seriously, and seek to learn from his or her religious experience. Anyone who approaches another with an a priori assumption that his story is "the only true story" kills the dialogue before it begins.

Third, and most important, this approach to theology will leave the door open for a more ecumenical and universal understanding of the significance of the Gospel. Traditional Christian theology simply ignores the greater part of the human race; it has only after-thoughts to offer concerning God's purposes for all those hundreds of millions of people outside the "Christian fold". The history of Christian mission is an outstanding example of the theological void created by the stubborn refusal of the Church to accept the religious experience of others. Aloysius Pieris in his article "The Church, the Kingdom and the other Religions," /5/ says that there have been four distinctive missiological moods in history: the conquest theory, the adaptation theory, and fulfillment theory and the sacramental theory. A close examination of all these theories shows a wilful reluctance on the part of Christian theologians to accept the religious experience of those outside the fold, and more seriously, a denial that human religious experience can be expressed and conveyed within thought forms other than that of traditional Christian theology.

The human predicament in other faiths

What does this mean in specific terms and how does it relate to the theology of dialogue? Let us take an example.

The human predicament is described in various ways in each of the different religious traditions. In Christian theology one speaks about, say, the "fall" of man, or rather, the "fallenness" of the human being or the state of "sin." The actual words "fall" or "sin" may not be used in modern theology, but words like "estrangement", "alienation" or whatever, eventually boil down to a particular idea of sin. It is within this predicament that we understand Christ as Saviour--as the one who gives us a new humanity.

The advaita, on the other hand, describes the predicament as avidya or ignorance that stands in the way of the realization of one's unity with the ultimate reality of Brahman.

The Saiva Siddhanta speaks of the human predicament in terms of anavam, the egoistic power of individuation, that clouds the love relationship between the soul and the Lord, bringing about ignorance and alienation.

Buddhism analyses the situation in terms of anicca, anatta and dukkha.

Is it not wilful blindness to insist that the "creation-fall-redemption" story or its modern counterparts are the only true description of the human predicament? Can we say that the idea of "sin" exhausts all descriptions of the state of man? After all, no one believes that there was an actual historical "fall" in which a man called Adam fell from the grace of God, thus affecting all human beings. Nevertheless, we believe in the "fall" because it speaks to us about our present human situation and gives us a framework within which we can speak about the significance of Christ.

What is essential to theology of dialogue is to take with absolute seriousness the analysis of the human predicament within other faiths. They are no more and no less valid than that within which traditional Christian theology is done. The tragedy of our past is that we have always compared the understanding of, say, avidya or anavam with the Christian concept of sin and passed judgment on their suitability or otherwise. Some have gone a step further to adapt these words, but only to pack them with Christian ideas. This is not dialogue, nor is it a responsible way of proclaiming Christ. Rather we have to get behind the Hindu and Buddhist stories to comprehend what is conveyed in their "story telling"; we must seek to listen patiently, and then, we might discover even a much fuller and sharper analysis of the human predicament within which Christ can have meaning.

Up to now the Christian proclamation meant that we first break down their "story" and present our "story" and then, having given them a new analysis, we present Christ as the solution. Is this the right way forward?

Telling our story in all stories

Theology of dialogue has to do with telling your religious faith and experience within all types of stories, within many different thought forms; for example, as mentioned earlier Buddhism has analysed the human predicament in terms of three signata (Tilakkhana): anicca, dukkha and anatta. Lynn de Silva claims that there is no point in attempting to impose the Christian conceptual framework on Buddhists. Rather, the Christian dialogue involves not simply listening to the Buddhist but being able to express the Christian experience within that conceptual framework. He says:

"The essence of the Buddha's teaching is summed up in the Tilakkhana, and this forms the conceptual framework of Buddhism. Anicca affirms that all conditional things change and are in a perpetual state of flux; anatta affirms that nothing changes, for there is no soul or any permanent entity in man; dukkha affirms that conditional nature, being transient and 'soul-less', is the source of conflict, pain and anxiety. At first glance this Tilakkhana concept appears to conflict with Christian belief, but closer examination will show that it offers an analysis of the human predicament which can provide a theological framework for an expression of Christian faith in the context of Buddhist thought." /6/

This in fact is the true meaning of religious dialogue. Unless we can tell our faith in our own culture and in our own language to our own people, there will be serious doubts about its validity and its power to change the human predicament. This does not of course mean that all "stories" are equally useful and that faiths can be expressed within any framework. The faith itself is always much larger than all thought forms. S. J. Samartha in his The Hindu Response to the Unbound Christ, for example, points out some of the problems and advantages of telling our faith within advaita:

"The quest for the ground of being culminating in the Brahman results in minimizing the significance of the world of History. Secondly, in its search for the essential nature of man culminating in the atman, there is a devaluation of the human personality. These two together in their mutual influence and interaction have contributed to the shaping of a particular outlook of classical advaita which has a tendency to ignore the social dimension of human life. It is suggested here that the insights of the Christian faith in Jesus Christ as Lord and Saviour would help in recovering the sense of the personal, the historical and the social in the structure of Hindu spirituality. At the same time, however, a narrow view of God's revelation in Christianity as being more or less exclusively confined to the historical, thus isolating it from nature on the one hand and human consciousness on the other, must be corrected by the Hindu insight into the larger unity of all life." /7/

Such mutual correction and enrichment is possible only when there is liberation from bondage to any one particular religion or theology that sits in judgment on the other.

Towards a new understanding of the Scriptures

What we have discussed so far raises many important questions but the one major question will be on the authority of the Scriptures. Many new attempts to do theology have fallen by the wayside because they failed in the first instance to see more clearly and state more definitely the relationship between theology and Scripture. Further, verses like: "No man shall come to the Father except through me"; "I am the way, the truth and the life"; "Baptizing them in the name. . ." etc. are often thrown in the face of the people engaging in dialogue. Or a Pauline understanding of the man or the salvation is held as the unalterable last word on the destiny of man.

Much has happened in New Testament scholarship to undo the belief that the Bible has the unchanging nucleus of belief and practice which is valid for Christians and others at all times and in all places. The school of demythologization of Rudolph Bultmann and his followers has shown how there should be a radical separation of the faith itself from the outmoded forms and language in which it is presented. But is it not right to say that in all our churches in Asia and Africa, Barth and Kraemer are still the abiding saints on the question of spiritual authority ? Is it not true that we still hold to the Scriptures as containing all "the doctrines that are necessary for salvation" ? Do we not seek scriptural authority for all statements and judge all new thoughts from the "point of view of Scripture"? Of all the bondages of the Christian church in Asia the bondage to a particular attitude to Scripture seems to be the most difficult to break away from.

Scripture not a dividing Wall

As early as 1938 the Indian theologian Chenchiah challenged Kraemer on this question and refused to accept the Scriptures as the only unfailing authority for our faith. "Was there a New Testament at all for Jesus (at his time) to speak of its authority ?" he asked. Some Asians speak of getting at "a core of the Scripture" to which one must try to be faithful. But this will prove to be another vain attempt. For recent scholarship has shown that there is not one Jesus in the New Testament, but at least five, the Markan, Lukan, Johannine, Pauline, etc. and that all the material we have can only be understood as "faith statements" by the writers. This does not mean, of course, that the Scriptures have no historical value or that they are to be totally set aside. What must be insisted on, however, is that we must develop a truer understanding of the nature of Scripture and its authority.

At best all Scriptures, including the Bible, are confessional material and they reflect the faith and belief of the people who composed them at a given time. It is of course important to understand and to appreciate the way in which faith was held at a given time. For a religion rooted in history like Christianity it may even be indispensable as a source of faith in Jesus Christ. But it does not mean, therefore, that the present understandings of Christ must be judged entirely by the Scriptural authority. In other words

Scriptures should not become the walls that limit theological reflection and divide one community from another, but the lamp posts that shed light and illumination on the religious experience of the community. This also implies that we need to have a different attitude to the Scriptures of other faiths which express and sustain their own faiths. No one Scripture is more valid or true than another. Each religious Scripture provides inspiration and lays bare the basis on which the faith of the fathers was founded. There is no reason why the Hindu Scriptures should not be meaningful and provide the context of faith in Jesus Christ for an Indian Christian. One realizes that there are many questions left unanswered here. But a theology of dialogue and dialogue itself will need to take a much more serious and closer look at the nature and authority of the Scriptures, both of the Christian faith and of others.

Such an attitude to Scripture, however, raises a very important question of authority in religion, which must also be re-examined in a theology of dialogue. It is becoming increasingly apparent that the traditional sources of authority--namely, Scripture and tradition--are not necessarily the only, or at any rate, the primary sources of authority to do theology today.

In the Indian religious context, for example, Scriptures are important sources of authority, but they are to be confirmed primarily by the anubhava of the faithful. Anubhava, inadequately translated as "experience", does not in fact deal with emotional experience, but with an inner certainty that grows and grips a person as he enters into a direct encounter with reality. This inner certainty is confirmed by scriptural authority and tradition but is never dependent on them for validity.

Again, a theology of dialogue will need to take into serious consideration the dynamic aspect of authority; Scripture and tradition as authorities are too static and refer only to the past. Can we, for example, develop criteria to judge theology by the dynamics it produces to change the human predicament? "By their fruits you shall know them."

In other words a theology of dialogue needs a new cluster of criteria in which Scripture and tradition will have to take only a proportional share of authority. We need to develop criteria that will hold together the historical and the experiential, the individual and the corporate, the traditional and the immediate aspects of the faith within which theology is done. This is is by no means an easy task but must engage our immediate attention. It can only be meaningfully entered into by those who have a theological understanding of the nature of the community we seek. Ultimately, dialogue is the question of the relationship of the Christian community to the human community, of which it is a part. The distinctiveness of the Christian community lies not simply in the faith that Jesus is Lord of its life, but primarily in the affirmation that Jesus Christ is the Lord of the whole created order. Therefore, the community we seek can never be the narrow church group of Christians but must be a whole new world order in which God will be "all in all."

Dr. Russell Chandran points out that "it is significant that in the New Testament the frontier for the Christian religion is not between Christianity as a religion and other religions The Jewish Christians never gave up their Judaism and the Council at Jerusalem decided that the Gentiles need not leave their religion either. All that was required was to refrain from what could be considered evil in relation to one's commitment to Christ. Neither Jesus nor the Apostles seemed to pay much attention to the problem of religious frontiers as such. Peter sums up his own experience on this question by saying 'God has no favourites, but that in every nation the man who is God-fearing and does what is right is accepted by him' (Acts 10: 34-35). The frontier mission, as the early Church sees it, is between good and evil, between righteousness and wickedness, between the kingdom of God and the powers of evil, not between one community and another." /8/ Again, does not the understanding so prevalent in our churches that the Christian community is the true community of God, cut across all that we know and believe about God in Jesus Christ ? Does not the divine love for all humankind, and the divine Lordship over all life, completely exclude any idea that salvation occurs only in one stream of human history which is limited in time to the last nineteen centuries and in space to those areas to which the missionaries went? The scope, the power and the means of the love of God can never be determined by any. If God is the God of the whole world we must presume, whatever its

42

implication for the understanding of the Christian religion, that the whole of humankind is a part of a continuous and universal relationship to him. Such a theological understanding of the relationship between God and all people makes dialogue not another option but an imperative for the Church. The most unfortunate aspect of the human religious life, John Hick says, is that most religions have divided themselves into "rival ideological communities." /9/, sometimes at each other's throats. Theology in this context has taken the place of some unalterable, divinely inspired truth to protect an ideology and is not the continuous process of reflection on the nature of the activity of God in his world which it rightly should be.

Discerning God's activity everywhere

A theology of dialogue thus should take the human community as the locus of god's activity. There is nothing particular about the Christian community except that it has come to accept the event of Jesus Christ as a decisively significant event in the whole history of humankind; but the message is about and for the whole community. The self-realization of the Christian community as one called to proclaim this message does not exclude God's purposeful activity in and through other faiths. Thus the Christian community must not only proclaim the Kingdom but must also seek to discern it everywhere, by entering into dialogue.

By this token the whole concept of "salvation history", understood as the history of the Jewish nation and the Church, is to be seriously challenged by the theologians of Asia and Africa. Without denying the importance of history itself, one must affirm that salvation history is the history of the whole of humankind. Dialogue cannot take place in a true spirit of discernment if the parties involved exclude each other's history from the mainstream of the salvation that God offers to all people.

Herein lies the greatest challenge and opportunity in relation to the theology of dialogue. If the Christian community is not the community that God intends but is the provisional, the sign-community, the leaven, the salt, the light, the servant, then what in fact is the community we seek ? What are the marks of the true community, that God intends and how do we arrive at it ?

If the whole realm of human discovery is the arena of God's saving purpose, what are the criteria by which we seek to discern his actions in history ? Here, one must admit, we are in infancy, taking the first few faltering steps, we must fail many times before we can even stand erect. But there is no other way to mature adulthood--to a genuine theology of community.

How can we speak about community and the struggle to achieve it, without taking seriously what God has been doing with the 800 million people of the Republic of China ? Or how can we seek to live in community with the people of other faiths wihtout understanding, in the first instance, the community they seek ? Here dialogue becomes desperately urgent.

A theology of dialogue does not surrender the particularity of the Christian faith, of Jesus Christ and of the community that confesses him and is committed to him. Such commitment, however, must lead us to a more open, generous and inclusive understanding of God and his ways. It must not separate us from our fellow human beings but must place us in the midst of their struggles and hopes so that we can together seek the community that God intends for all his people. It must not be an impenetrable fortress but a garden where there are many trees, flowers, colours and scents, above all a garden where there is light ands fresh air and where you feel free to be one with the whole creation of God.

NOTES

/1/   S.J. Samartha: "The Holy Spirit and People of Various F-iths, Cultures and Ideologies." In: Dow Kirkpatrick (ed.): The Holy Spirit. Lake Junaluska, N.C.: World Methodist Council, 1974.

/2/   Choan-seng Song: "New China and Salvation History: a Methodological Enquiry." South East Asia Journal of Theology, Vol. 15, No. 2, 1974, pp. 55-56.

/3/   Henry Fielding: Tom Jones.

/4/   Wilfred Cantwell Smith: The Meaning and End of Religion, p. 109ff. New York: Mentor, 1962.

/5/   Dialogue, October 1970.

/6/   Lynn DeSilva: "Theological Construction in a Buddhist Context." du G. H. A. ed.: Asian Voices in Christian Theology, p. 40, Maryknoll, N.Y.: Orbis, 1976.

/7/   S. J. Samartha: The Hindu Response to the Unbound Christ, p. 17, Madras: Christian Literature Society 1974.

/8/   J. Russell Chandran: "Christian Approach to Other Faiths."   Paper read at the refresher course on Evangelization, United Theological College, Bangalore, India 1974.

/9/   John Hick: "The Reconstruction of Christian Belief for Today and Tomorrow. 2: Other World Religions," Theology, vol. LXXIII, 1970, p. 400.

DIALOGUE: DOES IT COMPLEMENT

5

MODIFY OR REPLACE MISSION ?

Anton P. Stadler

In the missiological literature of recent years, it has become popular to associate the concept of dialogue with that of mission. Some advocate dialogue as positive modification of mission; others reject it as undermining the missionary commitment of the Church. Thus dialogue has contributed to the continuing polarization among Christians concerning the meaning of mission in the modern world.

This paper deals primarily with the positive reception of the dialogue theme by the World Council of Churches and the Magisterium of the Roman Catholic Church. For over a decade these bodies have devoted increasing attention to this issue, mindful of the question to which no satisfactoiry answers have yet been found: does dialogue complement, modify or replace mission?

This writer intends to attempt a clarification of the

Anton P. Stadler is a Roman Catholic theologian who graduated from the Theological Faculty of Luzerne, Switz - erland, in 1971 and earned his Ph. D. at Union Theological Seminary, New York City, in 1977. In the fall of 1977 he will be sent by the Basel mission to join the faculty of the Seminary of the Kimbanguist Church at Lutendele, Kinshasa (Zaire).

This paper is taken from The Occasional Bulletin of Missionary Research (now called The International Bulletin of Missionary Research), Vol 1, 3:29, July 1977. Reprinted by permission of the publisher.

relationship between mission and dialogue. He presupposes that the association of these concepts indicates, in the final analysis, the need for a rethinking of the traditional understanding of mission. For this task, two basic requirements must be met: The integrity of both mission and dialogue must remain intact and their intrinsic relationship must be made explicit.

The Mission-Dialogue Issue Since 1955: Contributions of the World Council of Churches

In 1955 the Central Committee of the World Council approved plans for a long-term study on the Word of God and the Living Faiths of Men. /1/ This initiative was not totally unprecedented as the study by Hallencreutz indicates, /2/ but it marks the beginning of a systematic inquiry into the possibilities of dialogue between Christians and people of other religious traditions.

In the first years, the question was discussed at intra-church levels under the guidance of two WCC agencies, the Department of Missionary Studies and Studies in Evangelism, and the Department of the Study Centers in Asia. Between 1955 and 1967 a number of consultations sought to identify the issues and explore relations between Christians and Muslims, Hindus, and Buddhists, respectively. Soon the need for a new understanding of mission was felt. /3/

The Mexico City Assembly of the Commission on World Mission and Evangelism in 1963 /4/ added a new dimension to the dialogue concern. The conference was particularly aware of the secular world, calling the Church to discern the will and work of God by teaching the will and work of God by reaching out to people--be they secular or religious wherever they live. At this meeting, "witnessing" and "meeting" were the key words.

Concluding the series of intramural gatherings, the Kandy (Sri Lanka) Consultation in 1967 considerably advanced the understanding of interreligious dialogue: Dialogue means a positive effort to attain a deeper understanding of the truth through mutual awareness of one another's convictions and witness....Dialogue implies readiness to be changed as well as to influence others. /5/

In the same year, the Central Committee recommended: continuation of the study project. It suggested, however, the exponents of Marxist and humanist thought also be included as partners in dialogue.

The first interreligious consultation was arranged at Ajaltoun, Lebanon, /6/ in 1970. A small number of Hindus, Buddhists, as Muslims met with a larger number of Christians to experience living in dialogue and to explore its future possibilities. The question of mission and dialogue was raised and listed among the topics referred to future meetings.

Immediately afterwards, a group of theologians convened in Zurich to evaluate the consultation. An Aide-Memoire /7/ was drafted. The mission-dialogue issue is prominent in this document which attempts to clarify misunderstandings and allay fear in this domain. The freedom of the partners to witness to their own faiths is advocated. Dialogue as a new missionary strategy is, however, rejected. Still, as "means of communication" dialogue considered "clearly part of mission and....to be undertaken within the context of God's mission." /8/

Since Ajaltoun, dialogue has become a central concern of the World Council. The Central Committee, which met in Addis Ababa in 1971, issued a three-part document entitled An Inter-Policy Statement and Guide-Lines. /9/ The document emphasizes the dialogue is "a dynamic contact of life with life, concerned with living together and acting together." /10/ It recognizes, furthermore, the tension arising from the simultaneous promotion of dialogue and of mission. The clarification of the connection between mission and dialogue is left to further theological study" and "actual experience of dialogue." /11/

In the following year, the World Council sponsored a fine bilateral encounter between Muslims and Christians at Broumana, Lebanon. /12/ Some forty-six participants, almost equally divided between the two faith communities, gathered together under the theme of "The Quest for Human understanding and Cooperation. Christian and Muslim Contributions." Neither the papers nor the Memorandum focussed on the mission-dialogue problem. The concerns of the

48

participants centered more on the challenges of the present socio-political situations to which both sides should respond.

At the Bangkok Assembly of the Commission on World Mission and Evangelism in 1973, /13/ the overarching theme "Salvation today" and the genius loci may have been conducive to pondering the mission-dialogue question. The report of a special discussion group argues that there need not be tension between mission and dialogue. Rather, it observes, "increasingly mission is being carried on in this spirit of dialogue without the subsequent decrease in the sense of urgency in evangelism." /14/ In view of renewed missionary activity of other religions, the report speaks of reciprocal mission. In his report, Philip Potter, General Secretary of the World Council of Churches, considered dialogue as the first of four methodologies appropriate to evangelization in our times.

The theme of the Colombo Consultation in 1974 (the second multilateral meeting) was "Towards World Community. Resources and Responsibilities for Living Together." /15/ The mission-dialogue problem did not surface in the interchange. There was, however, considerable interest in dialogue as a major resource toward world community.

The Nairobi Assembly in 1975 /16/ epitomizes not only the drive for dialogue that became manifest in the years after Uppsala, but also unresolved problems of a theological nature inherent in the dialogue concept.

The theme of Section Three documents the fact that the World Council has opened its doors to the people of various faiths, cultures, and ideologies who join in a common search for community. Again the dialogue issue is not much advanced except for the statement that dialogue is no alternative to mission. Lynn A. de Silva from Sri Lanka offered, however, a remarkable apologia for dialogue in Asia for the sake of authentic mission. He stated:

"Dialogue is urgent and essential for us in Asia in order to repudiate the arrogance, aggression and negativism of our evangelistic crusades which have obscured the gospel and caricatured Christianity as an aggressive and militant religion.... Above all, dialogue is essential for us to dis-

49

cover the Asian face of Jesus Christ as the Suffering Servant, so that the Church itself may be set free from its institutional self-interest and play the role of a servant in building community." /17/

Apart from these well-publicized events, the World Council engaged in contacts with exponents of contemporary Judaism, with Marxists and humanists, and with representatives of primal world views.

From its inception, the World Council manifested a particular concern for Jewish-Christian relations. /18/ Gradually it fathomed some of the far-reaching consequences of the Holocaust. It also became sensitive to the political aspects of modern Judaism.

In the new structure of the World Council, the Committee on the Church and the Jewish People moved from the Commission on World Mission and Evangelism to the Sub-Unit on Dialogue with People of Living Faiths and Ideologies. In 1968 official joint consultations between the committee and exponents of Judaism (later the International Committee for Interreligious Consultations) were inaugurated and held seven times through 1976. World problems in general and themes toughing Jewish-Christian relations in particular were discussed. Most recently, the Jewish side suggested a clarification of the meaning of mission or witness in connection with dialogue. Rabbi Henry Siegman formulated the question as follows:

"The principle of witness--Christian or Jewish--need not be offensive to religious sensibilities nor pose a barrier to Christian-Jewish relations. I do recognize, however, that it is a concept that leads to abuse. A clearer definition of the concept and of its limitations within the concept of dialogue is one of the major issues to which we need to address ourselves in future discussions...." /19/

In 1974 the first regional Muslim-Christian dialogues, cosponsored by the World Council were organized in Legon, Ghana and in Hongkong. /20/ Priority was given to the question of constructive relations between the two communities at the local levels. In this connection, the mission-dialogue issue was raised. It was stressed that the

right to witness one's faith does not, however, justify proselytism. Muslims and Christians alike advocated a peaceful
coexistence of the two communities.

Only lately, people of primal world views have been
considered as potential partners in dialogue. The report on
the first exploratory consultation at Ibadan, Nigeria, /21/ in
1973, does not mention the mission-dialogue problem.

Although the World Council perceived the urgency of
interchange with representatives of ideologies, particularly
with Marxists, /22/ only one Christian-Marxist Dialogue
materialized in 1968. At a later meeting, the question of
"Faith and Ideology" was constructively resumed. /23/ The
mission-dialogue question was absent there.

A Theological Consultation on dialogue in Community,
sponsored by the Sub-Unit on Dialogue with People of Living
Faiths and Ideologies, took place at Chiang Mai, Thailand,
April 18-27, 1977. The preparatory material recommended
the study of previous documents concerning the problems of
community, dialogue, mission, and syncretism. Thus the
consultation was very conscious of the mission dialogue issue,
and its report--published in the April 1977 issue of the
Occasional Bulletin of Missionary Research--said:

"We endorse dialogue as having a distinctive and rightful
place within Christian life, in a manner directly comparable
to other forms of service.... But by 'distinctive' we do not
mean totally different or separate....We do not see dialogue
and the giving of witness as standing in any contradiction to
one another. Indeed, as we enter dialogue with our
commitment to Jesus Christ, time and again the relationship
of dialogue gives opportunity for authentic witness... Thus...
we feel able with integrity to commend the way of dialogue
as one in which Jesus Christ can be confessed in the world
today." (Paragraph 20).

Contributions of the Roman Catholic Magisterium

In order to capture the development of the dialogue
question at the level of the Roman Catholic Magisterium,
conciliar, synodal, and papal documents as well as the
publications of two Vatican Secretariats must be reviewed.

51

We shall first focus on the pronouncements of Pope Paul VI in Ecclesiam Suam (1964) and Evangelii Nuntiandi (1975). Then, some of the major documents of Vatican II and the reports on the Third General Assembly of the Synod of Bishops (1974) will be considered. Finally, attention will be given to the work of the Secretariats for Non-Christians (1964) and Non-Believers (1965) and also to the Commissions for Judaism and Muslims (1974).

The encyclical Ecclesiam Suam, /24/ deals extensively with the question of the Church's dialogue with the world. Its theological presuppositions are the following: God's relation with the world is dialogical for the sake of the salvation of humanity (colloquium salutis); the Church is called to continue the God-initiated dialogue; for this purpose, the Church is placed at the center of the world, surrounded in concentric circles by the rest of humanity. This model allows an "inside" and an "outside" of the Church. Those outside are defined by their proximity to or distance from the center. The Church is sent to all people far and near. Dialogue greatly assists the Church in fulfilling its mission. Thus the relationship of dialogue to mission is one of subordination. Mission is the primary task of the Church and dialogue is a suitable method of evangelization. In particular, dialogue humanizes, as it were, the Christian approach to people of other religious or secular convictions.

It is not accidental that the latest papal document, the apostolic exhortation Evangelii Nuntiandi, /25/ is exclusively devoted to the theme of evangelization. It is a vigorous promotion of evangelization in the face of growing reluctance and indifference among Catholics to support the missionary involvement of the Church. The exhortation is concerned with the primary dimension of the Church's mission, i. e., the proclamation of the Gospel to all people of the inhabited world. It makes clear that evangelization aims at the conversion of the evangelized and at their incorporation into the Church. In contrast to Ecclesiam Suam, the mission-dialogue problem is not articulated here.

The documents of Vatican II /26/ manifest the concerted efforts of bishops and theologians to discern the signs of the times. The mission of the Church in the world is the

52

central concern of the Council. Dialogue is recommended in different pronouncements, but the mission-dialogue issue as such is not articulated.

The Dogmatic Constitution on Divine Revelation, Dei Verbum, offers the basis for a truly theological interpretation of the mission-dialogue question, for it speaks of the dialogical structure of the God-world relationship. According to biblical experience, God as pleased to disclose himself to the people he created and make known to them his innermost plans for the salvation of the entire human family (colloquium salutis). The human partners, in turn, are invited to participate in this dialogue by their response of faith.

God reaches his people through socially mediated means, ultimately through Jesus Christ and, subsequently, through the Church. In the process of handing on the revelation in Jesus Christ, the Church evolves and becomes itself a transmitting agent. Hence the missionary nature of the Church and the essential connection between mission and dialogue.

The Council's teaching on the mission of the Church is found in three documents: Lumen Gentium (Dogmatic Constitution of the Church), Ad Gentes (Decree on the Missionary Activity of the Church), and Gaudium et Spes (Pastoral Constitution on the Church in the Modern World).

Lumen Gentium mirrors the tension between the static and the dynamic ecclesiological concepts of, respectively, Vatican I and biblical and patristic theology. Thanks to the emphasis on the symbols of the Church as the "Pilgrim People of God" and as the "Universal Sacrament of Salvation," the ecclesio-centric views of mission are in principle overcome. The meaning and role of other religions and the relationship between Christians and people of other convictions can now be seen afresh in the light of the universal salvific will of God and in the perspective of salvation history.

By promoting the idea of dialogue, Ad Gentes attempts to mediate between the conflicting notions of salvation (hence the necessity of mission). Dialogue is understood as an approach to the missionary endeavor and as an important factor in the process of the Church's adaptation to other than Western cultures.

No other document is as outspoken on dialogue as Gaudium et Spes. It reflects awareness of the interaction between different cultures and manifold forms of international interdependence. In this Constitution, the Council is both offering and promoting dialogue. The Church wishes to participate in all efforts toward a truly human world and, accordingly, seeks to enter into dialogue with all who toil for the transformation of the earthly planet. Likewise, it rallies all people of good will to engage in dialogue in order to strive in a common effort for a better world. To achieve this goal, the Church declares its readiness to assist the world and also to learn from it. Thus the principle of mutuality in dialogue is openly recognized.

The Declarations on Religious Freedom: Dignitatis Humanae and on the Relationship of the Church to Non-Christians: Nostra Aetate, are particularly significant for the mission-dialogue problem. Both affirm the mission of the Church in the sense of evangelization, and, at the same time, clearly advocate dialogue.

With the recognition of the principle of religious freedom as human right, Dignitatis Humanae removed one of the major obstacles that for centuries had prevented the Church from meeting people of other religious traditions with respect and openness. The far-reaching consequences of the change in attitude for the mission-dialogue question are not spelled out in detail. The Declaration insists, however, on two basic things. On the one hand, religious freedom does in no way lead to religious indifference and relativism nor does it interfere with evangelization. To the contrary, this principle is an essential prerequisite for missionary work. Only if and where religious freedom is fully honored can there be a climate favorable to the Christian message.

While this document stresses the legitimacy of evangelization, Nostra Aetate emphasizes the desirability of dialogue and collaboration among the different religions. The reflection of the latter on the significance and function of other religions in the lives of people crystrallize in two essential statements. Firstly, the Church does not reject any of the values present in other religious traditions but regards their teachings and practices with esteem. Secondly, Catholics are encouraged to "acknowledge, preserve and promote" the spiritual and moral values of other religions by engaging in dialogue and collaboration with their adherents.

Aware of the historical and theological connections with and chasms between the Church, Islam, and Judaism, respectively, the Declaration (sections three and four) seeks a sincere approach to these faith communities by suggesting collaboration and dialogue, above all, in areas of common concerns. It also takes a clear stand against antisemitism. The issue of Christian mission to Muslims and to Jews is carefully avoided. Thus no clarification of the mission-dialogue problem has been achieved at Vatican II.

Evangelization in the Modern World was chosen by Paul VI as the theme for the Third General Assembly of the Synod of Bishops. /27/ In his opening address, the Pope made the problem under consideration the principal issue as he urged the Synod Fathers to study and clarify how universal mission and dialogue can be reconciled. Despite the papal mandate, the question did not receive adequate attention and was, at the close of the Synod, practically abandoned by the Pope himself. A few scattered voices from Africa and Asia advocated the concern for a dialogical approach to people of other religious traditions.

Two insights ensuing from the Synod are pertinent in future discussions on mission and dialogue. The assembly came to realize the fact that Europe, hitherto considered a Christian continent, had become a religiously pluralistic world (a description equally applicable to North America). It is, therefore, likely that Europe--and not the so-called Third World--will become the testing ground for the credibility of mission and dialogue in Asia and Africa. The second insight refers to the key role of the Holy Spirit in mission and to his active presence in other religions. Dialogue was in general closely linked with mission as a dimension or method of evangelization.

The commitment of the Roman Catholic Church to dialogue is institutionalized by the establishment of two Secretariats and two Commissions. The general purpose of these agencies is to implement the teachings of Vatican II, notably Nostra Aetate and Gaudium et Spes. Accordingly, the Secretariats promote dialogue with people of other convictions and assist the particular or local churches to engage in dialogue with their neighbors. The Secretariat for Nonbelievers is not directly concerned with the mission dialogue question. It is primarily interested in the study of atheism and of ideology in its various forms, particularly the Marxist variant.

The mission-dialogue issue has, however, been articulated from the beginning by the Secretariat for Non-- Christians. Dialogue and evangelization are seen as distinct activities of the Church, each having its own integrity, objectives and methods of work. Thus there can be no conflict or alternative between the two concepts. Despite their distinctiveness, mission-dialogue and dialogue are held inseparable. /28/ By its stance, the secretariat documents that for organizational reasons it does not interfere with problems concerning mission, although it recognizes the theological connection between dialogue and mission.

The Commissions for Judaism and for Muslims were founded for the purpose of promoting and fostering relations of a religious nature between Jews and Catholics and between Muslims and Catholics.

The mission-dialogue issue is urgent above all in the relations among these communities. Jews and Muslims are equally opposed to Christian advances in the sense of proselytism. Christians, on the other hand, feel the pressures of Muslim expansion in certain countries. The reverberations of the tragic history of Jewish - Christian and Muslim - Christian relations are still felt, partly in actual tensions and conflicts, partly in pertinacious prejudices. Dialogue is, therefore, utterly difficult and delicate.

The Commission for Judaism (attached to the Secretariat for Promoting Christian Unity) is officially entrusted with the furthering of Jewish-Catholic contacts. In 1975 it published Guidelines /29/ for Catholics on Jewish-Catholic relations. It focuses primarily on practical questions. Among other things, the necessity of evangelization is advocated in the context of religious liberty. In subsequent meetings of tbe Jewish-Catholic Liaison Committee (founded in 1970), the partners had to be assured that no proselytism was intended by these statements. Conversely, the document earned credit for its clear stand on antisemitism and its willingness to understand the Jews as they understand themselves.

In the discussion of the Liaison Committee, the concepts of people, nation and land in Jewish and Christian perspective were central. At the Jerusalem meeting in 1976, the Committee decided to place the problem of witness in the context of dialogue on the agenda of future studies and discussions.

The Secretariat for Non-Christians paved the way for the Commission for Religious Relations with the Muslims. From its inception, it sought contacts with representatives of the highest authorities of Islam and with Muslim scholars. At the local level, contacts with Muslims were initiated in various countries, e.g. Indonesia, Pakistan, the Arab world (Egypt, the Magreb). The Tripoli Seminar in 1976 on Islamic-Christian Dialogue, /30/ indicates that the prospects for future collaboration are promising, provided both sides abstain from proselytizing activities.

The problem of the compatibility of mission and dialogue emerged in both Jewish-Catholic and Muslim-Catholic encounters as a key factor in determining the future of these relations. Since Catholic as well as Muslim missionary activities are often defined in terms of proselytism, it is imperative for all involved in mission or witness, (or Islamic Da'wah), to clarify what they mean by this activity per se and in connection with dialogue.

Critical Comments

The mission-dialogue problem has been recognized, articulated and intensified by both the World Council and the Roman Catholic Magisterium. The issue became increasingly more acute the more the idea of dialogue was advanced. Gradually the churches realized there was something definitely wrong in their theologies that kept them from contructive interchange with their neighbors of other convictions and world views. They became conscious, furthermore, of the tendencies toward a world community owing to growing economic and cultural interdependence. No doubt, the churches have begun to change their attitudes toward people of other persuasions. Inevitably they had also to ponder the implications of this change for their understanding of mission.

If our impressions are correct, the churches felt attracted by the possibilities of dialogue but sensed its challenging implications for the traditional understanding of mission. In the World Council, a clear gravitation toward dialogue concurrent with a deemphasis on mission is evident. It can be observed, in contrast, that the Magisterium sought to rekindle missionary enthusiasm among Catholics and thereby let the concern for dialogue slip silently into the background.

Exploring the possibilities of dialogue in bilateral and multilateral encounters, the World Council came to the awareness that interreligious dialogue requires living together much more than talking together. Through the well-defined channels of its Secretariats, the Magisterium focussed its attention on the preliminary stage, i. e., the preparation of the potential Catholic interlocutors for dialogue.

It seems that in their own ways both sides avoided facing the conflict between mission and dialogue theologically. It is significant that the mission-dialogue problem was most strongly felt in Jewish-Christian and Christian relations. The Jewish request to study the issue evinces that gathering common concerns and insisting on the compatibility of mission and dialogue in no way suffice for a theological response to the question.

Outline of a New Approach

The following considerations are meant as mosaic pieces that may contribute to the formation of a new theology of mission made necessary by the emergence of the dialogue theme.

Today the call for a contextual theology is universally heard. It is, however less difficult to identify particular contexts /31/ than to sketch a universal context. To capture the true proportions of the mission-dialogue problem, we must gain a global view on the world in which we find ourselves today and which is in the making. Suffice it to signal the most conspicuous phenomena of our time.

58

Our world is one of extreme contrasts. Humanity moves forward toward a world community and yet is unable to stop the process of fragmentation. The phenomena of growing economic interdependence and cultural interpenetration indicate that humanity is approaching a crucial stage in its continuing transformation. Thomas Berry interprets this process as follows:

"We are presently creating the multiform human tradition as the effective and encompassing society in which each person and each particular society finds a comprehensive context for existence in the human order of being. Within this universal society of mankind each human person becomes heir to the fullness of man's past cultural achievements, participant in the convergent cultures of the present and, according to capacity, maker of the future." /32/

Two aspects of this interpretation are decisive. The resources for making this planet a place for all to live and breathe freely lie in the people themselves, and these resources are now available to all persons, ready to be tapped.

At the point of the convergence of the various cultures, people can no longer coexist at the level of superficial conversation. It becomes increasingly urgent that people learn to communicate with one another on a deeper level. In this endeavor, the religious traditions of humankind are destined to assume a significant role. From ancient times they articulate the yearnings and aspirations of the people and are themselves interpretations and responses to the human quest for purpose and meaning. The meeting of religious traditions promises, therefore, the release of immense spiritual energy needed for the transformation of this planet. The churches are called to leave their ecclesiastical ghettoes and share their resources with other religious and secular traditions in a common venture of constructing a world that will once more be inhabitable. It follows that the rethinking of mission should take place within the horizon of the global context.

The universalist biblical motifs, present already in the first chapters of the Bible, correspond theologically with this global perspective. For the Bible is the story of God's ongoing involvement in the history of humankind-the story of his mighty deeds among his people. As creator and redeemer, Yahweh is the Lord of history yet letting his human partner be the maker and responsible agent of history. The Torah is the authentic witness and normative interpretation of the divine-human interaction in history. The covenant with Israel is not an end in itself but is designed to be a blessing for all peoples on earth.

In formulating a new theology of mission we must remember that the divine promise is valid and effective for the entire creation. Hence the distinctions between universal and particular salvation history and similar theologoumena are questionable. Recent biblical research encourages us to approach the Bible with new questions. In view of the convergent cultures of our age, questions such as these are highly relevant: How did Israel relate to the surrounding cultures ? What did she learn from the wisdom of her neighbors ? How did she adapt the stories of other peoples ? Are the hermeneutics for interreligious encounter already available in the Old Testament ? Could it thus be said that the Bible serves as paradigm for the communication between various world view ? /33/

With respect to the dialogue question it may be advisable also to approach the New Testament differently. The beginnings of Christian mission in the context of the Mediterranean world of the first century /34/ may tell us more about the New Testament understanding of mission than certain logia of commission. The parallels and differences as to the patterns and methods between early Christian mission and Hellenistic and Jewish religious propaganda indicate that the Church originated in a religiously pluralistic world. In this situation, mission acquired the characteristics of apologetics. The dual nature of apologetics as reasoned defense of religious claims and as the art of persuasion (promoting one's faith among others and motivating one's own people) sheds some new light on the mission-dialogue issue.

The significance of apologetics is that it is contextual. This means that christians respond to the challenges of their contemporaries by rendering account of their faith publicly, in the arena of business, politics, and competing world views. Since apologetics has an affinity to both mission and dialogue, it may assume a mediating function between them. Although religious competition is well in business today and some would have interreligious encounter more in the sense of confrontation than dialogue, the signs of the times call for interreligious communication and communion. Apologetics properly speaking would, therefore not sufficiently clarify the mission-dialogue issue unless it were modified. Such modification could be initiated through the concept of dialogue. Apologetics in our time must become dialogical. Dialogue adds a constructive and conciliatory note to apologetics while taking away its aggressive aspects. Dialogue requires both mutual repect for the otherness of the other and openness to be changed by the other. Naturally this view needs to be unfolded. This cannot be done within the framework of this paper. Instead, two central ideas for a reorientation of mission will conclude this outline.

Firstly, the key insights of the Bible--no matter under which rubric (Revelation, Missio Dei, Incarnation)--converge in the recognition of the divine mystery according to which God chooses to communicate with humanity throughout its history. If the God-world relationship means divine communication with humankind, then the Church-world relationship must, analogously, be one of communication. Theology of religion, in particular, should see its task in the translation of this basic biblical datum into the modern situation of religious pluralism. Its primary task is to illuminate the disturbing fact that God's dynamic in the world in and through his Holy Spirit is absolutely boundless, extensively as well as intensively. As a consequence, all Christian superiority complexes must be eradicated.

Secondly, Christian mission started as a movement among Jews. After the Holocaust, Christian misssion to the Jewish people seems impossible and dialogue utterly difficult. Without intending to minimize the formidable obstacles between Christians and Jews, we propose that a reorientation of mission must begin, on the one hand, with a decided departure from the missionary concepts of the colonial era and, on the other hand, with the promoting of communication with contemporary Judaism. The tentative Jewish-Christian approaches of the past years suggest that any missionary attempt would be offensive in the eyes of the Jewish partners. Yet the question of identity, indeed for both sides, is at stake. Christians and Jews cannot truly communicate without freely telling their stories: the story of God's odyssey with his people to this day (the Torah story) and the story of this odyssey including the journeys of Jesus from Bethlehem to Golgotha (the Torah-Christ story). Is it not the destiny of the Jewish and the Christian people to keep these stories alive so as to live by them and in the hope that one day God will write the ultimate conclusion? Is it too bold to assume that the credibility of Christian mission as dialogical apologetics will depend upon the communication between Jews and Christians? Christians must ask themselves seriously whether they can make any significant contribution to the transformation and humanization of our world if they fail to reach those who gave them all they have, the Jewish people.

NOTES

/1/ Gerard Vallee, "The Word of God and the Living Faiths of Men. Chronology and Bibliography of a Study Process," in Living Faiths and the Ecumenical Movement, ed. S. J. Samartha (Geneva: World council of Churches, 1971), pp. 165-182.

/2/ Carl F. Hallencreutz, New Approaches to Men of Other Faiths 1938-1968: A Theological Discussion (Geneva: World Council of Churches, 1970)

/3/ Interim Statement, drafted at the Nagpur Conference in 1961: Vallee, op. cit., p. 172.

/4/ Witness in Six Continents. Records of the Meeting of the Commission on World Mission and Evangelism of the World Council of Churches, Mexico City, December 8-9, 1963, ed. Ronald K. Orchard (London: Edinburgh House Press, 1964).

/5/ World Council of Churches, Study Encounter, Vol. III, No. 2, 1967.

/6/ Dialogue Between Men of Living Faiths. Papers presented at a Consultation held at Ajaltoun, Lebanon, March

1970, ed. S. J. Samartha (Geneva: World Council of Churches, 1971).

/7/ Text in Living Faiths and the Ecumenical Movement, pp.
33-45. The sections of the document are numbered.

/8/ Ibid. No. 12.

/9/ Text in Living Faiths and the Ecumenical Movement, pp.
47-54. The sections of the document are numbered.

/10/ Ibid., No. 7.

/11/ Ibid., No. 11.

/12/ Christian-Muslim Dialogue. Papers presented at the
Broumana Consultation, 12-18 July, 1972, Ed. S. J.
Samartha and J. B. Taylor (Geneva: World Council of
Churches, 1971.

/13/ Bangkok Assembly 1973: Minutes and Reports on the
Assembly of the Commission on World Mission and Evangelism
of the World Council of Churches, December 31, 1972, and
January 9-12, 1973 (Geneva: World Council of Churches,
1973).

/14/ No. 8 of the group report on the special subsection
of the section on "Culture and Identity."

/15/ Towards World Community. The Colombo Papers, ed. S.
J. Samartha (Geneva: World Council of Churcees, 1974).

/16/ Breaking Barriers: Nairobi 1975. The Official Report
of the Fifth Assembly of the World Council of Churches,
Nairobi, 23 November-10 December, 1975, ed. David M.
Paton (London: SPCK-Grand Rapids, Mich.: Wm. B. Eerdmans,
1976).

/17/ Ibid., pp. 72f.

/18/ See the reports of the General Assemblies at
Amsterdam, Evanston, New Delhi (in particular), Uppsala, and
Nairobi; and Jewish-Christian Dialogue: Six years of
Christian-Jewish Consultations. The Quest for World Com-

munity: Jewish and Christian Perspectives; published by the International Jewish Committee on Interreligious Consultations and the World Council of Churches' Sub-Unit on Dialogue with People of Living Faiths and Ideologies (Geneva: World Council of Churches, 1975). Valuable for actual information: World Council of Churches: The Church and the Jewish People. Newsletter (1972 onward).

/19/   World Council of Churches: The Church and the Jewish People Newsletter, No. 2, 1976, p. 16 (emphasis added).

/20/   World Council of Churches, Study Encounter, Vol. XI, No. 1, 1975, pp. 1-5 (Legon): pp. 6-I3 (Hongkong).

/21/   World Council of Churches, Study Encounter, Vol. IX, No. 4, 1973.

/22/   World Conference on Church and Society. Christians in the Technical and Social Revolutions of Our Time. Geneva: July 12-26, 1966 (Geneva: World Council of Churches, 1967).

/23/   World Council of Churches, Study Encounter, Vol. XI, No. 4, 1975.

/24/   Latin Text in Acta Apostolicae Sedis (AAS), 56, (1964), 609-659. English edition: Washington, D.C.: National Catholic Welfare Conference, 1964.

/25/   Latin text in AAS, 8 (1976). English version in L'Osservatore Romano (Weekly edition in English No. 52, Dec. 25, 1975, pp. I6, 11-13.

/26/   Walter M. Abbott, gen. ed., The Documents of Vatican II, New York/London: America Press/Geoffrey Chapman, 1966. We refer to the texts by giving the Latin titles taken from the initial phrases of the documents.

/27/   Proceedings and Statements of the General Assembly are found in L'Osservatore Romano (Weekly edition in English). Nos. 41-48, 1974.

/28/   See P. Rossano's definition of dialogue as specific activity and as a methodology of approach and the affinity

64

of the latter to mission in Secretariat for Non-Christians, Bulletin 2 (1967, No. 6) 134-145.

/29/ Guidelines and Suggestions for Implementing the Conciliar Declaration "Nostra Aetate" (Number Four), in Secretariat for Promoting Christian Unity, Information Service, No. 26, 1975/I, pp. 1-7.

/30/ Report on the seminar in Secretariat for Non-Christians, Bulletin 10 (1976, no. 30) pp. 5-13.

/31/ A remarkable drive for contextual theologies is visible for instance in Asia. See Asian Voices in Christian Theology, ed. and with intro. by Gerald H. Anderson (Maryknoll, New York: Orbis Books, 1976).

/32/ Thomas Berry, Religious Studies and the Global Community of Man (Paper read at a Colloquium held at Zurich, September 2-9, 1973, on Intercultural Cooperation. (emphasis added). Professor Berry (Director of the Riverdale Center of Religious research, Bronx, New York), has varied the same theme in other important papers, available as manuscripts, e. g., Future Forms of Religious Experience; The Christian Process; Christian Humanism; Cosmic Person and the Future of Man.

/33/ Such questions are raised, for instance, by James A. Sanders whose contributions to canonical research and comparative Midrash are most valuable for a reorientation of theology of mission. See among other works of Sanders: Torah and Canon Philadelphia. Fortress Press, 1972, 1974, "Reopening Old Questions about Scripture," Interpretation 28 (1974) 321-330, "Torah and Christ," Interpretation 29 (1975) 372-390; "Hermeneutics in True and False Prophecy," in Canon And Authority, ed. G. Coats et al. (Philadelphia: Fortress Press, 1971 (Festschrift Walter Zimmerli): "Adaptable for Life: The Nature and Function of Canon," forthcoming in the G. Ernest Wright Memorial Volume.

/34/ See, e.g., Elisabeth Schussler-Fiorenza, ed., Aspects of Religious Propaganda in Judaism and Early Christianity (Notre Dame, Ind.: University of Notre Dame Press, 1976).

List of Recommended Books

Dean, Thomas, Post-Theistic Thinking: The Marxist-Christian Dialogue in Radical Perspective. Philadelpia: Temple University Press, 1975.

Evers, Georg. Mission-Nichtchristliche Religionen Weltliche Welt. Dissertation. Munster: Verlag Aschendorf, 1974.

Fleischner, Eva. Judaism in German Christian Theology Since 1945: Christianity and Israel Considered in Terms of Mission. Metuchen, N. J.: The Scarecrow Press, Inc. and the American Theological Library Association, 1975.

Friedli, Richard. Fremdheit als Heimat. Auf der Suche nach einem Kriterium fur den Dialog Zwischen den Religionen. Freiburg, Switzerland: Universitatsverlag, 1974.

Gensichen, Hans Werner. Glaube fur die Welt; theologische Aspekte der Mission. Gutersloh: Verlagshaus G. Mohn, 1971.

Hallencreutz, Carl F. Dialogue and Community: Ecumenical Issues in Interreligious Relationships. Swedish Institute of Missionary Research, Uppsala/Studia Missionalia Upsaliensia 31, 1977.

Hick, John, ed. Truth and Dialogue: The Relationship between World Religions. London: Sheldon Press, 1974.

International Review of Mission 65 (1976, No. 260): Christian Mission and Islamic Da'wah.

Jurji, Edward J., ed. Religious Pluralism and World Community. Interfaith and Intercultural Communication. Leiden: E. J. Brill, 1969.

Knitter, Paul. Towards a Protestant Theology of Religions. A Case Study of Paul Althaus and Contemporary Attitudes. Marburg: N. G. Elwert Verlag, 1974.

Kontexte, Vol 5 (Essays on Dialogue, ed. by HansJurgen Schultz). Stuttgart/Berlin: Kreuz Verlag, 1969.

Mann, Ulrich, Das Christentum als absolute Religion, 3rd ed. Darmstadt: Wissenschaftliche Buchgesellschaft, 1974.

Neill, Stephen. Salvation Tomorrow. The Originality of Jesus Christ and the World's Religions. Nashville, Tenn.: Abingdon, 1976.

Nys, Hendrik. Le Salut sans l'Evangile. Etude historique et critique du probleme du "salut des infideles" dans la litterature theologique recente (1912-1964), Paris: Editions du Cerf, 1966.

Rutti, Ludwig, Zur Theologie der Mission. Kritische Analysen und neue Orientierungen (Dissertation). Munich/Mainz: Chr. Kaiser Verlag/Matthias Grunewald Verlag, 1972.

Samartha, Stanley J., Courage for Dialogue. (Collection of Essays between 1968-1975). Maryknoll, New York: Orbis Books, 1980.

Telmage, F. E. Disputation and Dialogue. Readings in the Jewish-Christian Encounter. New York: KTAV Publ. House, Inc., 1975.

Thils, G. Propos et problemes de la Theologie des Religions non-chretiennes (Eglise Vivante). Tournai-Paris: Casterman, 1966.

Thomas, M. M. Man and the Universe of Faiths, Interreligious Dialogue Series: No. 7 Madras: The Christian Literature Society, 1975.

Wolff, Otto. Anders an Gott glauber. Die Weltreligionen als Partner des Christentums. Stuttgart: Kohlhammer Verlag, 1969.

BASES AND BOUNDARIES

6

FOR INTERFAITH DIALOGUE:

A CHRISTIAN VIEWPOINT

Monika Konrad Hellwig

This paper is written directly from experience. It is not a survey of previously published scholarly and official church statements. While in itself useful and necessary, such a survey scarcely seems to serve the purpose of the present

Monika Konrad Hellwig (Roman Catholic) holds an M.A. and a Ph.D. (1968) from Catholic University of America, and completed other graduate studies at the Universities of Notre Dame, Oklahoma, and Pennsylvania. From 1962-64, she was a ghost-writer/research assistant at the Vatican, then handled the English Language Desk at Pius XII International Center in Rome. She taught at Catholic University and at DePaul, then became a lecturer at the Theology Dept. of Georgetown University, where she is now a full professor. She has frequently lectured and conducted workshops for diocesan and parish groups, clergy, etc., in the U.S., Venezuela, Ghana, Uganda, and Kenya. She has written numerous articles and several books, most recently The Eucharist and the Hunger of the World; she is also contributing to an interfaith collection of Passover Haggadah (ed. Leon Klenicki) and to Alan T. Davies' forthcoming Paulist Press book, Anti-Semitism and the Foundations of Christianity. She is an Associate Editor of the Journal of Ecumenical Studies.

This selection is from the Journal of Ecumenical Studies, 14, 1977, pp. 419-431. Reprinted by permission of the publisher.

68

dialogue. A statement from experience, on the other hand, is useful only in proportion to its fidelity to what is actually taking place within the community as a whole. The task of this paper, therefore, is understood as one of discerning within the Christian communities at present the possibilities for a deeper engagement in dialogue with the Jewish and Muslim communities, and discerning likewise the factors that may restrain the Christian communities from such deeper engagement. /2/ What may be the possibilities and restraints operating with the Jewish and Muslim communities is understood here to be the task of the complementary papers.

It must be acknowledged clearly at the outset that Christianity is not a univocal tradition, and that Christian communities and denominations today will not all agree to particular proposals concerning dialogue. In order that there may be a clear and sharp focus, this paper is presented primarily from the point of view of the Roman Catholic tradition, with an acknowledgement of major differences with other groups where appropriate. The task is further complicated by wide doctrinal variation even within particular churches and denominations, especially the range of positions from a strictly fundamentalist to a radically critical interpretation of documents and doctrines. /3/

It might at first sight appear that it is our common convictions that propel us to dialogue and our unique convictions that set the limits to that dialogue. A more complex pattern is here proposed: it is the very nature of the Christian's commitment to proclaim the experience of Jesus of Nazareth as Savior and Word of God that propels the Christian community to dialogue with respect for the freedom and the truth of the others. /4/ More particularly it propels Christians to a dialogue with other communities claiming a message of universal salvation. Among these the dialogue becomes more immediately urgent with those whose proclamation of universal salvation stems from the same biblical roots but branches out into quite different interpretations of history. /5/

This will certainly appear as a highly contrary thesis. Yet it is evident that if Christians could regard Jesus as savior of a statically defined Christian sector of the human race, there would be little urgency or theological need for dialogue. Christians could then live side by side with those of other persuasions, quietly minding their own business, inquiring perhaps into the folkways and beliefs of other communities for diplomatic or purely academic reasons. Such dialogue would remain forever peripheral to Christian theology and Christian identity. It is precisely because they proclaim a universal salvation, and proclaim the centrality of Jesus of Nazareth as a saving power in the history of the whole human race, that Christians are driven to dialogue by a systematic and practical exigence that arises out of the very center of the Christian understanding and commitment. The Christian understanding and commitment can not be authentically maintained within the Christian community if it is not in fact engaged in the continuous dynamic of serious dialogue with outsiders.

The subject matter of such dialogue obviously is not a debate over the conflicting truth claims of different traditions. Sober reflection on the nature of religious language and religious experience and on the cultural and epistemological bases of religious claims has long since convinced thinking persons of all traditions that there is no "unbiased" procedure by which to judge among the conflicting truth-claims of different traditions. The subject of such dialogue from the Christian viewpoint must be concerned with the nature of salvation. Because Christians are committed to proclaiming salvation in Jesus the Christ, they are required by their own commitment to seek an understanding of what salvation is, why it is linked to the person of Jesus, and how it can be universally meaningful. Christians are bound to tell their story and to listen in order to learn what others hear in it. Likewise they are bound to listen to the stories of the other traditions, to try to find out what their understanding of salvation is; why it is linked to particular persons, events, and teachings; and how it can be meaningful in terms of their own experience. They are bound to this simply by the demands for inner coherence of their own stance.

Thus far the need for dialogue would direct Christians equally toward Hindus, Buddhists, and even Marxists. But the demands become very much more urgent in relation to Jews and Muslims, though the pattern is not quite symmetrical in these two relationships. The Christian community looks toward the Jews with the claim that the Christian community, though still looking forward to a final fulfillment, has already experienced through the person of Jesus the definitive realization of the promises and hopes of Israel. For its own self-understanding, therefore, the Christian community is required to search not only for the sense in which those hopes and promises were understood by Israel before the time of Jesus, but also for the way they are understood now by those who expect salvation in the Jewish tradition and not through the person of Jesus of Nazareth. In other words, without intent to proselytize but rather for their own understanding of their own position. Christians are driven to ask Jews what it is that they expect and do not see in the person and followers of Jesus of Nazareth. /6/

When Christians turn in the direction of the Muslims, their question and their quest are somewhat different. In effect they must ask themselves, and therefore they must ask the Muslims, why the message of salvation in Jesus the Christ with its universal claim has in the course of history been complemented by a vast people, gathered from many nations, coming likewise to worship the god of Israel, but in a distinctively different tradition that denies the universality of the Christian claim. For their own self-understanding, Christians must ask themselves what the experience of being called to salvation is for those who are brought into submission to the one god as followers of the Prophet. They must ask wherein lies the difference between Christians and Muslims in the interpretation of the ancient hopes and promises passed on to them from Israel.

Of course, these questions to Jews and Muslims could be asked simply in the context of ethnology and of social and political and cultural history, and within these contexts they could be answered. But if these answers were to be taken as complete, they could lead only to a sense of the cultural relativity of all convictions and a certain cynical indifference to the truth claims of one's own tradition. The questions must be asked seriously in a theological context, expecting further insight into the various ways that the need for salvation is experienced and understood, and into the various ways that persons, events, and teachings promising salvation have been experienced and understood.

The dialogue concerning the meaning of salvation can not and does not take place in a vacuum, however. It assumes the meaning of some common terms and understandings and the need to explain some unique terms. What follows is an attempt to set out the more important points in each of these categories from the Christian perspective.

Chief among the common points of departure is certainly our understanding of the One God, transcendent, benign, provident, all-powerful, intervening in history to judge and redeem, self-revealing to those who seek, forever mysterious but offering the possibility of personal relationship in prayer and the direction of one's life. /7/ To know that others claim self-revelations from the same God that we ourselves worship is an invitation to discover the content of the revelation as perceived by the others. To know that others worship the same God that we worship is to know also that somewhere in our experience there lie possibilities for common prayer, though it may only be a prayer of wordless quiet. To hold that this God intervenes in history to judge and to redeem implies a willing ear for testimonies expressing perceptions from other traditions of the judgments and the redemption.

The basis for assuming that the three traditions are in a sense on common ground here is that for all three God is ultimately inscrutable mystery, and the self-revelation that is received is never exhaustive of the reality. Nor is that self-revelation ever apprehended in strictly appropriate concepts or in univocal images; religious language can only be the language of poetry, of analogy, of subtle hints of the inexpressible. From a fundamentalist position in which this is not admitted, there can be but little meaning to dialogue with a tradition other than one's own. If the assumption is made that not only the revelation, but all the language in which it is apprehended and expressed, is divinely guaranteed as timeless, changeless, beyond critical examination, having intrinsic and exclusive validity quite independent of historical and cultural conditioning, then there can not be a common ground from which dialogue between traditions can take place.

A second common point of departure is the (often unspoken) assumption that history has a goal, that time is

72

not only cyclic (which it assuredly is) but also linear, that salvation is not only a salvation of the human spirit from the world but is quite comprehensively salvation of the world. The god of the biblical religions is not seen as other than Master of the Universe. Lord of history, Lord of all being, and Ruler of the day of reckoning. All history is under God's judgment, and all peoples are God's people summoned to find their own fulfillment in doing God's will. That will is recognized constantly as justice--justice on a grand social scale, not only a certain relative justice in one-to-one relationships. /8/

This common base seems to offer very clear grounds for dialogue among the three traditions on matters of social justice and the relief of large-scale human suffering and deprivation. At least in theory, it offers a basis for meaningful dialogue in matters as thorny and urgent as colonial oppression, racial oppression, remnants of slave trading, the State of Israel, the plight of the Palestinians, various liberation struggles, societal role restrictions on women, deprivation of civil rights of certain groups, and so forth. These obviously are not points at which dialogue might be expected to begin, but neither may they be categorically ruled out as possible areas of dialogue. The self interest and mutual distrust of power groups may pose almost insurmountable obstacles, but the religious bases for dialogue on these issues exist in the teachings concerning a goal for all history, the ultimate unity of the whole human race before God, and the divine demand for social justice that does not exclude the poor and powerless.

Again, it must be noted that such a common base does not appear so clearly from positions more or less approx-imating the fundamentalist one. When it is understood that the law of God and the plan of God have been set forth once and for all, explicitly and in every detail, there can be little room for moral questions about new situations that arise in the course of time, and obedience to the divine will is readily reduced to private lives of individual persons and to certain archaic patterns of association in groups within the tradition. For dialogue among traditions there can even less room. Yet it must also be noted that such a common base seems to be equally absent in certain liberal positions which see almost all elements of the tradition as culturally relative and expendable, simply because such positions adapt very readily to fit the national or partisan interests of their own group, and they read the situation from that vantage point.

A third common base or point of departure is closely linked to the second, but does appear to be a different point. This is the election or vocation of each person and the election or vocation of the community. It is a calling to a way of life that is a communion with God and a call to community or peoplehood with prescribed patterns of relationship and duties toward others. The three traditions make reference to the same basic vocation stories concerning Noah, Abraham, and Moses, which are models of individual election but also of the election of the people. Each tradition interprets history rather differently in the light of these stories, in applying the election or calling to itself. Yet this appears as a common point of departure and as a conviction that rather peremptorily impels the traditions to dialogue with one another (as has indeed happened, peacefully or otherwise, since early times).

A community which claims to have been chosen in some special way as God's instrument of redemption of the world is compelled to ask itself how it stands in relation to other communities that claim a similar election from the same God, if only because of the need to define its own claim for its own members. Yet each community can really only come to an authentic answer to its own question in the process of open dialogue that solicits testimony from the other communities as to how they interpret their traditions and their election in the changing contexts of the present. There is no other way to distinguish oneself or one's position from others than that which begins with an attentive inquiry into the nature and the characteristics of the others.

It may seem paradoxical, yet it seems that it is the very universality and apparent mutual exclusivity of our claims that provides the necessary basis for a fruitful and substantive dialogue. Any position that attempts to reduce or obscure the claim to a unique election related to the universal plan of God would seem to reduce rather than enhance the foundations for dialogue. So, of course, will any position that sees the doctrine of election as simple, fully explicit, and univocal, and as having attained a timeless formula capable of direct and universal application. Any position between these two moves naturally into a dialogue in its quest for a more comprehensive and coherent understanding in the contemporary context.

A fourth common base has been quietly assumed in the presentation of the preceding three. This is the common heritage of biblical lore and spiritual ancestors. There is an available common language of symbols (found in persons and events), and an available common pool of models and points of reference. The biblical stories that form the common lore seem also to be precisely those that offer the most basic and universal insights and understandings, the most archetypal images and visions. Moreover, these biblical stories with their symbolism have remained both foundational and explicit in all three traditions. They carry assumptions and attitudes that may not be underestimated, as to creation, the providence of god in history, the nature of the faith response, or submission and obedience. It is, for instance, quite clear to Christians that when Jews and Muslims speak to each other about Isaac and Ishmael, each may not like what the other is saying, but they both understand very well what it is that they are discussing. Likewise, when Christians invoke the Pauline understanding of Isaac as the child of the promise, and claim thereby to be the true children of Abraham, Jews may object to the exegesis, but they object because they understand it. All of this offers a not insubstantial base for effective dialogue on important issues for the three traditions concerned.

Having given brief consideration to these four points of common basis, one is left with the task of considering those unique convictions or positions of Christianity which are bound to affect the possibilities of dialogue with the other two traditions. First and most obvious among these is the Christian perception of revelation and redemption as focused in the person of Jesus of Nazareth. At first sight this seems to be primarily a hindrance to dialogue, something for which the Christian community should apologize, explaining that it can do no other than to hold and proclaim this, but that it nevertheless wishes to enter into dialogue with its biblical neighbors.

As pointed out in the beginning of this paper, however, such an admission and apology would seem to be premature. If the aim in dialogue is a fuller understanding of the position of the other, in order the better to grasp the inner logic of one's own position and in order to achieve some clarity and authenticity in relations with the other tradition, then the central and constitutive claim on which one's own tradition rests must be placed centrally in the dialogue also. As such, if offers a rather solid platform for an exchange of perceptions and perspectives. In confrontation with Jews and Muslims, Christians must either be silent or must give an account of what the revelation and redemption are that they have experienced in the person of Jesus of Nazareth, and they must attempt this account in language other than the technical "churchy" language which already assumes the experience. They must attempt to account for their ex-perience and conviction in language that is experientially meaningful to those who are outsiders to the Christian tradition. Such attempts can not but be sources of thoroughgoing renewal within the Christian community itself, although they will be regarded as dangers to "the Faith" by those holding more fundamental positions in which the technical "churchy" language stands in its own right as divinely guaranteed. Likewise, such dialogue can not but be a source of more coherent relationsips with the outsiders to the tradition, although certain more liberal elements within the Christian tradition will see a danger to the ecumenical dialogue or dialogic endeavor whenever the unique claims and teachings are put forth as subject matter for interfaith conversation.

At this point, some crucial limits or restricting boundaries to the dialogue may be noted. They are not doctrinal but practical. Chrtistians can not speak very clearly about revelation and redemption experienced in Jesus of Nazareth, in the presence of Jews, because centuries of anti-Semitism and oppression obscure the testimony. Likewise, Christians have considerable difficulty inquiring of Jews concerning the Jewish understandoimg of revelation and redemption, because Jews tend to suspect a proselytizing drive and are conscious of being a minority for whom the possibility of discrimination, contempt and outright persecution is never remote. Even in Israel today, the situation can not be said to be substantially more favorable;

Jews readily interpret such inquiry as judgmental on the conduct of the State of Israel and its relations with the Palestinians, while Christians are embarrassed by being unable in conscience to give the unconditional approval to everything Israel does, which is often demanded as a prelude to serious dialogue. /12/

When Christians address themselves to Muslims in dialogue concerning revelation and redemption experienced in Jesus the Christ, and revelation and redemption as experienced according to the teachings of the Prophet Mohammed, there are again obstacles which are not doctrinal or theological, but rather practical and historical. Christian voices are heard by Muslims in the context of the Crusades and of colonialism under Christian auspices, so that any message of peace, humility, reconciliation and forgiveness sounds quite hollow. Moreover, the Christian gospel advocacy of simplicity of life and the blessedness of the poor is seen in the context of the colossal economic imperialism of the Christian West against which all Third World nations must contend. At the same time, the situation is not much better in the other direction, because Christians are likely to hear anything the Muslims say in the context of a fear of Holy Wars, internal violence in Muslim countries, terrorism, despotic governments, oppression of women and harsh persecution of non-Muslims. Much as this may be a caricature, it does in practice tend to cloud and obscure testimonies concerning the true nature of Islam.

These practical considerations may not be underestimated. The possibility for any genuine dialogue at all certainly depends on the willingness of some scholars and religious representatives to achieve a psychological distance from these historical and practical stumbling blocks, by willingness to consider not the achievements of the other parties but the aims and desires intrinsic in the religious position of each. More habitually each group evaluates its own position by its ideals and the position of the others by their performance. From this nothing but further prejudice and failure of understanding can arise.

Yet even when these problems have been somewhat overcome by persons and groups particularly dedicated to dialogue, there remains at all times the question as to the extent to which they represent their respective communities. It is a frequent experience that groups with a mandate from their communities to engage in dialogue draw up a coherent and far-reaching statement that represents real progress in mutual understanding among the partners to the dialogue, only to find at the end of their labors that the respective mandating authorities in their own communities will not approve the statement. Such statements are then frequently reduced to rather unsatisfactory evasions and compromises that were already in vogue before the dialogue was set up. What seems to be at stake is the question whether dialogue with the other traditions can be delegated to specialized groups or whether it must be conducted at the heart of the religious and theological enterprise of each community.

Having noted the negative aspects that restrict dialogue concerning the central issue for Christians, one must note two further unique convictions from the Christian viewpoint which play an important role in dialogue. One of these is the role of the church or, more accurately, of the many Christian churches which exist today in a state of considerable ambivalence toward one another. Though the churches do act`jointly on some issues, and although there have been great ecumenical advances in the contemporary experience, it must frankly be admitted that the Christian churches, claiming to live by the same gospel of Jesus the Christ, are in a condition of rather extensive dissociation from one another. There is a double disadvantage for interfaith dialogue in this condition of dissociation. Not only does the dialogue tend to represent and speak for some churches and not others, but the very concept of church and the understanding of the role of the church in the society at large and in the redemption do in fact vary widely from church to church. The primary referent in this essay is the self-understanding of the Roman Catholic Church.

The role of the church is bound to present problems to Jewish and Muslim partners in dialogue inasmuch as it is not coextensive with a people racially, ethnically, culturally, or politically. In fact, theologically, the church can only be understood as that community of witnesses that mediates between Jesus the Christ and the final realization of the Reign of God among all human persons and peoples which Jesus proclaimed and promised. The church may be understood as an assembling or a movement of such witnesses in history, although it most obviously appears as an institution and usually as a rather powerful hierarchic structure. As many reflective Christians view it today and have viewed it in the course of history, the church is necessarily a counterculture force, a critique of any established regime and social structure, a radicalizing force that judges every situation in relation to the views of the promised Reign of God. Clearly this is by no means the way the church (or the larger churches taken as a group) has in fact conducted itself in most matters throughout the history of Christianity. Therefore, although it may puzzle and antagonize the outsider to the Christian tradition, Christian partners in the dialogue may say without any sense of hypocrisy or inconsistency that "the church does not condone" actions and situations which the outsider sees being done by Christians and perhaps even by those who appear as church representatives.

The church claims to be the gathering of those who have been "reborn" in the experience that Jesus who was crucified and died has burst forth again in irrepressible and unquenchable vitality that permeates the whole human race and all history with new and undreamed of possibilities of fulfillment, reconciliation, and community in a double sense: they have witnessed in the rebirth in their own lives the coming of the Reign of God, and they bear witness to others by their community life, their hope, their service, and their transforming impact. They do this, ideally, "from within," that is, in community with similarly "reborn" persons--all willingly and creatively changing their relationships with one another to express what they have experienced.

In this ideal picture, the "elect among the nations" who are called to this witness function are not thereby cut off from their diverse cultural and political affiliations, though these all become relativized in the light of an over-riding interest in the community of all the human race--an interest which is most particularly concerned with the poor, the outcast, and the suffering, as perenially represented by the Crucified. /18/ The issue is of course immensely complicated by the fact that through the centuries, sometimes by conquest, sometimes by princely "conversion" of whole peoples, there came about the identification of Christianity with the whole of Western culture and with the political

79

structure of Europe, which we named Christendom, which was in due time extended to the whole of the North and South American continents. It is quite common to speak of these as "Christian nations, " and indeed, governments often invoke Christian beliefs in their support, as in the power struggles of the West with the Communist countries, but from the point of view of most Christian ecclesiologies (which strongly favor separation of church and state) the term is almost meaningless. /19/ Most Christians spokespersons, whether church officials or theologians, will not accept the actions of their governments as attributable to the Christian community as such.

The clarification of this position is obviously rather important to interfaith dialogue because both Jews and Muslims envisage as the ideal an integrated peoplehood in which the religious convictions are expressed in political, legal, economic and cultural as well as religious ritual forms. This sets some limits or boundaries to the dialogue, which again involved practical, historical as well as theoretical problems. It may be very puzzling and irritating to Jews that Christian nations and even Christian churches have stood so aloof in the Lebanese civil strife, instead of leaping to the defense of their "Christian brothers and sisters" against the Muslims of that country. Israeli Jews may find it hard to undestand that the so-called Christian nations do not experience any particular bond with the Christians of Lebanon, while all Jews may be horrified that the churches have generally been more concerned to disentangle the questions of social justice involved in the conflict than to support "their own."

A parallel problem arises in dialogue with Muslims, who frequently ask why Christian nations and Christians churches express support for the State of Israel when they should be supporting and defending their Arab Christian brothers and sisters from aggression, land expropriation, exile, deprivation of political rights, and harsh oppression. Thus Jews and Muslims use the same argument as an obstacle to dialogue, though for diametrically opposed practical purposes. The strong and fairly monolithic alignments of interest in the case of both Jews and Muslims on a worldwide basis render it urgent, but also difficult, for Christians to represent their own total allegiance to the gospel as taking priority over their qualified allegiance to any particular group. It may well be that it is only in the context of a three-way interfaith dialogue that this particular element of dialogue can be put in its proper perspective.

The last and most crucial point to be made concerning the unique claims and teachings in the Christian tradition is of course that of the trinitarian conception of God and the claim of divinity made on behalf of Jesus of Nazareth. It may seem at first sight that the very admission of these two doctrines simply vitiates all that has gone before. It seems so because the history of previous encounters over the centuries may suggest that interfaith dialogue comes to an impasse at that point. But previous encounters were conducted with a frame of reference much closer to simplistic fundamentalist positions, and much less aware of the cultural relativity and analogous nature of all religious language. It would seem to be supremely worthwhile to re-engage in dialogue precisely on these points, remembering again that the point of the dialogue is not proselytizing but the clarification of one's perception of the position of the others, in order thereby to clarify one's perception of one's own position and engage in more realistic and authentic relationships.

It should be no secret to Jews and Muslims that the doctrines of the trinitarian Godhead and of the divinity of Jesus have been and are the subjects of searching inquiry, reflection, and renewed attempts at appropriate formulation by Christian scholars within their own circles, quite apart from the demands of interfaith dialogue. At the risk of over-simplification within this limited space, it may be said very briefly what the minimal formulations of these ancient doctrines are. As to the Trinitarian "image" or conception of God, one may say with Josef Ratzinger that Christian faith is at pains to preserve at all costs a paradox it is not able logically to resolve--a paradox that reflects as faithfully as it can certain irreducible elements of the Christian experience. Christians worship the transcendent God of Israel, yet they know that in Jesus they had a self validating experience of what it is to be in the presence of God uttered or expressed within history and within the human community, and at the same time they know that their experience of the presence and the power of God was not only in the person of Jesus long ago in history, but is in the Spirit that is alive and active now within the community of believers. Moreover, Christian faith is committed to the confident conviction that these divine self-revelations may be trusted, that God is in inner reality truthfully as God is revealed to us in history, though the reality clearly transcends what human knowing and imagining can grasp. Jesus is experienced as the fullest possible, and therefore the definitive, self-expression of God in history and within the human community. Yet it must be said quickly that Jesus is not seen dissociated from the rest of the human race, but rather as "heading" or incorporating the human race within his own person and experience--a process that is seen as being yet unfinished.

The scandal of the particularity of the claims made for Jesus certainly stands at the heart of Christian faith, and raises the question as to the possibility of dialogue. Inasmuch as the religious language of the divinity claim--Son, Word, image, light from light, one in being with the Creator, and so forth--is capable of the most varied and nuanced interpretations, much careful exploration of the meaning would seem to be appropriate in interfaith dialogue. However, the appropriate pathway into this exploration is by way of that which can be judged by outsiders by reference to their own experience. With reference to Christology that approach is through the experiential analysis of what is meant by salvation and why Christians claim a foretaste of salvation in their association with Jesus as the Christ.

It would seem to be suitable to conclude this essay with the question whether there is a language or a model that might serve in such interfaith dialogue as has been envisaged here. A language and model that would seem to be appropriate from the point of view of all three traditions is the biblical notion of the covenant or alliance of God with the people. As presented in the Hebrew scriptures, there appears to be only one covenant, expressed in various modes of participation--the covenant of creation realized in the Noachic covenant, very precisely focused and explicitly expressed in the intimate participation of the Abrahamic and Mosaic covenant. Jews have been willing to grant that Christians and Muslims participate in the Noachic covenant, but both Christians and Muslims claim rather a complementary participation in the Abrahamic covenant, and each claims in its own way to bring that covenant to its consummation. Inasmuch as all three traditions own and understand this language of covenant, it seems to provide an appropriate arena for an exchange of the alternative interpretations of the history of salvation (and the salvation of history).

There is a further image that seems to offer a very viable context for dialogue, and that is the image of the seed and the tree with the two great branches, proposed by Yehuda Halevi. Israel sees itself as a witness people for God and as situated at the heart of the redemptive process, yet does not generally reach out in proselytizing efforts. Christianity and Islam see themselves as rooted in the revelation and promised redemption inherited from Israel, but as sent out to embrace all the nations. This much has not changed since the time of Yehuda Halevi, and the image appears to be as generative now as it was then.

NOTES

/1/   Such surveys are available, though none cover the whole area of the three-way dialogue. Besides the documents listed specifically in note 2 below, current official or semi-official instances of dialogue are recorded in the periodicals, SIDIC, Origins, The Bridge (all reporting mainly those encounters with Catholic participation), and in the various publications of the World Council of Churches (reporting mainly Protestant initiatives organized on an international scale). On the history of Jewish-Christian relations, there exists a huge literature. A very comprehensive bibliography is available in Roy A. Eckardt, Elder and Younger Brothers, (New York, Scribner's 1967) pp. 179-184.   The history of Christian-Islamic and Jewish-Islamic relations is not as readily or extensively accessible to English-speaking readers. An excellent "Introductory Bibliography" is offered in James Kritzeck, Sons of Abraham (Baltimore: Helicon, 1965), pp. 117-126.

/2/   For the Roman Catholic Community, the Documents of Vatican II have been taken as setting out an official Church consensus. They are available in Walter M. Abbott ed., The Documents of Vatican II (New York: America Press, 1966). Of particular interest are Lumen Gentium (the Dogmatic Constitution on the Church), pp. 14-96; Nostra Aetate (the Declaration on the Relationship of the Church to Non-Christian Religions), pp. 660-668. This last is further developed in relation to the Jewish community by the Guidelines for Jewish-Christian Relations, issued December 1, 1974, by the Vatican Commission for Relations with the Jews (Origins, January 9, 1975, pp. 463-464); by a statement on Pastoral Orientations with Regard to the Attitude of Christians towards Judaism, (La Croix, April 18, 1973); and by a pastoral message of U.S. Bishops, The Church and the Synagogue, issued November 20, 1975 (Origins, December 4, 1975, pp. 384-386).

In relation to Islam, the Declaration, Nostra Aetate, is further developed in Guidelines for a Dialogue between Muslims and Christians (Rome: Edizione Ancora, 1969), promulgated by Paul Cardinal Marella on behalf of the Vatican Secretariat for Non-Christians. The Tripoli statement, "Moslem-Christian Dialogue" of February 6, 1976 (made jointly by Vatican delegates and Muslim representatives), Origins, March 18, 1976, was not endorsed by the Vatican Secretariat.

Outside the Roman Catholic Church, the principal documents available are from the World Council of Churches but represent papers read by individual participants at W. C. C. conferences rather than statements of the Council as such. They include Dialogue between Men of Living Faiths (New York: World Council of Churches, 1973); Christian-Muslim Dialogue (New York: World Council of Churches, 1972); Jewish-Christian Dialogue: Six Years of Christian-Jewish Consultations (New York: World Council of Churches, 1975); and Toward World Community (New York: World Council of Churches, 1975).

/3/ By "strictly fundamentalist" is here meant that understanding which insists on the literal sense of the words as self-evident to the contemporary believer, By "radically critical" is meant that style of interpretation which is willing to submit the words to investigation by any and all available scholarly criteria from any discipline.

/4/ The assertion is made in conscious contradiction of the positions usually taken in dialogue situations, e.g., in almost all the documents listed in note 2 above.

/5/ This theme has been noted frequently and probably should be attributed originally to Judah Halevi, The Kuzari. See translation by Hartwig Hirschfeld (New York: Schocken, 1964), p. 227.

/6/ This thesis is consonant with the potentially significant but actually little noticed dialogic ecclesiology set out by Pope Paul VI in his inaugural Encyclical Letter, Ecclesiam Suam, August 6, 1964, A.A.S, Vol. 56 (1964), pp. 609-659, available in English translation. His Church (Huntingdon, IN: Our Sunday Visitor, Inc., 1964).

/7/ Almost all joint statements resulting from interfaith dialogue begin at this point; a clear example is in the Tripoli statement, Origins, March 18, 1976, p. 617.

/8/ Cf. Ibid., resolutions 3-9, p. 618.

/9/ This theme is set out rather clearly by Kritzeck, Sons of Abraham.

/10/ Ibid.

/11/ Contemporary Christian theology is already well stocked with efforts to do this in relation to the existentialist perceptions (e.g., the writings of Bultmann, Tillich, Rahner), in relation to the Marxist experience (e.g., the works of Moltmann, J. B. Metz, G. Gutierrez, and J. L. Segundo), and in relation to many other currents of thought and experience.

/12/ This observation is based on the author's own experience in Jerusalem among academics well disposed toward and well prepared for interfaith dialogue, during the academic year 1975-76.

/13/ This can certainly be said for the Jewish -Christian statement that was drawn up before Vatican II, in relation to what appeared in the approved texts, and again for the repeated efforts of the Vatican's post-conciliar commission.

/14/ The author is indebted to Juan Luis Segundo for this insight, which is a recurring theme in the latter's writings.

/15/ These conflicting models are expressed very clearly in Lumen Gentium.

/16/ Cf. Hans Kung, Structures of the Church (Notre Dame, IN; University of Notre Dame Press, 1964), and The Church (New York: Sheed & Ward, 1967). Also, J. B. Metz, ed., The Church and the World of Politics (New York: Paulist Press, 1967).

/17/ For an analysis of the various models and perceptions of the church, see Avery Dulles, Models of the Church (Garden City: Doubleday, 1974). And cf. Pier Cesare Bori, Koinonia (Brescia: Paideia Editrice, 1972).

/18/ Cf. J. B. Metz, "The Future in the Memory of Suffering," in J. B. Metz, ed., New Questions on God (New York: Herder, 1972), pp. 9-25.

/19/ This has not always been so and is not universally so now. For example, Spanish and Portuguese colonialism were officially sanctioned by the Catholic Church, while the Church of England is nationally established in a bond of mutual support with the government.

/20/ The author has heard both positions expressed rather frequently.

/21/ Expressed vigorously to the author by Muslim Arabs both in the U.S. and during a stay on the West Bank.

/22/ E.g., in Paul Tillich, Systematic Theology (Chicago: University of Chicago Press, 1951); in Karl Rahner, Theological Investigations, especially Vol. 13 (New York: Seabury,1975); in Jurgen Moltmann, The Crucified God (New York: Harper, 1974): in the various Christologies of the "process theologians"; etc.

/23/ There is no possibility for present unanimity among Christians on this point; therefore, particular and generally accepted authors are followed here.

/24/   Josef Ratzinger, Introduction to Christianity (New York: Herder, 1970), Part I, Chap 5.

/25/   Cf. Ibid., especially Part II, and Piet Schoonenberg, The Christ (New York: Herder, 1971).

/26/   Cf. Kritzeck, Sons of Abraham.

/27/   Ibid., p. 227.

THE FAILURE OF DIALECTIC

7

IN HENDRIK KRAEMER'S EVALUATION

OF NON-CHRISTIAN FAITH

Antonio R. Gualteri

Introduction: Problem and Context

Careful attention to the thought of Hendrik Kraemer is warranted not only by the intrinsic merit and stimulation of his thought, but also by the historical fact that in the last three and a half decades reflection upon the Christian mission and the proper attitude toward other religions has

---

Antonio Roberto Gualtieri (United Church of Canada) is associate professor of religion at Carleton University, Ottawa, on whose faculty he has served since 1967. He was previously instructor and lecturer in religion and college chaplain at Vassar College; pastor of two congregations in Quebec and Ontario; and a summer chaplain for the Royal Canadian Air Force. He holds the B. A., B. D., S. T. M., and Ph.D. (in history of religions) from McGill University, and had a travelling fellowship to the Fascotta Valdese di Teologia in Rome. He has published a dozen scholarly articles and a chapter in Religion and Culture in Canada, ed. Peter Slater (1977). He was ordained in 1955.

This paper is a revision of one read at the International Association of the History of Religions, University of Lancaster, August 15-22, 1975. Taken from the Journal of Ecumenical Studies., 15, 1978, pp. 274-90. Reprinted by permission of the publisher.

proceeded by taking up a position relative to Kraemer's, either by way of endorsement or by way of repudiation. A former missionary in Indonesia, he was asked to prepare a study guide for the International Missionary Council Meeting at Tambaram in India in 1938. This was subsequently published as The Christian Message in a Non-Christian World, /1/ and became the standard against which to formulate one's own views of the relationship of Christian to non-Christian faith.

Subsequent to his missionary service in the then Dutch East Indies, Kraemer was appointed Professor of the History of Religions at Leiden University. This was followed by a period as the first Director of the World Council of Churches' Ecumenical Institute at Celigny, Switzerland. His academic career was resumed at Union Theological Seminary in New York and at Princeton Theological Seminary.

In the two decades or so following his Tambaran study of 1938, Kraemer published two large books (Religion and the Christian Faith and World Cultures and World Religions) on much the same subject, but they were concerned on the whole to clarify and amplify the positions already set out in the earlier work. Kraemer says explicitly:

"As a whole, notwithstanding my frank acknowledgment of deficiency in treatment, I continue to hold strongly to the main theses of The Christian Message in a Non-Christian World. The present book is partly an endeavour to remedy the deficiencies of that book and to treat the same subject in a different way, without any real change in my standpoints of 1938." /2/

In a later article, Kraemer challengingly declared: "A radical rethinking and re-shaping is...imperiously demanded, if we discern the signs of the time and are willing to learn to walk in new ways of obedience to the Lord Jesus Christ." /3/ In view of this promise of a radical reorientation to the non-Christian religions, the subsequent publication of his World Cultures and World Religions /4/ was a disappointing historical survey of religious communities that broke no fundamentally new ground for the theology of religions. Kraemer's judgements on the non-Christian religions remain, nevertheless, a powerful influence, as the allusions to his position in books on the theology of revelation and missions indicate. Given the prominence attained by his thought, most of the books on missiology published after 1938 are obliged to make reference to Kraemer's position and to indicate how their own resembles it or differs from it.

But Kraemer's thought continues to be important apart from his historical influence. It possesses inherent significance inasmuch as the type of theological position and missionary outlook exemplified by Kraemer continues to be an operative factor in the conservative Christianity that still abounds (and probably increases) in spite of the neo-liberal reaction to orthodoxy during the 1960's.

Although Hendrik Kraemer also approaches the study of religion as a phenomenologist, his writings reflect for the most part a theological method. Put simply, theology of religions entails raising evaluative judgments on religious traditions and faith according to norms derived from a particular tradition looked upon by the theologian as true in some sense. The burden of Kraemer's intellectual work has been to frame a theological statement of the attitude toward non-Christian religions which is consistent with the revelation in Christ as he apprehends it.

My approach in this study of Kraemer's thought is to subject it to a critical analysis which focuses on the validity of certain logical inferences he draws (or fails to draw) from some of his own theological assumptions. To anticipate the conclusion, my argument attempts to show that Kraemer's attitude toward non-Christian faith--on his own premises of what a dialectical judgment entails--is not in fact dialectical, but rejectionist. There is, nevertheless, a constructive implication in my program. The demonstration of deficiencies in Kraemer's conclusions at certain points and of contradictions within his own system should induce a reconsideration of his theology of religions and its application to missiology.

This, of course, entails as a precondition as fair and accurate a description of Kraemer's position as I am able to give. To avoid the tiresome repetition of qualifiers such as "presumptive," "alleged," or "putative," I have made what might at times seem bold normative statements about God,

90

humanity, and the world. At these points, my intent has been for the most part simply to describe Kraemer's understanding (and, to a lesser extent, that of other Christians) regarding Christian life and teaching.

I. Non-Christian Religion as Human Achievement

1. Subsumption of Non-Christian Religions under Category of Human Achievement

When Kraemer turns to the problem of the correct Christian attitude toward and evaluation of non-Christian religions, he adopts a perspective that irrevocably determines the solution at which he will arrive. He makes the judgment that the non-Christian religions are part of the world and must be understood and appreciated as such. "The attitude towards the non-Christian religions is to be seen in the context of the general problem of the relation of Christianity to the world and its spheres of life." /5/

By "the world" Kraemer means, basically, human achievements. More specifically, the non-Christian religions are examples of human creativity in its self-transcending aspect, that is, its attempt to overcome the limitations of human finitude and guilt. Religions are the effort and achievement of the human quest for a satisfying view of and relation to existence. In characterizing this natural human endeavor toward spiritual self-affirmation, Kraemer says, "All religions....are the various efforts of man to apprehend the totality of existence." /6/ This drive toward an apprehension of and integration with the totality of existence is analyzed as human effort and is ascribed to the universal religious consciousness that is part of the human constitution.

In his preface to Religion and Christian Faith, Kraemer acknowledges that this stress on the world religions as human achievements was overstated in his earlier book, The Christian Message in a Non-Christian World, and that he should have pointed out more fully how the religions outside the biblical sphere of revelation are loci of divine encounter. This omission he seeks to redress in the later volume, yet he asserts: "It does not mean, however, that I reject my former thesis that there is a great amount of human achievement in

91

all religions." /7/ It is very difficult, in fact, to discern much significant development in Kraemer's thought between these two books.

It is my view that, given Kraemer's theological judgment upon human nature, his initial stance--his decision to subsume non-Christian faith under human achievement--is incorrect and disastrous for a proper understanding of the faith of other people.

2. Implication of this Classification

It follows that once the problem of the attitude toward non-Christian religions is seen as a specimen of the general problem of assessing the world (understood here as human values and creativity), then its resolution lies in ascertaining the proper status of the world. Kraemer follows the logic of the argument for he says, "The question behind this root-problem is always in some form or another: What do you think about man, his nature, his possibilities, his achievements?" /8/ The judgment made about people and their works will also be the correct appraisal of non-Christian religions. As Kraemer says: "To define our attitude towards these religions virtually menas to affirm our conception of man and his faculties, to pass judgment on our fellow-man and his aspirations, attainments and aberrations." /9/

3. Grounds for Regarding Non-Christian Religions as Human Achievement

It is important to understand what leads Kraemer to make this judgment that non-Christian religions are human attempts at self-transcendence that remain tainted with human presumption and self-glorification. He gives three reasons:

a. Cultural Corollary of Religious Faith. The first is that religions are not restricted and isolated traditions; rather, they are exhaustive life enterprises. In this regard Kraemer writes: "These non-Christian religions, however, are all inclusive systems and theories of life, rooted in a religious basis, and therefore at the same time embrace a system of culture and civilization and a definite structure of society and state." /10/ Kraemer uses the fact that religion externalizes itself in comprehensive culture as an argument to justify the treatment of religious traditions and faiths as instances of human achievement rather than the result of revelatory acts of God. But surely such an inference is unwarranted. Its effect is to deny an incarnational principle to any faith. Faith that does not find expression in society, in law and culture, is not authentic faith even from a purely human or secular perspective. The very meaning of faith is that it is the ultimate conviction and value by which one organizes one's life and all its spheres. It must, therefore, by definition, externalize itself in all decisive human activities.

Indeed, one significant criterion for assessing the worth of respective faiths is precisely the degree to which they succeed in producing inclusive patterns of life. A faith that restricts itself to a religious or sacred sphere and attempts to remain aloof from the material and social travails of human beings would rank very poorly in a hierarchy of faiths. Kraemer's contention that non-Christian religion is a human achievement because it embraces culture and civilization and therefore must be judged as the "world" is--on his own incarnational theological premises--an untenable position.

b. Role of Natural Theology. Kraemer adduces a second reason for placing non-Christian religions within the category of the world. It is occasioned by his decision in his earlier work to deal with the problem of the attitude toward non-Christian religions in the traditional way, that is, by reference to the concepts of natural theology and general revelation. /11/ His train of argument then unfolds in this way:

First, it must be seen that extra-biblical knowledge of God--i. e., knowledge derived from natural creation--is patently a human activity. It is the employment of natural reason (i. e., reason unaided by supernatural grace) to establish belief in God's existence and activity, through inferences drawn from nature, history, and conscience. The results of natural reason's inferential activity are properly placed within the world, that is, they are human achievement rather than gracious divine action. The second move in Kraemer's argument is that such knowledge of God as may exist in non-Christian religions is the result of natural theology. It follows logically that if natural theology is a human achievement and if the non-Christian religions are natural theology, then the non-Christian religions must be human accomplishments and not, speaking in a strict biblical sense, revelation.

But both of these assumptions of Kraemer's are open to question as he himself begins to see in his later work in Religion and the Christian Faith. In the first place, is it true that all knowledge of God not derived through special historical revelation--that is, all knowledge received through nature, history, and conscience--is natural theology in its sense of inferences made by natural (supernaturally unaided) reason? The more probable answer among modern Christian theologians--certainly on the Protestant side--is that any significant knowledge of God that exists outside of special historical acts of revelation and redemption exists not in the form of rational inferences from creation but rather as the living communication of divine presence through the media of creation. /12/ In other words, natural theology and general revelation must be clearly distinguished. "Natural theology" may be retained to designate that intellectual activity that seeks to establish the existence of God (more precisely, a philosophical Absolute) and some divine characteristics, by drawing logically valid inferences from mundane existence. It is not our concern here whether such attempts are able to withstand logical scrutiny (I believe they are not); our pur- pose here is simply to designate a traditional way to an alleged knowledge of God.

The term "general revelation" serves most adequately to denote that knowledge of God that is seen as coming from creation, not as an inference, but as an immediate disclosure of the living God who uses creation to manifest constant presence, concern, and majesty.

This insistence upon the distinction between natural theology and general revelation is important. While it is an easy matter to regard natural theology as a human activity and, therefore, to judge it on the same basis as one judges any human accomplishments in the world--subject to demonic perversion and potentially instruments of self- glorification--one cannot make the same easy assessment of general revelation. For in general revelation the gracious activity of God is stressed; here the stress falls on revelation even though its locus is outside the history of Israel and Christ considered normative by Christians. This universal or general revelation is patently not (or not only) a human achievement.

The great non-Christian religions are not primarily theoretical explanations of existence in the manner of natural theology. They are ways of redemption that attempt to answer the existential crises of persons by putting them in touch with ultimate reality value, and meaning. Even if it were established that such came not through a special revelation in history and personality, such theological apprehension would still not be of the order of natural theology. It would, instead, be the result of general revelation. It would entail an experienced contact with ultimate reality and not a human explanatory hypothesis to account for the world and its phenomena. Accordingly, Kraemer's condemnatory appraisal of non-Christian traditions and faith that proceeded by classing them as natural theology and then invoking the theologically pejorative designation of human endeavor is unwarranted. They do not belong in that category.

Ultimately the foregoing analysis that distinguishes natural theology (a human endeavor) from general revelation (a divine initiative) is not directly relevant to the problem of the Christian's attitude toward non-Christian religions cannot be accurately viewed as natural theology, that is, derived from creation inferentially. But neither are they derived from creation as general revelation. Just as the Christian's primary inspiration is not the perception of God in nature, profane history, and personality but, rather, the historical Christ-event, so it is with the other great faiths. They may encounter God in creation, but their foundational inspiration is the emergence of an historical seer, teacher, prophet, or savior. /13/

Between the writing of Christian Message in a Non-- Christian World (1928) and Religion and the Christian Faith (1956) Kraemer came to see (though not clearly) the inappropriateness of regarding non-Christian religions as natural theology or even as general revelation. He rejects

95

the solution of the problem of the relation of Christian and non Christian faiths in terms of the general-special revelation formula because there is an historical specialty in all the non-Christian religions that prohibits their subsumption under the heading of general revelation. Each of the great religions has its own specific slant and genius. But though this specific reason for regarding non-Christian religions is called into question, Kraemer's theological assessment of non-Christian faith remains basically unaltered.

c. The Demands of Kraemer's Theological Starting Point. Kraemer's view of non-Christian religions as human achievement can be explained in part by his understanding of the Christian revelation. Kraemer seeks always to develop his thought consistently with his conviction that God, in Christ, has spoken a uniquely decisive revelatory and redemptive word to humanity. The judgment that the other great religions are essentially the results of human endeavor seems required, in his eyes, by the acceptance of Christ as the absolutely authoritative and final revelation. Christ is the norm for evaluating all human creativity and culture. Moreover the redemptive act in Christ is universally efficacious; it is for all people at all times who are summoned to respond to the announcement of the saving deed with faith. In the basis of these assumptions, Kraemer infers--it seems by depriving the non-Christian religions of the status of normative and effective revelation--that they must be fundamentally human creations. He concludes: "All religions, the so-called 'higher' as well as the so-called 'lower' ones, all philosophies and world-views, are the various efforts of man to apprehend the totality of existence." /14/

II. The Dialectical Character of Humans and their Achievement

1. The Dialectical Character of Human Achievement

Non-Christian religious tradition and faith having been classified as human achievement, Kraemer then poses the question: What is the spiritual value of human nature and its cultural and religious expressions? Human nature and its achievements, including the human religious consciousness and its expressions, have a dialectical quality: human beings are in the image of God but are also fallen. Our personal existence is the arena of impulses toward good and toward evil. "This fundamental disharmony is also manifested in all the spheres of life in which man moves, and in his cultural and religious achievements." /15/

This being the case, the evaluation of the non-Christian religions is dialectical. They are neither totally repudiated, nor are they favorably regarded without qualification as loci of divine encounter and salvation. A straightforward answer is impossible for the question: "Is God revealed--and if so, how and where--in non-Christian religious life?" For though God is in some sense operative in the universal religious consciousness that externalizes itself in the religions, so also is the downward pull of human sin. The resulting religious manifestations will, therefore, be highly ambiguous and of doubtful soteriological value.

Kraemer's dialectical evaluation of non-Christian religion is expressed in the following:

"The religious and moral life of man is man's achievement, but also God's wrestling with him; it manifests a receptivity to God, but at the same time an inexcusable disobedience and blindness to God. The world fails to know God even in its highest wisdom, although it strives to do so. Man seeks God and at the same time flees from Him in his seeking because his self-assertive, self-centredness of will, his root-sin always breaks through. /16/

2. Kraemer's Dialectical Anthropology

Kraemer brings out the ambivalent character of humanity's personal existence in his exposition of Genesis 1-3 to which he turns in his survey of the light that the Bible sheds on the problem of the true assessment of non-Christian faith. His examination of the myths of the human creation in the image of God and of the fall, leads him to conclude that humanity exists in a dialectical situation. Paradoxically, we are at the same time both in the image of God and fallen. Discussions about the degree to which the image has been defaced by Adam's rebellion and the fall are misguided. They are the result of applying an excessively rationalistic and schematic mode of thinking to concrete myths that are not primarily intended to serve as material for this type of approach. Their chief appeal is to the inspired imagination. They are not, therefore, properly understood by subjecting them to an analysis that seeks to specify what measure of the divine image remains to historical man and woman. Rather, as Kraemer tells us, "These conclusions are paradoxical: man is still in the 'image of God' and at the same time man has lost it entirely." /17/

Kraemer describes this historical dialectical condition more fully:

"The mythical story expresses far more effectively than theological or philosophical conceptual languages ever could, that the truth about man is that he, in religious, moral and psychological respects, i. e., in his total being, finds himself through the Fall in an inescapably dialectical condition; related to God--separated from Him; sought by God ("Adam where art thou: God's self-disclosure to man) and haunted by him--rebelling against Him and yet groping towards Him." /18/

The relevance of this understanding of the creation and fall myths for the problem of evaluating non-Christian faith is that the dialectical character of existential humanity to which they point enables Kraemer to assess the non-Christian religion as dialectical in nature themselves. The intermediate step in the train of reasoning that leads to this conclusion is, we have already noted, his subsumption of non-Christian religion under the classification of human achievement. We have also discerned that the reasons advanced for this postulate are problematic in the extreme. But throughout his work the premise that non-Christian religion is fundamentally a human effort and, therefore, the reflection of existential human nature, remains one of the assumptions that governs the direction of Kraemer's theological evaluation of non-- Christian faith.

If non-Christian religion is a human endeavor, then it will be infected with ambiguity that typifies its human creator. The non-Christian religions will exhibit an aspiration toward the transcendent source of their spiritually and morally edifying features. They will at the same time give evidence of the corruption that flows inevitably from human attempts at self-justification and the establishment of the human ego as the supreme authority in the universe.

In Religion and the Christian Faith this argument is modified only slightly by the more deliberate use of the concept of religious consciousness. There Kraemer writes that "This dialectical condition (exemplified by the Genesis myth)' is the constitutive element of man's religious consciousness." /9/ This means that the historical religious systems that issue from the human religious consciousness will reflect this dialectical character. They will be both good and bad, both godly and satanic.

Kraemer asserts that "religion and the religious conscious or unconscious responses to God (are) wrong, partly right, sometimes really right." /20/ And further: "The Bible speaks in unmitigated terms about the expressions of the religious and moral conscience of man as idolatry, spiritual adultery, manifestation of the divine wrath. And yet at the same time it hints at his response to God in various ways." /21/ This is to say that human religious responses have a dialectical quality; they are neither always false nor always true, nor are they simply a constant ambiguous mixture: Their value is not formulable in a permanent generalization.

Recourse to the notion of the dialectical religious consciousness, however, adds nothing substantially to the evaluative conclusions already formulated in The Christian Message in a Non-Christian World on the basis of Kraemer's anthropological doctrine.

3. The Revelational Implication of Kraemer's Dialectical Evaluation.

Kraemer's dialectical evaluation of non-Christian religion is in large part explicated within the context of his discussion of revelation. Saving knowledge of God, Kraemer argues, i. e., the morally authenticated presence of the divine in the believer, cannot be generated from within the nature and capabilities of humankind. To espouse this possibility is to capitulate to an autonomous humanism.

Religion of this sort, whatever its theistic pretensions, would truly be a human achievement and, as such, devoid of saving knowledge of God. Instead, knowledge of God must originate in God's gracious revelatory act. This could be conceived, as we have already noted, as universal revelation in creation or as a special historical disclosure through a religious savior or seer--akin, structurally, to the function of Christ. Kraemer, in Religion and the Christian Faith, rightly questions the category of general revelation as applicable to the historic individuality of the diverse religious traditions. He seems, however, unwilling to concede to them the remaining logical alternative of special, historical revelation.

And yet, the frank recognition of authentic divine revelation in the non-Christian religious traditions is necessary if Kraemer's dialectical evaluation is to be maintained. For it is revelation that imparts that objective knowledge of God which even when perverted by sin, retains some partial evidence of its divine origin. Only if the positive pole of the dialectical judgment is constituted by a genuine divine disclosure can we talk of a truly dialectical situation in which knowledge and worship of God are mingled with human blindness and self-worship. Otherwise, we have only the product of the transcendent human imagination and no true dialectic between gracious divine relevation and human auto-justification. The groping toward transcendence implanted in the hearts of human beings in virtue of our human nature must receive an answer in an objective act of divine revelation if there is to be such validity in religious life that would justify even a dialectical evaluation. Failing this, the correct evaluative category is not "dialectical" but "repudiation."

Kraemer sometimes maintains some sort of limited divine activity or revelatory quality in the non-Christian religions. It is, therefore, logically perplexing to find him referring to them as human achievements. He fails to see that if the religious life of non-Christians were explicable as human effort then his evaluational category of "dialectical" would be inapplicable. A dialectical view is only possible where there is true disclosure eliciting human response.

A considerable number of passages in Kraemer's work, however, suggest that the positive side of the dialectical judgment of non-Christian religious life is constituted not by the distorted-but-nevertheless-genuine revelation of God, but merely by the groping after God motivated by the transcendent restlessness occasioned in human beings by our creation with a spiritual nature (the imago dei). In discussing the possibility of points of contact between the revelation in Christ and non-Christian religious life, Kraemer speaks of "discovering in the revealing light of Christ the fundamental misdirection that dominates all religious life and at the same time the groping for God which throbs in this misdirection." /22/

If the positive side of the dialectical relationship to God is composed merely of this inherent human groping for transcendence, then it remains from the standpoint of revelation only a formal characteristic with no material content of revelation. In this case the products of the religious life can accurately be described as human accomplishments with the attendant strictures upon them from the Christian theological premise of justification by grace.

What then is Kraemer's final judgment on the nature of the positive side of his dialectical judgment? Kraemer's failure to distinguish divine revelation in non-Christian religious life from an immanent human disposition toward self-transcendence is evidence of his dismaying lack of precision which makes a clear answer difficult. Ultimately, certain verbal protestations to the contrary, the main direction of his thought conveys a negative verdict on non-Christian religious faith. It is not a place of redemptive meeting with God in any meaningful sense.

In an "Appended Note" in Religion and the Christian Faith, Kraemer attempts to meet some of the criticisms leveled against his earlier book, The Christian Message in a Non-Christian World. He concedes that "We have far too one-sidedly characterized the religions as human performances and achievements, good or bad, and dealt with them too unilaterally as purely human products. Only in short parentheses have we expressed the opinion that God is somehow active in these religions too. /23/

And yet Kraemer has done little to rectify this generally negative judgment on other religions. His declaration of a dialectical evaluation is unsubstantiated and inconsistent, since we are not given an unequivocal answer to the crucial question: Are the non-Christian traditions and the religious selfhood they inspire responses to divine initiatives and continuing vehicles of God's saving grace and of redemptive knowledge? Where the attempt is made to extract a dominant motif from Kraemer's ambiguous thought on this issue it still appears ultimately as a disavowal of the revelatory and redemptive power of non-Christian religious faith. Though Kraemer refers to his position regarding non-Christian religious faith as dialectical, thus encouraging his readers to believe that it entails a qualified positive estimate of non-Christian faith along with its partial rejection, his resultant view is, in reality, one of repudiation. /24/ His claim that he now (in 1956) takes "a far more dialectical view" may have expressed his growing doubt about the adequacy of his theology of religions, but he had not moved beyond doubt to systematic reformulation. /25/

III. Empirical Christianity and the Non-Christian Religions

1. The Concept of Empirical Christianity

An important but perplexing clue to understanding Kraemer's appraisal of non-Christian religion is the relation of what he terms "empirical Christianity" to the non-Christian religions. On numerous occasions Kraemer states that the non-Christian religions and empirical Christianity are correctly classed together and are, from the perspective of the biblical revelation, evaluated identically (i.e., dialectically). He writes: "We have learnt --or at least ought to have learnt--that empirical Christianity is just as much an example of religion in general as the other religions are. /26/ Their appraisal is, accordingly, essentially the same: "We have acquired the freedom to apply to empirical Christianity the same dialectical and 'totalitarian' view as to other religions." /27/

2. Ambiguity in the Source and Evaluation of Empirical Christianity

It is illuminating to apply Kraemer's understanding of the dialectical character of empirical Christianity to

102

non-Christian religions to ascertain whether their designations as dialectical are, in fact, congruent. There is, unfortunately, considerable ambiguity in Kraemer's analysis and estimate of empirical Christianity. This is readily detected by inquiring into the source of empirical Christianity. Here we meet a contradiction.

On the one hand, he tells us that empirical Christianity is, like the non-Christian religions, a manifestation of the universal religious consciousness. Kraemer further maintains that as such it is essentially a human achievement. In this regard he writes:

"Whosoever has learnt, with the aid of the science of comparative religion, to look honestly in the face the empirical reality of Christianity--I am not now speaking about the Christian revelation and its reality--and of the other religions, and has understood that Christianity as an historical religious body is thoroughly human, that is, a combination of sublime and abject and tolerable elements, will feel deeply that to speak glibly of the superiority of Christianity is offensive." /28/

This suggests a view of empirical Christianity as a human affair, essentially of the same order as the non--Christian religions. There are, on the other hand, indications that empirical Christianity, though not to be identified with the original revelatory events which alone are absolutely authoritative, nevertheless derives from them and is an expression in history of their revelatory character. The following statement supports this conclusion: "We have also, fortunately, unlearned the rash and erroneous identification of empirical Christianity with the revelation in Christ in consequence of which this empirical Christianity, which belongs to the relative sphere of history, was wrongly regarded and treated as of absolute character." /29/ To this must be added:

"This revelation, this repeated divine initiative has in the course of history engendered many ideas, concepts and experiences that are subject to the vicissitudes of ordinary human development; but they are never adequate to or to be identified with the revelation from which they flow. The ideas and concerns are derivations from and not the genuine content of this revelation." /30/

Further evidence supporting the judgment that Kraemer believes (though not consistently) that empirical Christianity, because of its character as a product of true historical revelation, enjoys a different and superior status over the non-Christian religions is found in the following: "There is only one great difference between empirical Christianity and the other faiths. Empirical Christianity has stood and stands under continuous and direct influence and judgment of the revelation in Christ and is in virtue thereof in a different position from the other religions." /31/ This sense of standing under the judgment of the revelation in Christ leads to a reforming self-criticism when the discrepancy between the actual practice of the Christian community and the perfection of the righteous and holy God disclosed in Christ is discerned:

"The truly remarkable thing about Christianity as an historic and empirical reality, which differentiates it from all other religions, is rather that radical self-criticism is one of its chief characteristics, because the revelation in Christ to which it testifies erects the absolute superiority of God's holy Will and Judgment over all life, historical Christianity included." /32/

Analysis of these two theories regarding the source of empirical Christianity sheds light on the sense in which Kraemer conceives Christianity to be dialectical. It can be discerned that two different meanings are possible. If empirical Christianity has its source in religious consciousness, then it is only a reflection of the dialectical tension within human nature between an aspiration toward self-transcendence and one toward self-aggrandizement. However, if it has its source in an objective act of divine revelation, then it is dialectical in another more theologically significant way--both as a genuine response to the revelation in Christ and as historical perversion through prideful self-assertion of this prevenient revelatory truth.

Kraemer's statements, in fact, support both inter-pretations and it appears that, though he intends to function with only one sense, he sometimes slips into divergent meanings. When he classes empirical Christianity and non-Christian religions together, he is functioning with the first understanding of dialectical, that is, religion as expressive of an ambivalent human nature torn between a quest for transcendence and self-worship. This, in reality, reflects his dominant assessment of non-Christian faith. But when he is dealing with the concrete reality of the church's life and mission, he has in mind the second sense, that is, the polar tension between divine grace and human rebellion. This, in turn, evinces his judgment upon Christian experience which originates in God's revelation in Christ and yet is distorted by sin.

If the first is held to be a true statement of the case (i.e., empirical Christianity as deriving from human consciousness), then the common grouping of empirical Christianity and the non-Christian religions is logically intelligible, even demanded by Kraemer's assumptions about non-Christian religion. They are both fundamentally human spiritual achievements marked with the ambiguity characterizing all human historical endeavor. If, on the contrary, empirical Christianity is the historical expression of the Christian experience of revelation in Christ, then it should enjoy a certain privileged status as the only historical embodiment of authentic revelation, even though vitiated by human sin.

The question now needs to be raised: which of these interpretations is normative in Kraemer's thought? His dominant view regarding the source of empirical Christianity is that it indeed derives--albeit imperfectly--from the revelation in Christ taken in Christian faith to be the final decisive redemptive disclosure of God to humanity. It should follow (on Kraemer's premises) that empirical Christianity ought not be collated with non-Christian religions either structurally (i. e., descriptively) or in worth, so long as they are viewed only as human achievement.

As a church theologian concerned with truth (which in the context of Christian theology means divine, salvific revelation), Kraemer's paradigm of dialectics is the Christian instance where revealed grace and human sin comprise the dialectical poles of the religious life.

1. Do Non-Christian Empirical Traditions Derive from Revelation?

It may well be that ultimately both phenomenologically and theologically empirical Christianity and non-Christian religions should be classed together (I believe they should), but this cannot be logically done if one is viewed as deriving from special historical revelation and the other from an ambivalent human consciousness. If Kraemer wishes to designate non-Christian religion as dialectical, he must postulate a correlate of revelation for non-Christian religion analogous to the way in which empirical Christianity is correlated with the revelation in Christ from which it derives and which it mediates.

A grave objection to Kraemer's scheme is that it does not show why the distinction between revelation and subsequent empirical expression and historical development ascribed to Christianity does not apply to other faiths and traditions. On the basis of his own experience and faith he affirms this distinction for the Christian case. The grounds on which this contrast between original, divine revelation and human historical manifestation of faith elicited by it is denied to the others remain obscure. Whereas, in Kraemer's view, empirical Christianity is favorably balanced off by the revelation in Christ, the claim of historical non-Christian religions to a normative divine epiphany which is the well-spring of their mundane history is disallowed--it appears solely for dogmatic reasons.

In spite of Kraemer's frequent references to the dialectical character of non-Christian religion, it seems clear that he ultimately eschews the conclusion which alone would qualify the non-Christian religions as dialectical; namely, that they are historical expressions of revelation, just as empirical Christianity is the manifestation in time of the meaning for Christians of the revelation in Christ. For Kraemer the non-Christian religions are not the result of revelation, of a saving intrusion of God into the lives of a people. They are classified with empirical Christianity, not because both derive from a revelation, but because both are not revelation. But whereas empirical Christianity has the virtue of being a reflection in history (albeit a humanly distorted one) of an authentic, historical divine disclosure, the non-Christian religions are essentially human products of the religious consciousness.

106

Conclusion

To summarize: Kraemer's conception of a dialectical judgment on religion is essentially correct. Religion is potentially both a response and channel to God (or, the sacred; ultimate reality; transcendence) and an instrument of human self-aggrandizement and idolatry. This is true of all religion--Christian and non-Christian. It is to Kraemer's credit that he groups empirical Christianity with the other religions, though--as we have had occasion to note--this ascription of a common character common character coexists with contrary claims.

But though Kraemer's insight is sound when he groups empirical Christianity with other religions, he fails to see that the parallelism also extends to the revelational element in Christian experience. For how can Kraemer speak of the religious faith of the non-Christian (as he does on occasion) as responses to God if they are not predicated on a revelation of God to which they are a response? Moreover, we cannot properly speak of a dialectical view unless we postulate the reality of revelation. To be dialectical, religious tradition and faith must, in some degree, be revelational

Kraemer's alleged dialectical assessment is, practically speaking, a negative judgment since it is not thoroughly and consistently dialectical. A truly dialectical view discerns the positive disclosure of God through the diverse religious traditions even as their distorted and demonic side is conceded.

NOTES

/1/ First published by James Clarke and Company, London, 1938. References in the work are to the third edition, 1956, cited as Christian Message.

/2/ Religion and the Christian Faith (London: Lutterworth Press, 1956), pp. 232-233, cited hereafter as Religion.

/3/ "Islamic Culture and Missionary Adequacy," The Muslim World, Vol. 50 (October, 1960), p. 250. Italics in original.

/4/ (London: Lutterworth Press 1960).

/5/ Christian Message, p. 110.

/6/ Ibid., p. 111.

/7/ Religion, p. 8

/8/ Ibid., p. 102

/9/ Ibid., P. 110.

/10/ Ibid., p. 102.

/11/ "The course usually followed "and which we shall follow too--when discussing the attitude of Christianity towards the non-Christian religions is that of expressing the whole problem in terms of the problems of general revelation and natural theology" (Christian Message, p. 102-103).

/12/ William Temple in Nature, Man and God and John Baillie in Our Knowledge of God have given paradigmatic expressions of this view.

/13/ The problem of identifying founders of religions is a vexatious one which is not pursued in this essay. Nevertheless a tentative generalization may be attempted. Religious traditions both historically and religiously refer back to historical founders as the source of their knowledge of the divine. By historically I mean that historical science is able to discern the lineaments of a figure who stands at the head of a tradition as its primary originator. Some instances are more obvious than others, e.g., Jesus, Muhammad, Confucius, Joseph Smith. By religiously I mean that from within a tradition a particular figure is acknowledged and revered as the inspiration of truth in the tradition. These may not always be the same persons. To illustrate: Toynbee, speaking as a historian, claims that Hinduism as we know it emerges in the ninth century A. D. in response to Shankara. From within the Hindu tradition we learn that it originates in the visions of the rishi or seers who first perceived the eternal Vedas.

/14/   Christian Message, p. 111.

/15/   Ibid., p. 112.

/16/   Ibid., pp. 126-127.

/17/   Religion, p. 251

/18/   Ibid., pp. 251-252; italics in original.

/19/   Ibid., p. 252.

/20/   Ibid., p. 257.

/21/   Ibid., p. 341.

/22/   Christian Message, p. 139.

/23/   Religion, p. 316.

/24/   My conclusion is confirmed by the interpretation of
Kraemer formulated by others as the following examples
show: "Kraemer's two major theses in that book (The
Christian Message in a Non-Christian World) were: (1) the
Bible presents God's revelation in Jesus Christ as God's
solitary act for the redemption of mankind and therefore as
the life or death crisis of all religions, and (2) the
scientific study of the world's religions forbids us from
conceiving a relation of preparation and fulfillment between
these religions and the revelation of Jesus Christ" (Edmund
Perry, The Gospel in Dispute, p. 11: "I do not find in Dr.
Kraemer's book any clear statement of what he conceives
will happen to those who do not follow his prescribed path.
I do not find any discussion of what the ultimate and grave
alternative is although, as he must see, the significance of
everything he says depends on this. Without clarity here,
there is no literalness, and no realism. The same fatal
weakness appears to pervade the words of all those who now
represent the method of Radical Displacement. It is as
though they did not quite believe in the danger which they
imply without defining. Their words have a hollow sound.
They evade the issue, and run off into figures of speech"
(William Ernest Hocking, Living Religions and a World Faith,
pp. 170-171.

/25/   Both Wilfred Cantwell Smith and Raimundo Panikkar have reported in conversation with me discussions each had with Kraemer toward the end of his life. They testify to his growing doubt about the adequacy of his ultimately exclusivistic theology of religions..

/26/   Christian Message, p. 145.

/27/   Ibid.

/28/   Ibid., p. 108.

/29/   Ibid., p. 145.

/30/   Ibid., p. 61.

/31/   Ibid., p. 145.

/32/   Ibid., p. 109.

SOME RECENT DEVELOPMENTS

ON THE QUESTION

OF CHRISTOLOGY

8

AND WORLD RELIGIONS

Lucien Richard, O. M. I.

The body of literature resulting from the encounter of religions has gained clarity and focus in recent years. The question of other religions has emerged as an important dimension of contemporary Christian theology. Many theologians have concluded that theology cannot continue to be made in isolation from an interior dialogue with other religious traditions, that in fact the future of Christian theology lies in the deepest possible assimilation of the spirit and finding of other religions. /1/ The data from non-Christian religions has become an essential element for theological reflection, which has to grapple with the existence and value of other religions and to account theologically for religious pluralism.

Fr. Lucien Richard, O.M.I. taught in the Oblate Seminary in Natick, Mass. before joining the faculty of the Weston School of Theology in Cambridge, Mass. He has a Ph.D. from Harvard Divinity School has published a book on Calvin and has written a number of important articles on both Christology and World Religions.

This selection is taken from Eglise et Theologie, Vol. 8, 1977, pp. 209-244. Reprinted by permission of the publisher.

Theology has to come out of a faith experience, where other religions in the world are actually questions posed and possibilities offered to every believer. Other religious traditions have become part of the theologian's existential situation. He may experience them, not simply on a theoretical level, but in the concrete as realities which put the absolute claim of his own Christian faith in question.

Certain theologians have defined the task of theology from within the framework of the encounter with World Religions. According to R. Whitson, the work of theology is to open one's religious tradition to another, both theologically and experimentally. /2/ The other religious tradition is to be perceived from within one's own tradition, one's own commitment. /3/ A type of cross-fertilization must take place where the spiritual wisdom and experience of another's religion affects one's own religious outlook.

This article is intended as a survey of recent contributions on the question concerning Christian attitudes to other Religions. The intention is to focus on the way in which the fundamental challenge of World Religions to traditional Christology is understood and dealt with. This present survey cannot be a comprehensive treatment of all the recent literature. It focusses on certain seminal contributions and attempts to span denominational lines, while ultimately indicating certain possible directions for future development.

In the context of a critical dialogue with non-Christian religions. /4/ Christianity's claim to the uniqueness and finality of Christ needs to be re-evaluated. Christology has to come to the fore. /5/ According to J. Cobb, it is:

"precisely through deepening its central conviction of incarnation that Christian faith moves toward its own transformation through openness to all faiths. The creative transformation of theology that leads toward universality can responsibly be identified as Christ." /6/

Precisely in faithfulness to Christ are the theologians being asked to transcend their Western and Christian parochialism. /7/ Now it has been claimed that Christology, at least since Nicea, has made Christianity one of the world's great exclusivist religions. /8/ One of the most fundamental affirmations of the Christian tradition concerns the uniqueness, the sole supremacy, and the finality of what God has done in Jesus Christ. This conviction is, according to Don Cupitt, expressed in a variety of ways: "That Jesus is God's only Son; that only through him can men be saved; that God acted in him once and for all; that world history will be wound up by him..." /9/ The emphasis on the centrality and uniqueness of Christ has introduced in Christianity a rhetoric of exclusion in regard to other people, and other faiths.

It becomes apparent that any real dialogue with other religious traditions is dependent upon a renewal in Christology.

It has become necessary today to formulate a Christology according to which Christ, as God's manifestation of reconciling love, is related not only to Christians but to all men, so that the language about him actually comes to serve the unification and humanization of the whole human race. /10/

Any constructive reflection on the fact of religious pluralism must deal with Christianity's claim to the uniqueness and universality of Jesus Christ. A Christian's basic attitude toward world religions is directly correlated to his understanding and interpretation of the significance of Jesus Christ.

The questions of Christology and of religious pluralism are systematically interdependent. According to G. Rupp, the question which the existence of other traditions poses for Christian theology may be formulated specifically as how the works or efficacy of Christ is related to those traditions.

It is evident not only that a given Christian theological approach to interpreting the fact of religious pluralism is correlative with definite Christological commitments, but also that a theologian's evaluation of other traditions, in turn, has implications for his understanding of the significance of Christ. /11/

In surveying contemporary christologies that have dealt seriously with religious pluralism, it has become apparent that the basic classical questions about the person of Christ are being debated within the context of the theologians' evaluation of other religious traditions. Questions about the uniqueness and finality of Jesus Christ inevitably lead to the question: "Is Christ different in degree or in kind?" This leads to the more important questions: How can we understand that in the event of Jesus Christ a reality of ultimate worth and meaning made its appearance within our midst? How is the divine revealing activity in Jesus Christ understood? What about the long Christological tradition stemming from Chalcedon affirming that in Jesus we have him who is truly God, truly man, and truly one? These questions are the challenging problems of a new Christology now emerging out of the faith experience that has taken seriously the vital existence of other faiths. Both Catholic and Protestant theologians are contributing to this emerging Christology.

These contemporary contributions, however, are not without preparation and antecedents. In fact, in examining contemporary christologies, Hegel's continued relevance becomes apparent. /12/ It also becomes apparent that Hegel's focus on the question of the relationship between the historical, individual Jesus of Nazareth, and the absolute truth claims made in reference to the Christ of faith, is still the basic question for twentieth century thelologians. /13/ One of Hegel's major theological interests concerned the connections between Christ and the course of the historical process; for Hegel, the Christian symbols provide a comprehensive interpretation of the whole scope of historical development. There is no attempt on Hegel's part "to provide a secure shelter for religious truth outside of space and time." /14/ There is no final end for created reality that is not in continuity with the present. Here the intimate relation between culture and religion is emphasized. In affirming Christ as the supreme appearance of the unity between man and God, Hegel advocated a universal dimension to Christianity which jeopardized the Jesus of history.

The most lucid expression of the Christological debate following Hegel is to be found in David Freidrich Strauss' book, The Life of Jesus Critically Examined. /15/ Strauss argues here that certainty about the truth of Christianity is not dependent upon historical knowledge of facts. Strauss cannot accept that the hypostatic unity existed in a single, historical individual, and offers his position in the form of rhetorical questions:

"And is this no true realization of the idea ? is not the idea of a unity of the divine and human natures a real one in a far higher sense, when I regard the whole race of mankind as its realization, than when I single out one man as such a realization ? is not an incarnation of God from eternity, a truer one than an incarnation limited to a particular point of time ?" /16/

The division of the Christ principle from the historical Jesus is accompanied by a deep skepticism about the historical realiability of the Gospels. F. Schleiermacher, in his The Christian Faith, had already rejected the metaphysical and ontological aspects of Chalcedon and had approached the interpretation of the meaning of Christ from the side of his manhood, inaugurating the modern humanistic approach to christology. According to John Macquarrie:

"It would be difficult to think of another century in the history of Christian theology when the structure of orthodoxy was subjected to such a series of shocks as beat upon it in these works.." /17/

Ernst Troeltsch, in his essay on the significance of the historicity of Jesus for Christian faith, /18/ understood Jesus' centrality simply as fulfilling the necessary require- ment for the development of any tradition.

Decisive for the appraisal of the significance of Jesus is, therefore, not the unavailability of salvation for non-Christians but rather the need of the religious community for a support, a center, and a symbol of its religious life. /19/

Troelsch saw Christiantiy as historically relative and conditioned as any other tradition:

"In all moments of its history Christianity is a purely historical phenomenon with all the conditionedness of an individual historical phenomenon just like the other great religions." /20/

One may not claim absolute validity for Christianity: the "criteria of its validity" can only be "the evidence of a profound inner experience." /21/ In dealing with Christianity's claim to the uniqueness and finality of Christ within the context of its own historical particularity, Troelsch argued for a provisional pluralism, and a better appreciation of other religious traditions. /22/

The contemporary Christologies we are focussing on have emerged in the context of a radical historical skepticism, and a radical humanistic approach to Christology. /23/

GEORGE RUPP

We begin our survey with George Rupp's book, Christ-ologies and Cultures: Toward a Typology of Religious World-views. /24/ While the author has not constructed a new christological model, he has established a typology of christological models and correlative worldviews, and has dealt with several contemporary authors. /25/

G. Rupp's basic contention is that past attempts at explaining the nature of Christ's redemptive work demonstrate different worldviews. The author argues for the possibility of relating systematically the various christological controversies to opposite worldviews. Rupp sees clear implications between various Christological types and different ways of interpreting "the fact of religious pluralisms." /26/ Interpretations of religious pluralism can be differentiated in reference to variables in Christology. /27/ These variables concern primarily the significance attributed to the redemptive work of Jesus Christ.

To take the point at which the connection is most direct, the way in which a given interpreter of the atonement treats the ephapax - the once-and-for-all claim for the work of Christ - cannot but have implications for his approach to non-Christian religious tradition. /28/

Rupp has chosen here to deal primarily with soteriology, affirming that doctrinal definitions concerning the person of Jesus are directly related to the perception of the nature of his work. /29/

He sees two major focusses to post-medieval inter-pretations of the significance and consequence of Christ's redemptive action: as a transaction of universal implication, or as the significance of an historical event. /30/ While the author sees these two alternatives as deficient and polarizing, his typology is grounded in these two positions. It employs two sets of variables: the Realist vs. the Nominalist, the Transactional vs. the Processive. /31/

According to Rupp, the realist perceives Christ as having assumed a universal human nature and his redemptive work as having altered the general and universal situation of mankind. The nominalist focusses on the influence of the historical Jesus on the individual believer. The significance of Christ is seen here as inseparable from the influence of his teachings. The emphasis is on a universally valid truth and on Christ as teacher and as example.

The transactional and processive variables are not directly concerned with the value of the work of Christ, but with the manner in which this redemptive work affects individuals and the world. While a transactional model sees the effect of Christ's atonement as transcending the normal, historical process, and as a-temporal and independent of historical mediation, the processive model respects the norms of spatial-temporal existence. Both sets of variables are therefore, concerned with the classic question of subjective and objective redemption - a question which has deep epistemological ramifications.

It is Rupp's contention that religious pluralism is inadequately interpreted if based on a Realist-transactional or Nominalist-transactional Christology. The author advocates a processive approach which allows an appropriation of the realist and nominalist commitments, and respects the historical context and the concrete data of all religious traditions including the Christian. /32/

A processive view considers the entire action of atonement as taking place in time and "emphasizes the fact of development and a belief in increase in being and/or value in individual selves, in the cosmic process, or even in God." /32/ The processive model respects social and cultural forms of mediation of Christ's influence. /34/

The change which Christ's work effects is not in principle complete apart from the temporal appropriation of this work, and the realization of salvation cannot abstract from historical development. The processive position attempts to do justice to the thoroughly historical character of human existence. It attends specifically to the questions of the historical mediation of Christian teaching.

In opting for a processive model which appropriates what is relevant both in the nominalist and realist position, Rupp accepts very consciously, Hegel's Christological and metaphysical position that "rejects every form of cosmological dualism or otherworldliness." /35/ there is no attempt to consider religious truth outside of space and time, nor any fundamental discontinuity between God's reconciling the world in Christ and historical development. "The kingdom or rule of God not only impinges on the present life of man; it is also the destiny of that definite historical existence. /36/

Rupp sees Hegel's position as most able to adequately interpret contemporary human experience:

"This Hegelian perspective is remarkably congenial to twentiety-century man's conception of himself and his world, especially once the contrast between "material" and "spiritual" is recognized as a useful distinction only on a microscopic scale." /37/

In fact, for Rupp, the crucial question of whether or not a religious system is viable in the twentieth century is dependent on its capacity to interpret as religiously significant man's increasing capacity to shape his personal and corporate life within the sphere of phenomenal existence. The "truth" question becomes an

"appraisal of the degree to which the religious system offers a coherent interpretation of the whole of human experience and, thereby, effectively shape man's thoughts, affection, and action in what is deemed a constructive direction." /38/

Rupp's interpretation of the significance of Christ does not require or imply an exclusivism which makes all religious

118

attainment or value dependent on or as derivative from his work.

The universality of Christ is a derivative one. "It arises only if and insofar as definite individuals and specific historical communities advance more comprehensive claims for the change or renewal which they experience." /39/

Rupp is speaking here again, basically about the power of the historical figure of Jesus shaping the religious consciousness of the Christian community and of others. Therefore, the biblical portrayal of Christ is essential. "...the Biblical portrayal of Jesus continues to inform man's religious imagination whether or not it represents an accurate record of past occurrences." /40/

While in the realist-transactional approach, no one attains salvation apart from Christ, /41/ a position which results in an ecclesiastical exclusivism, a processive view can entertain the possibility of salvation apart from Jesus Christ.

There is no fundamental metaphysical connection between Christ's work and successive generations of individuals. The transformation mediated by Christ is one which displaces individuals frmom a self-centered preoccupation with their concerns to a "loyalty to this ultimately all encompassing rule or kingdom of God." /42/ This transformation favors the process of interaction between traditions.

As previously mentioned, Rupp does not develop a Christology nor does he deal explicitly with the classical questions about the nature of Jesus' special relation to God. But in expressing his position on the significance of Christ, perceived primarily as an indirect significance, via the power of the historical Jesus to shape up our vision of reality, Rupp has expressed his difficulty with the Chalcedonian tradition.

JOHN B. COBB

John Cobb's basic affirmation in his new book, Christ in a Pluralistic Age, /43/ is that the process of transformation needed for theology to be open to all religious traditions can be identified as "Christ", for, according to Cobb, Christ is the Way that excludes no Ways.

Cobb sees the various religious traditions as claims and opportunities for Christian theology and the context in which Christ must be reconceived. /44/ In fact, much that was meant by Christ in the past, when we did not acknowledge pluralism, becomes destructive in our new situation.

The universalizing and absolutizing of Christianity's claim relative to Christ's work "is in opposition to our real need today." /45/

Cobb claims that it is in the deepening of our understanding of Incarnation that "Christian faith moves toward its own transformation through openness to all faiths." /46/

Pluralism must be recognized as significant for Christology since it is now impossible to continue to affirm "that Christ names the reality that is, in fact, supremely important for all, whether or not it is recognized as such." /47/

A positive appreciation of pluralism is a necessary correlate of any authentic christology. Faithfulness to Christ requires immersion in a pluralistic consciousness, /48/ because Christ breaks the relation to himself as objectified figure and becomes the principle of liberation at work in theology itself. /49/ Every sacred form must be relativized and that process is in fact itself Christ. /50/

Both Pannenberg and Whitehead seem to play an essential role in Cobb's evolution from Jesuology to Christology. This influence can be seen in terms of the understanding of faith and reason and in the concept of self and person.

Cobb does not see faith as a source of special knowledge. /51/ Faith cannot be the last and final bastion of the sacred. The correlation of faith and the sacred must be broken, and the relativizing consequences of such a break have to be fully accepted by the Christian. No longer is it necessary to choose between theology on the one side and the objective study of religion as a phenomenon on the other. /52/ This understanding of faith and reason leads to a reappraisal of classical Christology. Cobb wants to affirm literally and seriously the incarnation of the Logos, but without any supranaturalist or exclusivist implications of traditional theology.

Cobb's reappraisal of classical christology involves a Whiteheadian understanding of self and person. /53/ While Whitehead does not see the person as the total human organism, but the psyche, Cobb does not identify the self even with the psyche but only with one element within it. The self is that "relatively continuous center within human experience around which the experience attempts more or less successfully to organize itself." /54/ Selfhood is constituted when the "I" transcends the affective and rational dimension of the psyche. Cobb is advocating a complete rejection of any substantist categories relative to the self and the person. Selves conceived as substances can act upon each other only externally, and there is always an inherently negative element in being acted upon in this way. In substances, only accidents or attributes change; substances remain identical; they can only relate to one another externally, while experiences can be genuinely present to one another. /55/ Self-identity does not need to be explained by a numerical identity uniting past, present, and future experiences.

The Incarnation or the immanence of a transcendent reality cannot be understood in a substantialist context. The transcendent reality here is the Logos, "the cosmic principle of order, the ground of meaning and the source of purpose." /56/ The Logos is fully incarnated when it constitutes not only a necessary aspect of existence, but the self as such. /57/ "In Jesus there is a distinctive incarnation because his very selfhood was constituted by the Logos." /58/ The Logos shares in constituting selfhood. The Logos is identical with the center or principles in terms of which other elements in experience are ordered. The Incarnation means: a human "I" fulfilled through its identity with the immanent Logos. There is no confrontation of an "I" by a "Thou", for the Logos does not come from outside the "I," nor is self-identity lost by identifying with the Logos but perfected thereby.

While the Logos is incarnate in all human beings, Jesus is a paradigm case of Incarnation. The Logos not only constitutes a necessary dimension of his existence, but Jesus' self as such. "In Jesus there is a distinctive incarnation because his very selfhood was constituted by the Logos." /59/ Cobb sees here the difference of Jesus' selfhood from that of all others.

The distinctiveness of Jesus can be spoken of in terms of Christ. Christ is the incarnate Logos. As such, Christ is present in all things. The degree and the kind of Christ's presence varies. The fullest form of that presence is that in which he co-constitutes with the personal past the very selfhood of a person. In that case, Christ is not simply present in a person but he is that person. Cobb sees the special presence of God in Jesus in that way. Christ does not designate Jesus as such, but refers to Jesus in a particular way; namely, as the incarnation of the divine. It does not designate deity as such but refers to deity experienced as graciously incarnate in the world. /60/

In Jesus, the Logos was normatively incarnate, and For Christians, then, Christ names what is supremely important, and as such is found in Jesus. "Those who experienced what is supremely important as bound up with Jesus as Christians." /62/ But that recognition is not simply passive; it implies a creative transformation. Christ has to be realized in each and every one. "If the content of our hope is Christ, then it is the hope that Christ be perfectly formed in us." /63/ Our goal is the structure of existence already realized in Jesus. "The fulfillment of this movement in the co-constitution of our selfhood by our personal past and the Logos would be that perfection of incarnation already attained in Jesus." /64/

Within a processive framework, Cobb has revived the Logos Christology. While the Logos has always been operative in human history and is still operating, it is still important to recognize and name him. Christians know in naming the Logos "Christ" that the divine has constituted itself toward the world as Love, and that this love is creative transformation. /65/

SCHUBERT M. OGDEN

Schubert M. Ogden has characterized Christianity's claim to uniqueness and its christocentric exclusivism as mythological. /66/ Myth is taken as expressing an existential self-understanding, an understanding of one's existence in its constant structure and in relation to its ultimate ground and end. The point of Christology for Ogden is strictly existential. "The only meaning the event Jesus Christ has is

122

a purely existential meaning." /67/ To believe in Jesus Christ and to understand oneself authentically are one and the same thing. Contrary to Bultmann, Ogden claims that authentic human existence is possible in fact, not only in Jesus, but elsewhere. The word spoken in Jesus is addressed to all. /68/

The content of this possibility is man's ontological possibility of authentic historical existence before god. /69/ This ontological possibility of authentic human existence leads Ogden to universalize the Christ dimension of Jesus. Jesus' life, his historical existence became a

"witness to the truth that all things have their ultimate beginning and solely in God's pure unbounded love, and that it is in giving ourselves wholly into the keeping of that love, by surrendering all other securities, that we realize our authentic life." /70/ The life of Jesus is significant because it confronts us with the possibility of self-understanding. What is of major importance here is not the past event of what occurred between Jesus and God, but the present event that occurs between us and God through our encounter with the Christian witness to Jesus as the Christ. Ogden refuses to say that Jesus realized in his person complete authentic existence.

The office of Christ is that of being the bearer of God's eternal word. /71/ Jesus is Christ because he represents the possibilities of faith and, for Christians, represents it decisively. In Jesus' word and deed, the ultimate truth about human life before God can be understood. /72/ There is a normative dimension to this representation in Jesus for "...in distinction from all other historical events, the ultimate truth about our existence before God is normatively represented as revealed." /73/

For Ogden, the concept of representation which is a result of his reflection on Whitehead's statements that "speech is human itself," /74/ and that "expression is the one fundamental sacrament," /75/ is of crucial christological importance. The various religions, including the Christian religion, are but representations of a deeper faith that precedes them.

123

"Logically, prior to every particular religious assertion is an original confidence in the meaning and worth of life, through which not simply all our religious answers, but even our religious questions first become possible or have any sense. Hence the different historical religious questions first become possible or have any sense. Hence the different historical religions, again including Christianity, can be thought of only as several attempts at a more or less self-conscious understanding of this original confidence. They are the results (...) of that original faith itself in search for a more fully conscious understanding of its own nature... Because all religions are by their very nature representative, they never originate our faith in life's meaning, but rather provide us with particular symbolic forms through which that faith may be more or less adequately reaffirmed at the level of self-conscious belief." /76/

Religions are more or less valid inasmuch as they enable men and women to understand their confidence in the meaning of life. /77/ Jesus as the Christ is normative for Christians because of his ability to represent our ultimate significance. /78/

For the ground of faith and its object is not the Jesus who perfectly actualized the possibility of authentic faith and love, but the Jesus who decisively represents that possibility to us because through the Christian witness of faith, he represents the primal word of God's grace, to which our own faith and love are always only the response. /79/

According to Ogden, to perceive the significance of Jesus Christ as the representation of the truths of human existence is not to reduce Christ to be the exemplificator of timeless truths. But it is to insist on the responsibility of individuals to bring about the given possibility for human authenticity. But here the tension lies between affirming authentic existence as a factual possibility for all, mediated and communicated through any event, and its normative representation in the Christ Jesus who is also historical,

"The real meaning of the exclusiveness of Jesus Christ's Lordship is not that divine lordship is exercised solely in that particular life, but rather that whereever such lordship is exercised, and that naturally is everywhere, it can take no other form than the same promise and demand for us in Jesus." /80/

While for Ogden, the ultimate meaning of Christology is strictly existential, yet the New Testament's insistence on the historicity of Jesus, its actual assertion about Jesus, seems to indicate that Christology cannot remain simply existential. Relative to this aspect, Ogden makes a distinction between the factual question about a fact - "What are the facts?" - and the metaphysical question -"What is it to be a fact?" - While on the factual level one may be mistaken, this may not be so on the metaphysical level. Ogden relates that dichotomy to the historical level by making a distinction between empirical-historical and existential-historical. The existential is not essentially linked to the empirical. The fact "Jesus" is not taken with reference to the empirical-historical question: "What actually happened?" but to the existential-historical question: "What is the significance of what happened (or is taken to have happened) for human existence?"

"...the Christian witness of faith takes certain things about Jesus to be empirically true solely in order to proclaim through them the very meaning of human existence." /81/ What is important here is the assumption of fact, not the assertion of fact. /82/ To affirm that Jesus is human, is to be confronted in and through an historical existence with a demand to one's own existence. /83/ In all of Ogden's arguments, there seems to be a clear implication that Jesus as the Christ cannot be viewed as the final or supreme or unique revelation of God. God's action in Jesus did not differ from his action in other events. The specialness of God's action must be attributed to the beholder - the believer.

WOLFHART PANNENBERG

Wolfhart Pannenberg has attempted to revive the idea of a Christian understanding of universal history. /84/ His theology and Christology is a reaction to the existentialism of Rudolf Bultmann. In his Jesus - God and Man, Pannenberg initiates his Christology with a polemic against a soteriological approach to Christology which, in his mind, leads to a subjective reduction of Christology. /85/ A

125

soteriological approach is always in danger of a-priorism, and "is not far removed from Feuerbach's thesis that all religious concepts are only projections of human needs and wishes into an imaginary transcendent world." /86/

The starting point of his Christology is Jesus in himself. What is important is the significance of Jesus "in himself, in his history, and in his person constituted by this history." /87/ A transcendental existential approach does not found objectively our faith in Christ. For Pannenberg, Christological questions are best approached "by Christologies from below to above" and not "Christologies from above to below." /88/ In the context of a "from below" approach, Pannenberg understands Christ as the prolepsis in which God reveals the end and in which God brings men and women to salvation. Pannenberg holds to the finality and the universality of Christ and his revelation. Christ brings a final revelation insofar as he proleptically contains the end of all history which is the origin and driving force and end of all religion. "...in the fate of Jesus, the end of history is experienced in advance versus an anticipation," /89/ and in "the fate of Jesus as the anticipation of the end of all history, God is revealed as the one God of all mankind who had been expected since the times of the prophets." /90/ The Christ-event is an event for all peoples since in Christ "God is finally and fully revealed," /91/ and "no further revelation of God can happen."/92/ Christ's finality places him both within and beyond the history of religions. In a sense, non Christian religions cannot break out of their questionableness, they cannot know God sufficiently to receive the salvation effected in Christ. Although God is experienced in other religions, He is not really known.

JOHN HICK

John Hick has outlined on several different occasions a position challenging traditional claims for the uniqueness of Christ. /93/ Hick advocates a Copernican revolution in theology, a radical transformation in our conception of the universe of faith, "a shift from the dogma that Christianity is at the centre, to the realization that it is God who is at the centre, and that all the religions of mankind including our own serve and revolve around Him." /94/ Hick is advocating a shift from an ecclesiocentric to a theocentric understanding of the religions. In the context of this revolution, one cannot affirm Christianity to be true and all other religions false. This is ruled out by the Christian understanding of God whose love is universal in scope. "If God is the God of the whole world, we must presume that the whole religious life of mankind is part of a continuous and universal human relationship to Him." /95/ Hick is sharply aware of the theological implications of other religions. "Whereas, it was hitherto reasonable to develop our theology in disregard of God's dealings with the non-Christian world, it now ceases to be reasonable to do that." /96/

Religions, and this includes Christianity, are human cultural forms; it should not be assumed that their different apprehensions of God are mutually exclusive. /97/ It becomes imperative for Christian theology to take stock of the fact that our literal interpretations of the Incarnation have divisive and exclusivist consequences. The images, through which the Incarnation is expressed, have no literal meaning; they are mythological. /98/

Christianity's claim for the universality and uniqueness of Christ is based on the absoluteness of its experience. But this should not entail exclusiveness. Christ should be seen as mediating the presence and saving power of God in such a unique sense that no other religious figure has ever mediated it. The uniqueness of Jesus Christ has a purely devotional and subjective function. "That Jesus is my Lord and Saviour is language like that of the lover, for whom his Helen is the sweetest girl in the world." /99/ For a Christian, the claim to Christ's theological uniqueness is the product of a personal response to a way of life and salvation. /100/ The Christian must not absolutize his point of view, assuming that it is a knowledge of things as they are in themselves, but it is a view of things as they are for him, things as they appear from his conditioned spatial-temporal standpoint. One community's affirmation does not contradict the affirmations of other communities, since each can be understood as expressing how God is related to them and this involves only one aspect of God's nature.

Hick's position on the uniqueness of Christ has its correlate in his theology of the Incarnation. In explaining the Incarnation, he is unwilling to use substantive language. Instead he adopts dynamic categories of thought and derives his knowledge of God's nature from his knowledge of his deeds: "We know who and what He is insofar as we know what he has done." /101/ Everything that Christianity knows concerning the divine attitude and activity towards mankind can be summarized in the assertion that God is AGAPE.

God's nature is an operation, that of agape, which is revealed in the life and death of Jesus. In the life of Jesus, we find "not divine substance injected into a human frame, but divine action taking place in and through a human life." /102/

Jesus' agape is not simply the representation of God's agape; it is the eternal divine Agape made flesh, in-historized, operating in a finite mode; but it is not identical with the whole of the infinite Agape-ing. /103/ The continuity between the divine Agape-ing and the agape-ing of Jesus is one of event rather than of entity, of activity rather than of substance. Christ is the Christian's image of God and the Incarnation is an effective mythic expression of the Christian's appropriate attitude to God.

DON CUPITT

Don Cupitt has written about the uniqueness of Christ in a different vein. /105/ He sees the uniqueness, the sole sufficiency, and the finality of what God has done in Christ as the most fundamental affirmation of the New Testament. /106/ Christianity regards the life, death, and resurrection of Christ as in some way essentially unique and unrepeatable.

The classical foundation for the finality and uniqueness of Christ is faith's perception of Christ's unique relation to God, the perception that there is a unique embodiment of God in Christ. Cupitt has difficulty with this foundation. "The eternal God and a historical man are two beings of quite different ontological status. It is simply unintelligible to declare them identical." /107/ In the Gospels, Christ does not appear as one who embodies God, "but as one who with the whole of his passionate nature witnesses to God." /108/ According to the author, "it was always a mistake to make Jesus himself the direct object of worship." /109/ His mission was not to draw attention to himself, but to be a signpost, to point to God. "Jesus' legacy to mankind is an urgent appeal to each of us to acknowledge above all else the reality of God." /110/

To obviate the danger of absolutizing Christianity's claim to Christ's uniqueness, Cupitt prefers a Christology of Jesus as the Word of God instead of Jesus as God's Son. According to Cupitt, we should not think of Christ as Son or Image, but as Word and Witness. Jesus' finality does not lie in himself but in what he proclaims, and in the way he bears witness to it. "He is final because of the way he bears witness to what is final and unsurpassable." /111/ By separating the way he bears witness to what is final and unsurpassable." /111/ By separating Jesus' uniqueness from his person and relating it to his witnessing, Cupitt attempts to avoid pure religious relativism and the absolutist language in which traditional Christian faith has so often been expressed:

"God can be believed in and served in as many ways as there are people. In the Christian tradition, Jesus is the paradigm of faith, but that paradigm may be re-enacted in a great variety of ways, and we need not labour to reduce their number." /112/

JOHN A. T. ROBINSON

John A. T. Robinson has attempted to express his Christology in his The Human Face of God. /113/ While it is not written specifically from the viewpoint of World Religions, the author has spelled out in Chapter Seven his understanding of Christianity's claim for the uniqueness of and finality of Christ. Robinson accuses Christian theologians of having turned the finality of Christ "into a static, finished, and therefore, dead reality." /114/ The author would rather speak of the "provisionality of Christ." /115/ Christ is unique "not for any thing exclusive to himself or finished in the past, but, in Teilhard's phrase, as the 'budding shoot' of the next development not only in man but in God." /116/ The finality of Christ lies as much in the future as in the past. The Christian claims finality for Christ because he sees in Christ the all-embracing principle of interpretation of his experience:

"...the Christian sees in Jesus the clue to (though not the exclusive embodiment of) the Christ, who in turn is the clue (though not the exclusive embodiment of) the nature of God as personal..." /117/

Robinson's understanding of Christ's finality and uniqueness is underpinned by a specific understanding of the Incarnation. He refuses to see the Incarnation as an inbreaking of God into the human situation except in a symbolic sense. "The Incarnation does not mean insertion into the living stream, an intervention by God in the form of a man, but the embodiment, the realization of God in this man." /118/ There is here an explicit rejection of the doctrine of total immanence. The "realization of God" is a progressive one. "The Christ has been in the process -yes, in process - from the start, and in this sense we may speak of the 'eternal generation of the Son.'" /119/ The Logos is "personalized" rather than hypothatized; God is made dependent upon man's response. /120/

In addressing the question whether Jesus is different from us in degree or in kind, Robinson states: "If one had to choose, I should side with those who opt for a degree-christology." /121/ For Robinsin, christology is unhinged from the historical Jesus, and can be found everywhere - in other religions.

In recent years, a number of theologians, from within the Roman Catholic tradition, have used Vatican II as a door through which to pass further elaboration of the Church's new respect for non-Christian faiths and further exploration of their implications of that attitude. /122/

CHARLES DAVIS

For Charles Davis, Christian theology must find itself within the global context of religious man. /123/ Religious pluralism has entered our consciousness and deprived the Christian religion of its "unquestioned monopoly even when it remains our personal claim." /124/

The author sees a tension between claims for the universal active presence of Christ and the particularity of Jesus, the one who died on the cross. The historical

130

particularity of Jesus, Lord and Christ, is the source of Christian exclusivism. In the context of this exclusivism, Davis is interested in the possibility of relating Christianity to other religions. /125/

At the heart of every religious tradition lies a complex of symbols. /126/ Symbols are dynamic images that have been inspired by historical persons and situations, and are, therefore, culturally conditioned. It becomes difficult to transfer symbols from one culture to another. /127/ Davis is implying that although insight and understanding into another's symbol complex is possible, this complex does not open itself necessarily to an outsider on the level of experience. Remaining within a particular relgigious symbolic complex, complementarity becomes even more necessary.

Within the Christian tradition, the possibility of perceiving the need for complementarity involves Christology. Davis does not present a full Christology but attempts to deal with Jesus Christ as the symbolic center of the Christian faith. He speaks about Christ as a symbol, "as a dynamic image, focussing the imagination, releasing the emotions, and moving to action." /128/ "He is the embodiment of meaning, expressing both the objective content of God's supreme revelation and the subjective union of man with God." /129/

The author claims that Christ fulfills the function central to the symbolic complex of every religion, but in a distinctive manner. As the central symbol of the Christian faith, Christ is a real person and can never be substituted by a set of propositional beliefs. He is also an event perceived by the Christian community as the culmination of Sacred History. "The event of Jesus Christ is the final, irrevocable reconciliation of mankind with God." /130/

Christ is also a living person, a presence, the presence of God. "This implies a unique relationship between Christ and God. Christology is an attempt to formulate this." /131/ As the central symbol of the Christian religion, Davis claims that faith in Christ "implies granting him an unusual and final role in regard to human existence and human history." /132/ I do not see how the universality and finality of Christ can be denied without emptying the Christian tradition of meaning." /133/

131

But this universality and finality does not mean that other religions no longer have a function in God's purposes. "If Christ is truly universal Saviour, then religions other than Christianity, which are in fact still the vehicles for the religious faith of most men, must have a positive place in the divine schema of salvation through Christ." /134/ Davis sees a pluralistic situation as best in order to preserve and promote truth and to ward off corruption.

RAYMOND PANIKKAR

Raymond Panikkar has recently underlined an emerging tendency in the comparative study of religions: complementarity must be achieved with the individual himself: /135/

"The burden of our tale is this: any interreligious and inter-human dialogue, any exchange among cultures has to be preceded by an intra-religious and intra-human dialogue, an internal conversion within the person. We can only bridge the gulf between so many abysses, between East and West in this case, if we realize the synthesis and the harmony within that microcosm of ourselves." /136/

Any encounter between religions demands this internal conversion which Panikkar describes as a process of death and resurrection. /137/

The meeting of religions is a religious art, an art of incarnation and redemption. The laws of the interrelation of cultures are not the same as those of the meeting between religions. A certain kenosis is needed in any fruitful encounter:

"Christian faith must strip itself of the 'Christian religion' as it actually exists and free itself for a fecundation that will affect all religions both ancient and modern. What we call Christianity is only one among other possible ones of living and realizing the Christian faith." /138/

In his book The Unknown Christ of Hinduism, Panikkar suggested that the meeting of religions must be an existential one, that it must take place in Christ, in a Christ who does not belong to Christianity but to God. The finality and universality of Christ is not to be identified with the finality or universality of the Christian religion. In fact, it would be nearer the truth to say that Christ is the end of Christianity, as he is of Judaism.

What is needed, according to Panikkar, is a universal Christology. "Could we not develop an authentically universal Christology? (...) a fundamental Christology which would make room not only for different theologies but also for different religions ?" /139/

Christ answered the question about himself, not directly, but by describing what he was doing, bringing savation to the world. The identity of Christ should not be located in the categories of singularity and individuality, but in the reality "which is found in the encounter with a person, that knowledge which springs up when we really know and love somebody." /140/

What is important about Jesus is not simply his historical reality, but his personal dimension which can only be appropriated in love. /141/ Our Jesus "is not simply the historical Jesus, but the Risen One, a Jesus who as a person enters into the very structure of our own personal existence." /141/ Therefore:

"Christ as Saviour is, thus, not to be restricted to the merely historical figure of Jesus of Nazareth. Or, as we have already said, the identity of Jesus is not to be confused with historical identification." /143/

While Christ is the universal saviour, there are more saviours "embodying that saving power which Christians believe to be the spirit of Jesus." /144/

The reality of Jesus as the Christ affirms his "hidden" presence in the religious history of man-kind. It is the presence of Christ which opens the world religions and their individual adherents to the experience and reception of the "Christ event" and its efficacy. But this presence is manifold, as varied as the concrete forms of human religious history. Christ, then, is already the point of the encounter of Christianity and the world religions. In consequence,

Christianity has a sui-generis relationship, not an artificial one, with each of the world religions.

Since Christ is universal, he finalizes not just one but every great religious tradition. He is the ful-fillment of the aspirations of India as much as Israel. It is unrealistic and unnecessary to require any tradition to renounce their heritage in order to accept Christ. /145/

Panikkar is suggesting a form of Logos christology developed by the early Fathers. The dialogue with other religions does not begin with the historical Jesus, but with the non-historic Logos. There is a shift from the humanity of Christ to Logos who by his relation to humanity is the center of the universe.

KARL RAHNER

Karl Rahner has developed an important theological approach to non-Christian religions. /146/ Religions other than Christianity can be perceived as, however, a positive significance. As institutions, these religions can be seen as positive means of gaining the right relationship to God, as means positively included in God's plan of salvation. We must rid ourselves of the prejudice that we can face world religions with the dilemma that it must either come from God in everything it contains and, thus, correspond to God's will and positive providence, or be simply a human construction. /147/

According to Rahner, Christianity does not simply confront the member of an extra-Christian religion as a mere non-Christian, but as someone who can and must already be regarded in this or that respect as an anonymous Christian. Rahner interprets the non-Christian religions and the individual non-Christian as defined in a situation of anonymous or implicit Christianity. This attitude towards non-Christian religions is the result of Rahner's doctrine of the omnipresence of grace. According to Rahner, God's will to save all beings is really God's will to bestow himself on the creature who is endowed with spiritual faculties. Salvation is not essentially a created gift, but God himself; it implies the self-bestowal of God, and the possibility for the creature to receive what is offered.

The divine self-bestowal penetrates to the ultimate roots of a person, to the innermost depths, radically re-orientating this person towards the immediate presence of God. It imparts to human nature an inward dynamism and an ultimate tendency towards God himself, a mode of being inserted into human nature which becomes an abiding element in its spiritual mode of being, as something that is a living force always and everywhere, whether accepted or rejected. It radically influences the ultimate development of a person's existence as spiritual. The transcendentality of a person as spiritual does not remain a separate department of human life over and above the historical context in which he/she is involved. The call to share supernaturally in God's life determines ontologically the nature of each human being. /148/

While Rahner is proposing our uncompromising universalism, he qualifies it by his statements relative to the necessity of the Incarnation. "The possibility of the Creation depends on the possibility of the Incarnation." /149/ Creation as God's self-utterance of the Logos. "It is the Logos who appears and must appear if God wishes to show himself personally to the world." /150/

Both creation and incarnation have their possibility within the immanent Trinity. For Rahner there is an intrinsic metaphysical connection between the processions "ad intra" and the processions "ad extra." Creation and incarnation are understandable only in terms of their relation to the procession of the Word within the Godhead. /151/ While the possibility of change in God is grounded within the Godhead, the self-giving of God demands a line from below; the open transcendence of the human subject as spiritual being oriented to the absolute being of God. The essence of man as obediential potency constitutes in its own way the transcendental presupposition for an incarnation. Human nature should be conceived as an "active transcendence" as opening "toward the absolute being of God." /152/

"If human nature is conceived as an active transcendence towards the absolute being of God, a transcendence that is open and must be personally realized, then the Incarnation can be regarded as the (free, gratuitous, unique) supreme fulfillment of what is meant by 'human being.'

Christ's humanity can be seen as that which results when God in his Word literally becomes other to himself in a creature. In this way, Jesus Christ is the summit of creation, the Lord and Head of the human race because he is one of its members, the 'Mediator between God and creatures.'" /152/

The absoluteness of Christianity can only be accepted if one understands that Christ is the chief exemplification of God's gracious giving of himself and the actualization of man's own response. /154/ Rahner's christology is an attempt to affirm both exclusivism and universalism, to safeguard the uniqueness of Christ and also respect God's universal salvific will. /155/

The consequences of Rahner's doctrine of the omnipresence of grace is that Jesus is the complete and definite expression of a relationship between God and man already present potentially from the beginning and capable of being acknowledged at different times and different places. There is a single history of the dialogue between God and the world. /156/

CONCLUSIONS

The contemporary christologies that have taken seriously the challenge of world religions, have made clear the difficulties underlying the construction of a universal christology. These christologies incorporate one or more elements and difficulties resulting from the development of modern christology. /157/ This development began with the humanistic thrust of Schleiermacher's christology. Christology is held in the closest relation to anthropology. The second important moment is the christology developed by Hegel. The importance here is the global approach taken to Christology and the importance given to the Trinitarian pattern.

It is through the Son that the Father enters the world and the world is led back to the Father in the Spirit. While Hegel sees the eternal as prior to the temporal, yet he does not devalue history since the Spirit can only be actualized in the movement of history. Yet, many Hegelians have played down the value of the historical and the particular in their own christologies. Certain forms of Hegelianism lead to the

swallowing-up of history in timeless truths, of the particular
and concrete in the universal and abstract.

A third important moment in the development of
Christology is Bultmann's existential approach. The decisive
question according to Bultmann's existential christology is
whether Christ helps me because he is God's son, or whether
he is Son of God because he helps me. Christology is
subsequent to soteriology. A Christological pronouncement is
not primarily a description of Jesus Christ, but a confession
of his meaning for the follower.

Contemporary Christologies, emerging in the consciousness of other religious traditions, are characterized by
their concern for the correlation of Christology to
anthropology, for the universal dimension of Christ as Logos
and for the existential meaningfulness of Christ for every
contemporary Christian. These characteristics focus sharply
on the basic problem of contemporary christology - the
relationship of the historical Jesus to the Christ of faith, or
of the universalization of religious meaning, and the
radicalization of the special occasion itself. /158/ They
bring to the fore the basic questions being asked about
Christianity's relation to other religious traditions. Does the
grounding of the universal possibility of salvation derive from
the historical work of Jesus or from the divine intention as
is expressed in the ongoing process of creation? All three
elements have been objected to since, in different ways, they
appear to trivialize the historical dimension of the Christ
event. Self-transcending anthropology is seen as inadequate
because it leaves out the indispensable element of history.
Christology cannot be reduced simply to an extension of
anthropology. An anthropological approach leads to a-priorism
where Jesus becomes the occasion of faith, not the subject
nor the cause of faith. The call to faith does not come from
history, but from an apriori existential. The revelation in the
Jesus event is verified on the basis of its ability to meet
the requirements of a person's pre-understanding of him-her
self. Jesus as the Christ event is true because he fulfills
human needs. /159/

This anthropological approach to Christology gives rise
to different theories of "anonymous Christianity." /160/ Some
see in this concept the danger of seeing Jesus Christ simply

as coming in order to give a name to a reality which existed before him as nameless. They see the danger of explaining Christ in the light of the religions instead of the religions in the light of Christ. The tendency is to interpret the Incarnation as the historization of an archetype which is alraeady found throughout the history of religions. /161/ Would the reverse of anonymous Christianity be also true? Could the Christian be an anonymous Buddhist, Muslim, Hindu ?

The renewal of Logos christology, while deeply rooted in tradition, has been strongly influenced by Hegelian thought and the humanist approach.

The Logos is the cosmic principle of order, the ground of meaning, and the source of purpose. The Logos, in its transcendence is timeless and infinite; its historical effects are dynamic and ever changing. According to J. Cobb, "...the Logos is immanent in all things as the initial phase of their subjective aim, that is, as thèir fundamental impulse toward actualization." /192/ Logos Christology claims that the divine Logos is present in all things and that it is incarnate in Jesus of Nazareth.

There is an on-going danger to all Logos Christology of denying value to the concrete and the historical humanity of Christ. The manifestation of the Logos in the concrete historical individual of Nazareth has no uniqueness of its own.

The existential dimension of contemporary Christology has insisted on the "for us" aspect of God and Christ. This has been objected to as a dehistorization of the kerygma, the breaking of the continuity of history into existential moments, the dissolution of the history of salvation into the historicity of existence. /163/ Jesus is made Christ through a value-judgment.

The objections to all three dimensions of contemporary Christology may be reduced to the following: they reduce Christ to a symbol of some timeless truths and, therefore, trivialize his historicity and his uniqueness. Jesus and the event of salvation history become mere symbols of a wider universal truth about God rather than a once-and-for-all unique manifestation of God otherwise unknowable.

According to Van Harvey, /164/ these objections rest on the crude juxtaposition of symbol and event, that in turn rests on an unhistorical view of human nature. The distinction between timeless truths and events is too crude for theological purpose.

The power of a paradigmatic event is precisely the fusion of universality and particularity. Once this principle is grasped, then symbol and history are not perceived as opposites. /165/

It is also the characteristic of a symbol that it speaks most directly and persuasively when it reflects the structure of our own psyche. The symbols which speak to us most meaningfully are those of which we have inner experience, those which tell us of reality by telling us of ourselves. /166/

The Christ-event as symbol is the outward expression that calls to life and feeds what is already part of our own inner disposition. It shows us what we are and thus enables us to actualize our potentialities as sons of God.

While the criterion for the truth of a symbol is ex- istential verification, and the existential certitude of the believer lies in the finite givenness of the experiential, it cannot be totally one's subjective response that constitutes Jesus as "revelation of God," as paradigmatic event, as a symbol of mankind's unity/identity with God. Otherwise the reason for a special relationship to Jesus as Christ would be problematic. What is it about the historical Jesus independently of any appropriation, that grounds his symbolic and transforming nature ? What is the nature of the "fact" of Jesus ?

Different authors and lately David Tracy make a dis- tinction between fact as actualization and fact as repre- sentation. Tracy distinguishes between two different ways that possibilities can become fact: (a) through actualization of a human possibility in human action or (b) through the representing of a possibility in a disclosive symbolic language and action. In this sense primordial symbols are not mere possibilities, but facts; not as the actualization of possibilities, but facts possibility and not mere possibility.

The title Christ represents a certain possibility not explicitly an actualization of that possibility by the one who holds the title. The question about Jesus as the Christ is "not a primary question of fact" but of "meaning and truth of the claim that Jesus is in fact the Christ; that the representation really present in the office of Messiah may be found in the words, deeds, and destiny of Jesus of Nazareth," /167/ and that the truth of human existence is represented "with factual finality in the singular history of Jesus of Nazareth." /168/ In the affirmation of Jesus as Lord, we find the factual symbolic representation of a new agapeic possibility for existence.

While the Christian community cannot disavow its own historical past, where the Christ event is the decisive one for its self-understanding, yet this cannot mean that only in and through the Christ event the divine has been disclosed. Jesus as symbol cannot be confused with the reality he symbolizes - the presence of the universal and eternal God in the Human history. To say that Jesus as symbol for the Christian community is exclusive and has an overwhelming power of meaning is not the same as claiming that the reality being symbolized by Jesus the Christ cannot be conveyed by another symbol for another tradition.

The finality and uniqueness of Jesus Christ involves a personal response; the judgment about the person of Jesus Christ is a deeply personal matter. As all personal matters, it demands the freedom of faith and it is always open to an eventually deeper revelation. Questions of finality and uniqueness do not fit into finished categories, "once-and-for-all" realities. Rather, they imply a dynamic process and are basically developmental as faith itself. In the context of greater emphasis on the personal, the human, and the immanent, the confession of Jesus' uniqueness and finality comes more easily in the framework of a Christology "from below" than of one "from above."

NOTES

/1/   Cf. Paul TILLICH, The Future of Religions (N.Y.: Harper & Row, 1966); James M. CARMODY, "Towards a Comparative Christology," in Horizons, Fall, (1974), pp. 15-33; J. M. CARMODY, "A Next Step for Catholic Theology," in Theology Today, 32 (1976), pp. 371-383; Klaus KLOSTERMAIER, "A Hindu-Christian Dialogue on Truth," in Journal of Ecumenical Studies, Vol. 12, No. 2 (1975), pp. 157-173; Richard H. DRUMMOND, Christian Theology and the History of Religions," in Journal of Ecumenical Studies, 12 (1975), pp. 389-405.

/2/   Robley E. WHITSON, The Coming Convergence of World Religions (N.Y.: Newman, 1971).

/3/   Cf. John S. DUNNE, The Way of All the Earth (N.Y.: Macmillan, 1972).

/4/   Cf. Raymond PANIKKAR, "Inter-Religious Dialogue: Some Principles," in Journal of Ecumenical Studies, Vol. 12, No. 3 (1975), pp. 407-411.

/5/   Cf. CHOAN SENG SONG, "The Role of Christology in the Christian Encounter with Eastern Religions," in Christ and the Younger Churches, ed. by Georg F. VICEDOM (London: S.P.C.K., 1972), pp. 63-83.

/6/   John B. COBB, Christ in a Pluralistic Age (Philadelphia: Westminster Press, 1975), p. 24.

/7/   Cf. K. KLOSTERMAIER, "A Hindu-Christian Dialogue on Truth," in Journal of Ecumenical Studies, Vol. 12, No. 2 (1975), pp. 157-173.

/8/   Charles DAVIS, Christ and the World Religions (N.Y.: Herder & Herder, 1971), pp. 39-44.

/9/   Don CUPITT, "The Finality of Christ," in Anglican Theological Review, 78 (1975), p. 618.

/10/   Gregory BAUM, "World Congress at Brussels: Liberalism," in The Ecumenist, 8 (1970), pp. 97-98.

/11/   George RUPP, Christologies and Cultures: Toward a Typology of Religious World Views (The Hague: Mouton, 1974), pp. 199-200.

/12/   G. RUPP, Ibid., pp. 140-161.

/13/   Van A. HARVEY, The Historian and the Believer (N.Y.: MacMillan, 1966).

/14/   G. RUPP, Christologies and Cultures..., p. 188.

/15/   D. F. STRAUSS, The Life of Jesus Critically Examined. Translated by M. EVANS (N.Y.: Calvin Blanchard, 1860).

/16/   Quoted in G. RUPP, Christologies and Cultures..., p. 142.

/17/   John MACQUARRIE, "Kenoticism Reconsidered," in Theology, 77 (1974), p. 117.

/18/   Ernst TROELTSCH, Die Bedeutung der Geschichtlichkeit Jesus fur den Glauben (Tubingen: J. C. B. Mohr - Paul Siebeck, 1911).

/19/   Quoted in G. RUPP, Christologies and Cultures..., p. 222.

/20/   Quoted Ibid., p. 223.

/21/   Quoted Ibid., p. 225

/22/   E. TROELTSCH, "The Place of Christianity Among the World Religions," in F. von HUEGEL, ed., Christian Thought: Its History and Application (London: University of London Press, 1923), p. 29.

/23/   J. MACQUARRIE, "Kenoticism Reconsidered," in Theology, 77 (1974), p. 121.

/24/   George RUPP, Christologies and Cultures: Toward a Typology of Religious World Views (The Hague: Mouton, 1974).

/25/   Karl RAHNER, John B. COBB, Schubert M. OGDEN.

/26/   G. RUPP, Christologies and Cultures..., p. 199.

/27/   Ibid., p. 200

/28/   Ibid., p. 4

/29/   This is clearly in opposition to W. PANNENBERG'S position. Cf. Jesus - God and Man (Philadelphia: The Westminster Press, 1968), pp. 47-53.

/30/   G. RUPP, Christologies and Cultures..., p. 3.

/31/   The realist and nominalist variables are derived from the medieval debate about the status of universals: whether universals exist extramentally or whether only individuals exist. The transactional and processive variables relate to the dimension of history: a static or developmental concept of history.

/32/   G. RUPP, Christologies and Cultures..., p. 203

/33/   Ibid., p. 47.

/34/   Ibid., P. 188

/35/   Ibid., p. 189.

/36/   Ibid., p. 189.

/37/   Ibid., p. 188.

/38/   Ibid., p. 255.

/39/   Ibid., p. 162.

/40/   Ibid., p. 163.

/41/   Ibid., p. 201.

/42/   Ibid., p. 263.

/43/   John B. COBB, Christ in a Pluralistic Age (Philadelphia: The Westminster Press, 1975).

/44/   Ibid., pp. 20-21.

/45/   Ibid., p. 21.

/46/   Ibid., p. 24.

/47/   Ibid., p. 18.

/48/   Ibid., p. 187.

/49/   "Theology knows that it must serve Christ, but it' is only now learning that it does so by allowing itself to be creatively transformed by that discipline which revitalizes and desacralizes every form in which Christ has previously been known" (Ibid., p. 62).

/50/   "Christ has been the symbol of Christian exclusive superiority whereas the word is here appealed to as identifying the principle of critical overcoming of any such exclusiveness" (Ibid., p. 54).

/51/   Ibid., p. 27.

/52/   Ibid., p. 51.

/63/   John B. COBB, "A Whiteheadian Christology" in Process Philosophy and Christian Thought, Edited by D. BROWN (Indianapolis: Bobbs-Merrill, 1971).

/54/   Ibid., p. 391.

/55/   "Buddhists have stressed that there is no such self-identical substance enduring through time and especially that the self has no such status. Christians should agree. They should more fully appropriate the recent stress on a social self, that is, on a self that emerges out of a social matrix." John B. COBB, Christ in a Pluralistic Age..., p. 212.

/56/   Ibid., p. 71

/57/   Ibid., p. 138.

/58/   Ibid., p. 139.

/59/   Ibid., p. 139.

/60/   "What is incarnate is the transcendent Logos: so it is not false to attribute to Christ the transcendent character of deity as well, but Christ as an image does not focus on deity in abstractions from the world but as incarnate in the world; that is, as creative transformations" (Ibid., pl. 77).

/61/   Ibid., p. 257.

/62/   Ibid., p. 16.

/63/   Ibid., p. 257.

/64/   Ibid., p. 257.

/65/   "There is a more subtle point. "Christ" names Logos as that by which Christians orient themselves, that to which they commit themselves.   Wholly abstracted from this existential dimension, the Logos is not Christ at all in actuality, although it would remain a potentiality for becoming Christ. Yet Christians can name as Christ the unrecognized or misunderstood working of the Logos in the world if they thereby mean to identify what they name with what they intend to serve. In this sense Christians can name as Christ creative transformation in art, in persons of other faiths, and in the planetary biosphere" (Ibid., p. 87).

/66/   Schubert M. OGDEN, Christ Without Myth (N.Y.: Harper & Row, 1961).

/67/   Ibid., p. 124.

/68/   "To be sure, the church stands by the claim that the decisive manifestation of this divine word is none other than the human word of Jesus of Nazareth and thence of its own authentic proclamation. But the point of this claim is not that the Christ is manifest only in Jesus and nowhere else, but that the word addressed to all men everywhere, in all the events of their lives, is none other than the word spoken in Jesus and in the preaching and sacraments of the church" (Ibid., p. 156).

/69/   "Christian existence is always a 'possibility in fact' as well as a 'possibility in principle.' This may also be expressed by saying that the specific possibility of faith in

Jesus Christ is one and the same with a general ontological possibility belonging to man simply as such (...) This possibility is not man's own inalienable possession, but rather is constantly being made possible for him by virtue of his inescapable relation to the ultimate source of his existence. To be human means to stand coram deo and, by reason of such standing, to be continually confronted with the gift and demand of authentic human existence." (Ibid., p. 140).

/70/   S. M. OGDEN, The Reality of God (N.Y.: Harper & Row, 1966), p. 186.

/71/   S. M. OGDEN, Christ Without Myth..., p. 160.

/72/   S. M. Ogden, The Reality of God..., p. 184.

/73/   Ibid., p. 184.

/74/   Alfred N. WHITEHEAD, Modes of Thought (N.Y.: Macmillan Co., 1938), p. 52.

/75/   A.N. WHITEHEAD, Religion in the Making (N.Y.: Macmillan Co., 1926), p. 131.

/76/   S. M. OGDEN, The Reality of God..., p. 116.

/77/   Ibid., p. 116.

/78/   Ibid., p. 69.

/79/   S. M. OGDEN, "The Point of Christology," in The Journal of Religions, 54 (1975), p. 392. "The task of Christology today is to elaborate the claim that Jesus is the truth of human existence made fully explicit, meaning by this claim that the possibility of faith working through love that Jesus represents to us through the Christian witness of faith is precisely our own authentic possibility of response to God's grace" (Ibid., p. 393).

/80/   S. M. OGDEN, Christ Without Myth.-., pp. 162-163.

/81/   S. M. OGDEN, "The Point of Christology" in The Journal of Religions, 54 (1975), p. 382.

/82/ "Consequently, if empirical-historical research should prove that Jesus did not in fact say or do what he is taken to have said or done, this need not the least affect the truth of what the Christian witness of faith asserts, as distinct from what it assumes. For, whatever the empirical truth of the matter, it could still be existentially true that man's only authentic possibility is the possibility that this witness takes Jesus to represent by his words, deeds and tragic death" (Ibid., p. 387).

/83/ "Thus, what I properly mean when I assert that Jesus is "divine" is that the possibility here and now represented to me in the Christian witness of faith is God's own gift and demand to my existence. On the other hand, what I properly mean when I assert that Jesus is "human" is that I am here and now actually confronted with this possibility, that it is actually represented to me as an historical event and hence is not merely an idea as general truth" (Ibid., p. 385).

/84/ W. PANNENBERG, Basic Questions in Theology (London: SCM Press, 1970), Vol. I.

/85/ W. PANNENBERG, Jesus - God and Man..., pp. 21-46.

/86/ Ibid., p. 47.

/87/ Ibid., p. 48.

/88/ Ibid., pp. 33-37.

/89/ W. PANNENBERG, Ed., Revelation as History (N.Y.: Macmillan, 1968), P. 134.

/90/ Ibid., p. 134.

/91/ Ibid., p. 142.

/92/ Ibid., p. 143.

/93/ John HICK, God and the Universe of Faiths (N.Y.: St. Martin's Press, 1973).

/94/ Ibid., p. 131.

/95/ Ibid., p. 101.

/96/ Ibid., p. 106.

/97/ Ibid., p. 106.

/98/ "...to call Jesus: God, Son of God, God incarnate, etc. is to use poetic (or if you like, mythological) language which appropriately expresses loving devotions and commitment but which is misused when it is revealed as a set of literal propositions from which to draw further literal conclusions. That the imagery of incarnation has no literal meaning was made clear by the history of the Christological heresies, most of which were misguided attempts to give literal content to the idea of incarnation instead of leaving it in the realm of mystery and religious myth." (John HICK, "Christ's Uniqueness," in Reform, 1974, p. 19).

/99/ John HICK, "Christ's Uniqueness," in Reform, 1974, p. 18.

/100/ Ibid, p. 19.

/101/ John HICK, The Universe of Faiths..., p. 152.

/102/ Ibid., p. 152.

/103/ Ibid., p. 153.

/104/ Ibid., p. 174.

/105/ Don CUPITT, "One Jesus, Many Christs ?" in Stephen W. Sykes - John P. CLAYTON, Editors, Christ, Faith and History (London: Cambridge University Press, 1972), pp. 131-144; Don CUPITT, "The Finality of Christ," in Theology, 78 (1975), pp. 618-629.

/106/ Don CUPITT, "The Finality of Christ," in Theology, 78 (1975), p. 618.

/107/ Ibid., p. 625.

/108/   Ibid., p. 625.

/109/   Don CUPITT, "One Jesus, Many Christs"..., p. 143.

/110/   Ibid., p. 143.

/111/   Don CUPITT, "The Finality of Christ", in Theology, 78 (1975), p. 626.

/112/   Don CUPITT, "One Jesus, Many Christs ?"..., p. 144.

/113/   John A. T. Robinson, The Human Face of God (Philadelphia: The Westminster Press, 1973).

/114/   Ibid., p. 216.

/115/   Ibid., p. 216.

/116/   Ibid., p. 220.

/117/   Ibid., p. 229.

/118/   Ibid., p. 203.

/119/   Ibid., p. 203.

/120/   Ibid., p. 218.

/121/   Ibid., p. 209.

/122/   Paul KNITTER, "European Protestant and Catholic Approaches to the World Religions: Complements and Contrasts" in Journal of Ecumenical Studies, vol. 12, No. 1 (1975), pp. 13-29.

/123/   Charles DAVIS, Christ and the World Religions (N.Y.: Herder and Herder, 1971).

/124/   Ibid., p. 14.

/125/   Ibid., p. 65.

/126/   Ibid., p. 67.

/127/ "Again, while the meaning immanent in two sets of symbols may be complementary, this does not mean that they can be combined in their functions as dynamic images in the religious life of a person or group." (Ibid., p. 112).

/128/ Ibid., p. 124.

/129/ Ibid., p. 124.

/130/ Ibid., p. 126.

/131/ Ibid., p. 126.

/132/ Ibid., p. 127.

/133/ Ibid., p. 127.

/134/ Ibid., p. 128.

/135/ Raymond PANIKKAR, The Unknown Christ of Hinduism (London: Darton, Longman and Todd, 1961).

/136/ R. PANIKKAR, Asia and Western Romance (N.Y.: Collier Brooks, 1969).

/137/ "Christianity in India should not be an imported, fully-fledged and highly developed religion but Hinduism itself converted - or Islam, or Buddhism, whatever it may be... The process of conversion implies a death and resurrection, but just as the risen Christ or the baptized person is the same as previously and yet is a new being, likewise converted Hinduism is the true risen Hinduism, the same and yet renewed, transformed. In one word, the Church brings every true and authentic religion to its fulfillment through a process of death and resurrection which is the true meaning of conversion" (R. PANIKKAR, "The Relation of Christian to Non-Christian Surroundings," in J. NEUMER, Ed. (London: Burns & Oates, 1967), p. 144).

/138/ R. PANIKKAR, The Trinity and World Religions: Icon-Person-Mystery (Bangalore: C.I.S.R.S., 1970), p. 3.

/139/ R. PANIKKAR, "The Category of Growth in Comparative Religion: A Critical Self-Examination," in Harvard Theological Review, 66 (1973), p. 128.

/140/ R. PANIKKAR, Salvation in Christ: Concreteness and Universality (Santa Barbara, 1972), pp. 32-33.

/141/ Ibid., p. 39.

/142/ Ibid., p. 40.

/143/ Ibid., p. 51.

/144/ Ibid., p. 50.

/145/ "....Because the human person is not just an individual, but also has a sociological and a historical dimension, salvation, through an inner and personal act of Christ, Is prepared and is normally carried out by external and visible means which we call sacraments. The good and bona fide Hindu is saved by Christ and not by Hinduism, but it is through the sacraments of Hinduism, through the message of morality and good life, through the Mysterion which comes down to him through Hinduism, that Christ saves the Hindu normally. This amounts to saying that Hinduism has also a place in the universal saving providence of God" (R. PANIKKAR, The Unknown Christ of Hinduism..., p. 54).

/146/ Karl RAHNER, "Christianity and the Non-Christian Religions," in Theological Investigations, Vol. V. transl. by Karl H. KRUGER (Baltimore: Helicon Press, 1966), pp. 121-132; "Anonymous Christians," in Theological Investigations, Vol. VI, transl. by Karl H. and Boniface KRUGER (Baltimore: Helicon Press, 1969), pp. 390-398; "Anonymous Christianity and the Missionary Task of the Church," in IDOC International, 1:1 (North American Edition), Arpril 4, 1970, pp. 70-99; Karl RAHNER, "Atheism and Implicit Christianity," in Theological Investigations, Vol. IX (N.Y.: Herder & Herder, 1972), pp. 145-165; Id., "Church, Churches and Religions," in Theological Investigations, Vol. X (N.Y.: Herder & Herder, 1973), pp. 30-50.

/147/ K. RAHNER, "Anonymous Christianity and the Missionary Task of the Church," in Theological Investigations, Vol. XII (N.Y.: Seabury Press, 1974), pp. 161-181.

/148/ K. RAHNER, "Membership in the Church," in Theological Investigations, Vol. II (N.Y.: Herder & Herder,, 1960), p. 3.

/149/   K. RAHNER, "Nature and Grace," in Theological Investigations, Vol. IV (N.Y.: Seabury Press, 1974), pp. 176-177.

/15/0   Ibid., p. 177.

/151/   K. RAHNER, "Trinity," in Encyclopaedia of Theology (N.Y.: Seabury Press, 1967), 1758-1762.

/152/   K. RAHNER & H. VORGRIMLER, Dictionary of Theology (N.Y. Herder & Herder, 1965), p. 24.

/153/   Ibid., p. 24.

/154/   K. RAHNER, "On the Theology of the Incarnation," in Theological Investigations, Vol. IV (N.Y.: Seabury Press, 1974), pp. 105-121.

/155/   "If, on the one hand, we conceive salvation as something specifically Christian, if there is no salvation apart from Christ (...); and if on the other hand God has really, truly and seriously intended this salvation for all men - then these two aspects cannot be reconciled in any other way then (sic) by stating that every human being is really and truly exposed to the influence of divine supernatural grace" (K. RAHNER, "Christianity and the Non-Christian Religions," in Theological Investigations, (N.Y.: Seabury Press, 1974), p. 123.

/156/   Ibid., p. 123.

/157/   John MACQUARRIE, "Some Problems of Modern Christology," in The Indian Journal of Theology, 23 (1974), pp. 155-175.

/158/   David TRACY, Blessed Rage for Order (N.Y.: Seabury Press, 1975), p. 206.

/159/   Hans Urs von BALTHASAR, Word and Redemption (N.Y.: Herder & Herder, 1969,), pp. 23-48.

/160/   Cf. Anita ROPER, The Anonymous Christian (N.Y.: Sheed & Ward, 1966).

/161/   Cf. Ulrich MANN, Theogonische Tage (Stuttgart, E. Klett, 1970).

/162/   John B. COBB, Christ in a Pluralistic Age (Phila-delphia: Westminster Press, 1975), p. 76.

/163/   Cf. W. PANNENBERG, Jesus - God and Man..., pp. 47-53.

/164/   Van A. HARVEY, The Historian and the Believer (N.Y.: Macmillan, 1966), p. 286.

/165/   This is affirmed by Helmut R. NIEBUHR: "For history may function as myth or as symbol when men use it (or are forced by processes in their history itself to imply it) for understanding their present and their future. When we grasp our present, not so much as a product of our past, but more as essentially revealed in that past, then the historical account is necessarily symbolic; it is not merely descriptive of what was once the case: (The Responsible Self (N.Y.: Harper & Row, 1963), p. 156).

/166/   Paul RICOEUR, The Symbolism of Evil (Boston: Beacon Press, 1967), pp. 353-357.

/167/   D. TRACY, Blessed Rage for Order, p. 216.

/168/   Ibid., p. 217.

DOES COPERNICUS HELP ?

REFLECTIONS FOR A CHRISTIAN

THEOLOGY OF RELIGIONS

J. J. Lipner

I want to consider in this paper a question that is looming large in the theology of most world religions, not least in the Christian tradition. The following discussion will be confined to the Christian standpoint, though I hope mutatis mutandis the main points will be seen to apply to other religious perspectives as well. Specifically then, this question can be expressed in two ways. We may ask, (i) in the context of the contemporary dialogue situation, how is the committed Christian to regard the adherents of non-Christian religions? and (ii) what status do these alien belief-systems have with respect to the Christian faith-response? Both forms of the issue are often discussed it seems to me without due attention being given to an important distinction between them. So, at the outset, it will be useful to make one or two observations about this. First of all, it is inevitable, I think, that an evaluational factor is implied by both formulations. We are pondering a basically Christian assessment of religious traditions that are non-Christian, and any solution suggested which eventually eliminates a one-sided overall perspective will apparently put us in a dilemma. For, on the one hand, a Christian theology

Religious Studies, Cambridge Univ. Press, 13, 1977, pp. 248-258. Reprinted by permission of the publishers.

of religions will be expected to produce a Christian (and therefore evaluational) result; on the other hand, a finally non-evaluational solution seems unable to be called a Christian view of things at all. In the event of such a "neutral theology" as the latter resulting (by no means a purely speculative question as we shall see), is a dilemna that becomes apparent a genuine one, or can it be resolved by a more stringent analysis of the relevant issues ?

Secondly, the difference between the two formulations becomes clear from a scrutiny of the language in which they are expressed. For in the first case, the use of the word "adherents" suggests a personalist stress to the answer given, while the second mode speaks not in terms of "adherents" or members and therefore persons, but rather of beliefs and propositions: a very different emphasis indeed.

Now it is quite true that people's beliefs can often be seen to be isolated elements in their lives, divorced from the sort of people we experience them to be, and playing no significantly influential role. We have all met "nominal" or "token" believers of a religious tradition. But there is a real sense, I submit, in which the distinction drawn between person and belief, in the original question, is not as crucial as all that, for when we talk in terms of committed believers this dichotomy no longer obtains simply because it is of the nature of religious faith (and this includes beliefs informing religious experience and practice) to penetrate the whole man and require a full personal commitment of the individual. The believer seeks to establish as close a correspondence as possible between theory and practice. There is an important sense, then, allowing for the validity of the distinction in many individual cases, in which our opening question is an undivided one, and remains an integrated problem for us to tackle. If one adds to this the consideration that official policy-making bodies of any religion usually tend to emphasize the theoretical beliefs and teachings of alien religious traditions when promulgating authoritative proclamations on behaviour towards these for their own members (thereby affirming the wholeness of our question), the importance of working out a theology of religions on a theoretical level for any vital religious tradition, can more readily be appreciated.

Having shown, I hope, its validity and importance, let us return to our specific inquiry, I will not discuss the great ambiguity inherent in the very term "Christian" (or "Hindu" or "Buddhist") or the general dissatisfaction that prevails when definitions of these expressions acceptable to those who profess to be covered by them are sought. I shall make the working assumption not only that at least the main religions are indeed genuinely different with respect to one another, but also that Christians and Hindus and others regard each other as being sufficiently disparate in religious viewpoint to make the enterprise of dialogue a worthwhile and complex one. At least this is a reasonable starting point for our discussion and one which the course of history amply vindicates.

Now the Christian theologian or philosopher of religion ought to be in his work reflective as a Christian and it is justly expected of him to shed some light on how we might go about a theology of religions. What are the alternatives that confront him ? There seem to be two extremes in this regard which for some reasons which will become apparent need to be avoided. On the one hand there is the absolutist viewpoint, championed by most - not all -fundamentalist - evangelist groups; on the other, there is the relativist stance most clearly illustrated and articulately defended by Professor John Hick. Let us examine each position in turn.

In effect, proponents of what I have called the absolutist extreme regard a theology of religions, and consequently any attempt at inter-religious dialogue as essentially missionary in aim. The overriding purpose of "dialogue" becomes the ultimate conversion of one's counterpart or at least convincing him of the deficiency of his views. From the Christian angle, underlying this approach we have the assumption, on the one hand, that Jesus Christ and biblical, especially New Testament texts, are theologically exclusivist to the point of an almost face-value interpretation of the latter; and on the other, that non-christian systems of belief and practice have no intrinsic value at all. There may indeed be individual insights and teachings in these alien faiths which appear to correspond to certain basic Christian truths and are thus laudable in themselves, but the system as a whole is radically perverted and these insights as part of their contexts can be seen to have no theologically redeeming function. So far as Jesus is concerned, it seems that proponents of this view require an explicit and formal submission of the non-Christian to the Jesus of the gospels, as the necessary condition for final salvation. Thus on the personal level, all non-Christians who either refuse this allegiance or find that they are unable to consider it as a viable religious option in their lives (perhaps because of the nature of their contact with the kerygma), are regarded as lost. The number of individuals in this category, then, simply applies to the majority of the human race. One does not joust at windmills in outlining this extraordinary theology. The following quotations cited by Professor Hick in this book <u>God and the Universe of Faiths,</u> /1/ forcefully reveal how current and alive it is. Thus the Frankfurt Declaration of 1970 had this to say to all those who are not Christians: "We therefore challenge all non-christians, who belong to God on the basis of creation, to believe in him (Jesus Christ) and to be baptized in his name, for in him alone is eternal salvation promised to them." /2/ This statement illustrates the requirement of an explicit and formal recognition of Jesus as universal saviour. In the following quotation the view that all non-Christian religions are fundamentally theologically misguided is expressed: "The adherents of the non-Christian religions and world views...must let themselves be freed from their former ties and false hopes in order to be admitted by belief and baptism into the body of Christ." /3/ Finally, the extremism such a blanket condemnation generates comes home to us when we read in one of the Messages given in 1960 at the Congress on World Mission in Chicago that "In the years since the war, more than one billion souls have passed into eternity and more than half of these went to the torment of hell fire without even hearing of Jesus Christ, who He was, or why He died on the cross of Calvary." /4/ The view underlying these admittedly extremist expressions is not confined to relatively minor Christian sects. Illustrious theologians, who have wielded great influence in their time and continue to do so today, have embraced standpoints much more temperate in the judgement of their fellow men but close enough to the theoretical position discussed hitherto. Thus Karl Barth and Hendrik Kraemer for example, for all the disclaimers made on their behalf both by some of their disciples and in their own writings, find no way to attribute salvific validity to religious beliefs that stand outside their own tradition. "Dialogue", if one can still use the word in this context, no longer remains an open conversation between two participants based on mutual respect and understanding but an exercise in missionary activity.

In days gone by, in the aftermath of the pioneers of Empire, the naked imperialism of this approach was much more in evidence. Like the expansionist aims of its political counterpart, the policy followed was one of confrontation with the newly encountered religions, a conflict sharpened by the widespread ignorance, on the part of most of the protagonists, of the actual teachings and scriptures of their opponents. Today the mechanics of this approach has changed somewhat, but not the underlying theology. Now Christians who subscribe to these views come prepared to "dialogue", armed with information about the religious beliefs and observances of their co-dialogists. Indeed, many are open to and appreciative of non-Christian insights that can be seen to correspond recognizably to their own understanding of Christian truths. A sincere attempt may even be made to enter as sympathetically as possible into the faith-response of one's partner. But this form of dialogue, which regards the contributions of one's counterpart as acceptable only to the extent that he is a crypto-adherent of one's own viewpoint, has the same overall objective - if not the explicit conversion ultimately of the other, then the demonstration that his religious tradition is not salvifically viable. The assumption seems to be that God does not, or should I say, cannot, save non-Christians in and through their own faiths.

There are a number of other assumptions usually implied in this way of thinking. Thus the close attention paid to the literality of the sacred texts and their face-value interpretations generally results in a tendency on the part of the believer to identify the religious kerygma with the cultural (especially conceptual) matrix in which this kerygma has been traditionally expressed and developed. Now I am quite aware that we have entered upon a very knotty issue, namely, the relationship between the import of a religious message and its cultural environment. While it is quite clear that this nexus is an extremely intimate one, the validity of the distinction, I submit, must be squarely faced. Any religious tradition which claims some universal value, transcending the barriers of time and place, is thereby committed to enforcing a dichotomy between its kerygma and the conceptual setting in which the message arose. In his Religion and the Christian Faith, /5/ Kraemer states this unequivocally. He avers: "The Church is, by its nature and calling, in the first and last instance an apostolic body...It has a message for the whole world that must be heralded...This message has to go out to all men, in all lands, in all situations and civilizations, in all conditions and spheres and circumstances of life, so witnessing to God's redemptive order in Jesus Christ, by word and deed." /6/ Now how this distinctive spirit is to be captured or poured into alien contexts remains, and rightly so, the subject in much discussion and research. I do not want to make a case for a clear-cut "essence" of Christianity, or for a generally acceptable (to Christians) core of formulations that characterize Christian faith. It is quite possible that there is no Christian (or Hindu, or Islamic) conceptual core that can be so disentangled and planted in traditionally foreign terrain. And I suspect that to view the issue thus is to make a wrong-ended approach. But what I do want to suggest here is that instead of talking in terms of conceptual overlap or correspondence in a dialogue situation (on the discursive level), it will be much more fruitful to look for converging patterns of spirituality and/or frameworks of insight between different religions, the particular cultural milieu filling out so to speak such structures with the conceptual flesh of available tradition. The divergences in these patterns too must not be overlooked. For the last thing I wish to do is to advocate a universal, syncretistic Religion of Man, through a process of jettisoning or demythologizing all that is distinctive and considered valuable in each tradition. Re-interpretation in the light of the changing mosaic of human experience is all very well, and often quite necessary, but it must be purposeful and responsible. It may be that dialogue centering on a one-to-one correspondence between the ideas of two different religions (e. g. the Christian notion of "incarnation" and the Hindu notion of "avatara") has only a limited future. But however one looks at it, some disengagement of a religious vision from its original cultural context is necessary for a religion claiming to look upon reality as a whole, and it is in this regard that absolutist theologies tend to prove inadequate. Speaking more concretely, I do not think that it is necessary for a

Hindu either to unlearn his Hindu tradition or to disavow root and branch, as it were, his traditional experience of the Absolute in order to accept Jesus as the supreme value in his life and become a committed Christian. There is sufficient basis in the multifaceted historical phenomenon we call Hinduism not only to enable him to understand and penetrate the Christian vision, but also to enable him explicitly to make it his own should the occasion arise (he would then no longer remain a Hindu in designation) and even enrich it from the store of his former Hindu insights. To counter that the fragments of "saving truth" in Hindu belief are really Christian in essence is to avoid the issue. For it might well be the case that such beliefs have informed an integral part of Hindu theory and practice from earliest times, and if the Christian can talk of the "unknown Christ" (or Christianity) of Hinduism, the Hindu can just as well speak of the unacknowledged Gita or Vedantic teachings of Christian tradition. Certainly, if such a conversion should take place one of its manifestations would be a repudiation of perhaps many once-accepted religious truth-claims (e. g., "The path to moksha is through progressive physical rebirth" or "Salvation comes through the Lord Krishna") in favour of characteristically Christian ones. But this does not necessarily entail a notation of the inherent salvific validity of Hindu experience as such. For even from the Christian viewpoint, there might be sufficient in a major strand of Hindu belief to engender an acceptable approach to God, and to reflect the workings of his divine providence in Christ. We shall take up this point again later, but this conclusion, I submit, is compatible with the accepted Christian understanding of the gospel kerygma and its supporting texts, as well as with the inner reasonableness of Christian belief, whereas the absolutist theology we have been considering is deficient in both these respects. As to the first limb of this refutation, the matter is partly exegetical, partly pheno-menological, and in part historical, and beyond making the statement that the great weight of contemporary theological discussion comes down firmly in my favour, I will not go. As for the second claim of my argument, viz. that the absolutist position is incoherent from within Christian belief itself, the point Professor Hick is concerned to make in his writings on the subject will be sufficient to show this. "We say as Christians that God is the God of universal love, that he is the creator and Father of all mankind, that he wills the ultimate good and salvation of all men...Can we then accept the conclusion that the God of love who seeks to save all mankind nevertheless ordained that men must be saved in such a way that only a small minority can in fact receive salvation ?" /7/ We can add to this that any positive content to the notions of divine providence and concern for man cannot permit a sweeping dismissal of the salvific value of all non -Christian religious belief.

It must be said in partial extenuation of the absolutist viewpoint, however, that in the past from very early times Christian attitudes tended to favour it. In his extended essay on "Membership of the Church according to the teaching of Pius XII's encyclical 'Mystici Corporis Christi,'" /8/ Karl Rahner makes the following observation: "we have to admit nevertheless that the testimony of the Fathers with regard to the possibility of salvation for someone outside the Church, is very weak," /9/ but this was because, according to him, "the early Church during the period of the preaching of the Gospel more or less took it for granted that every pagan remained a pagan through his own fault, and that every heretic and schismatic was a formal heretic and schismatic." /10/ In any case, Rahner is careful to point out that the magisterium of the Church never officially accepted this stance, and from very early times the harshness of this attitude was tempered by a positive approach, discernible in the writings of Justin Martyr and others, towards non-Christian belief, which was then continued in the middle ages through the development of such concepts as "baptismus flaminis" and "baptismus in voto." The absolutists have not followed the spirit of the progressively more generous and optimistic interpretation of the Gospel message and doctrinal texts. They have chosen to retain an a priori, almost face value rendering of the Scriptures, thereby landing in a static theology of religion, with the inflexible consequences we have recounted. The result of this, further, is a tendency to neglect a dynamic re-evaluation of source material with the help of modern forms of Gospel exegesis so necessary for a relevant and vital theology today. For reasons given above then, I do not think an absolutist theology of religions can pass muster, and I shall leave it now for a consideration of a view at the other extreme of the pendulum's swing, i.e. that proposed by Professor John Hick.

At the outset it must be said that no one is more acutely aware of, or more persistent in exposing, the unpalatable consequences of an absolutist approach to other religions. But whereas the latter form of Christian theology claims to have primarily a biblical basis, Professor Hick's position lays greater store by the role of reason in the matter (though he does think that contemporary New Testament exegesis supports his views). Not only must be seen to be such. This is why his writings on the subject stress the (logical) untenability of conclusions he thinks arise from exclusivist theologies of Christ (and Christianity). I have already illustrated his distinctive approach to the question when quoting from him to object to the absolutist viewpoint. The rationalistic approach he brings to this issue is well brought out in an autobiographical statement made by him, reflecting an earlier phase of his thinking:

"I believed that God has made himself known to mankind with unique fullness and saving power in Christ, and has ordained that all men must come to him through Christ. And although it follows from this that those who do not become Christ's disciples have missed the way to salvation; yet I did not explicitly apply this conclusion to the hundreds of millions of inhabitants of the globe. I believed by implication that the majority of human beings are eternally lost; but I did not believe this explicitly and wholeheartedly, so as to have to come to terms with its consequences for my other beliefs. This was of course a thoroughly illogical state of mind to be in." /11/

Now in passing it might be said that reason certainly has an important role to lay in interpreting the Christian vision, but whether the perceived rationality of a religion is the chief criterion of its validity seems to be another question. Thus Christian tradition has, in various ways, made much of such insights as "Has not God made foolish the wisdom of the world ?" (I Cor 1:20), the "folly" of Christ crucified (I Cor 1:21f.), and the inscrutability of God's ways. But this is not a point I will directly consider here. Let us examine rather, with the help of his own words, Professor Hick's solution to our central problem, a solution he has named the "Copernican revolution" in theology. The traditional standpoint, according to him, is embodied in the Roman Catholic dogma "extra ecclesiam nulla salus" (outside

the Church there is no salvation) and its Protestant
equivalent "outside Christianity there is no salvation," /12/
and this openly teaches that it is either the Church or
Christianity (or both) which must act as the only door for
any saving experience for mankind. Following the (now
obsolete) Ptolemaic model of the solar system, the Christian
Church /13/ has set itself up as the sun of the religious
universe around which all the other world religions must
gravitate and be evaluated. This Ptolemaic theology lands the
Christian, says Hick, into "a paradox of gigantic
proportions," /14/ the paradox that a God of universal love
who is called "Father", nevertheless is responsible for the
perdition of the majority of the human race by appointing a
theologically exclusivist role for Jesus Christ in the economy
of salvation. Before we go on to consider the solution Hick
proposes for this "moral contradiction," an observation
concerning the way he poses the problem can usefully be
made. First of all, there seems to be some confusion in his
formulation, between the Church in so far as it purports to
represent and extend the person and role of Christ on earth,
and the Church as a cultural and historical phenomenon.
Consider the following quotation "we...say, traditionally, that
the only way to salvation is the christian way. And yet we
know, when we stop to think about it, that the large
majority of the human race who have lived and died up to
the present moment have lived either before Christ or
outside the borders of Christendom." /15/ Here reference is
made to "Christ" and "the borders of Christendom" and the
two are juxtaposed as it were, in one breath. Again when
criticizing recent attempts of the Catholic Church to
formulate a theology of religions, Professor Hick makes a
similarly misleading conjunction. He mentions "This
presupposition of Vatican II that human salvation is only in
Christ and his church..." /16/ The same ambiguity resides,
I submit, in Hick's use of the well-known expression "extra
ecclesiam nulla salus" (and the Protestant dictum "outside
Christianity there is no salvation"). But mainstream
Christian theology, as I understand it, has always preserved
the distinction, whatever the ups and downs of emphasis in
this regard, between "Church" in so far as it represented
Christ's person and role on earth (and to this effect
"Church" was used more or less synonymously with such
expressions as "bride of Christ," "body of Christ," etc.) on
the one hand, and on the other "Church" as a historical

development. Now such a distinction appears to me crucial not only for a correct understanding of the historical aspect of the matter, but especially for a view of religions which seeks to maintain an irreducible theological uniqueness for Christ, as well as find place for God's saving role through him in the non-Christian religions of the world. Yet Hick's formulation of the problem loads it from the start, for we are thereby led to form the impression that it has been traditional Christian teaching that outside the cultural manifestations that go to make up "Christendom," whether these be at conceptual or more surface levels, there is no hope of salvation.

But Hick's overall solution to our question is an interesting one, and is put forward with much conviction. He writes: "the needed Copernican revolution in theology involves...(a) radical transformation in our conception of the universe of faiths and the place of our own religion within it. It involves a shift from the dogma that Christianity is at the centre to the realization that it is God who is at the centre, and that all the religions of mankind, including our own, serve and revolve around him." /17/ Now it might well be pointed out, as I have done already, that the suggestion made here misses the point, for "Christianity" is a culture connotative word, and whatever may be said of individual members or groups of the faith, Christian theology has never insisted that it is Christianity so understood which is at the centre of the universe of faiths. The Church has always proclaimed the truth so aptly expressed by Wilfred Cantwell Smith in his valuable book The Meaning and End of Religion, that it is not Christianity she believes in or Christianity that saves but God and Christ that are the centre of her hopes and worship. /18/ However, Professor Hick has written sufficiently on the subject to imply clearly that not even the Logos (in so far as this name refers to the historical figure of Jesus) ought to occupy a central position in the religious universe, even from the standpoint of a Christian theology of religions. And his attack on this traditional doctrine seems to be made on two fronts, though these are never formally distinguished as such in his writings. First, we are called upon to effect a conceptual reconstruction of our traditional vision; secondly, we are urged to undergo a change of heart, to redirect our attitudes from "some vestige...of the imperialism of the Christian West in relation to 'lesser

164

breeds without the law."' /19/ With regard to the first, in so far as this is a call to repudiate a cultural norm whereby we evaluate the beliefs or practices of alien faiths, or a recommendation to take seriously the methods and their discoveries of modern New Testament exegesis, I am in profound agreement with Professor Hick. I fully endorse too, the appeal to recast former attitudes expressed towards non-Christian religions and their adherents. But I submit that all this is quite compatible with the Christian's claim for some basic theological uniqueness for the person of Jesus and that the unprepeatable transcendent relationship he bore to the God he called "Father," a central element in traditional faith, is not jeopardized by this renewal. Professor Hick does not agree. The Christian must relinquish his claim for Christ's theological irreducibility if it is to be even logically possible for him to work out a viable theology of religions, and he asserts this as emphatically as the absolutist asserts that an explicit avowal of Jesus is the necessary condition for salvation. To this effect is his challenge for a Copernican revolution in religious thinking made. I propose to criticize Hick's view first by attempting to show that his proposed theological reconstruction is basically incoherent and misleading, and secondly, by trying to point out how our problem need not be viewed as a simple either/or issue, i. e. either accept the Copernican revolution (and the consequent repudiation of Jesus' unique position) or endorse the absolutist standpoint and reject the possibility for God to act savingly from wthin non-Christian faiths. There is another way.

My criticism centres around the expression "God" in Hick's statement. How are we to understand its use here? Now the word "God" is usually employed in two kinds of contexts: (a) it is used as a term in philosophical discussion and stands for the Supreme Being. As such, God is commonly thought to be the creator, omniscient, omnipotent, truth itself, gracious and so on. (b) But "God" is also often used in expressly religious contexts, and a different cluster of propositions holds the attention of the believer. In this case "God" is given a very specific content which flows from the distinctive name attributed to the deity or Absolute by different religious groups. Thus for Vaishnavite Hindus he is Vishnu-Narayana and all that this appellation implies in a particular theological system; by Christians God is looked upon as "the Father of the Lord Jesus Christ" and this has its own specific connotations; for Muslims the appropriate name is "Allah," and so on. And while it is true to say that in most particular theologies a philosophy of God is also contained, these different philosophico-theological conceptions are by no means coincident one with another. Further, even within one particular tradition, while some ingredients in its conception of God may be claimed to be based on reason, the religious meaning is filled out and made whole from "divine revelation" or its equivalent. Now revelations vary from religion to religion, and the main point being made here is that the different religious conceptions of God are intimately bound up with, indeed, are regarded as definitive expressions of their individual revelations and underlying theologies. To return now to Professor Hick's use of "God" in the above quotation. I take it that he is not speaking in terms of the distinctive and mutually divergent religious notions of God here. Indeed, he is concerned to do away with such divisiveness. Is he then referring to the God of the philosophers as the hub of his universe of faiths? Not only is such a notion extremely vague and contentious, but it is of its very nature inadequate for what a religious understanding of God is all about. Religions regard a revelative event of some sort as the source and mainstay of their understanding of the Absolute, philosophers as philosophers do not; and while a religion may be perfectly justified in trying philosophically to substantiate the primacy of its revelative experience remains unchallenged. There can be no question of "purifying" this religious conception by philosophical analysis and so arriving at a universal consensus. For one, many basic philosophical presuppositions of say, Indian and Western religion are non-convergent (e.g. the Christian doctrine of a temporal "creatio ex nihilo" is totally foreign to Indian thought); for another, the very idea of "God" in a particular religious tradition depends in the revelation and underlying theology that produce it. Any drastic refinement of the notion by philosophical analysis totally changes its character, results in a loss of vitality, and the religion as such collapses. There can then arise no "theology of religions" or "universe of faiths." A further objection can be seen to follow from this. The practical consequences of its implementation will certainly not end in accord, for the understanding of God thus reached will either be too broad to give any impetus to inter-religious dialogue, or too narrow for a Copernican perspective as suggested by Professor Hick. Now that Professor Hick does speak as a Christian to Christians cannot be gainsaid. The whole problem is discussed within a Christian framework, he identifies himself with Christians by a frequent use of the first person plural in that context (cf. for example, God and the Universe of Faiths, p. 122); he appeals to the Christian notion of God as an all-loving creator and Father of mankind (a description that neither Theravada Buddhists nor Muslims, for example, for different reasons, will accept) to draw conclusions against what he regards as the traditional Christian stance. It is then surprising that he cannot see the fundamental difficulty in his own position. Is "God" at the centre of the universe of faiths a Christian God (and then we regress once more into the "Ptolemaic" standpoint so emphatically criticized by him), or is this Copernican understanding of the deity, whatever it turns out to be, neither Christian nor religious in the sense of belonging to any of the living faiths of the world? In other words, it seems impossible to argue meaningfully in a way that is not self-defeating for a theology of religions, or global theology, or universe of faiths, without the conclusion implying what Hick rejects as a Ptolemaic perspective, i. e. a perspective from within a particular religious tradition considered as normative in some sense for the others.

Another objection to Hick's choice of terminology, and one implied in the foregoing discussion, may now be more clearly stated. Where do those religions which accord no final standing to "God" in the minimal sense of a transcendent, unconditioned, existent reality, fit into the Copernican reconstruction ? When criticizing one "epicycle" theory which involved the notion of the baptism of desire, he noted that "since presumably only theists can have a sincere desire to do God's will, the doctrine of implicit desire does not extend to adherents of the non-theistic faiths, such as Buddhism and an important part of Hinduism; and thus does not go far enough." /20/ Can it be said with equal justification that Professor Hick's own use of the word "God" in his statement falls under the same charge? For, advaitavadins or proponents of undifferentiated monism for whom the idea of a God has validity only as the furthermost stage of maya in the unveiling of Brahman, or Theravadins who refuse to regard as conceptually valid an ultimate transcendent process or being in contradistinction to the empirical order, appear to have no place in this form of theology of religions. And even if Hick extends the notion of God to embrace such concepts as "Absolute", "Transcendent," etc. /21/ the force of the preceding objections is not met. He will still either have to reckon with the vagueness of such a comprehensive notion, or pack it with the flesh and blood of particular and mutually divergent religious conceptions. The process will still imply a contradiction between the approach employed and the objective sought; and some important religious traditions will just not fit into the picture.

Nor will it do, of course, to insist that it is not intended to stress any concept of "God" or "The Absolute" or whatever in this reconstructed theology, but the reality underlying this concept. For all the old objections crop up again. It is impossible to have a religious tradition, or theology, or sustained religious experience even, without a conceptual framework, and a study of the faiths of the world bears this out. It is the whole point of revelative encounter with the Transcendent, on which almost every religion takes its stand, that this otherwise inscrutable, mysterious reality has in some sense made itself known definitively in the particular religion under consideration. It is only too well known that the revelations of different religious traditions diverge in significant areas and become expressed in a shower of often exclusivist truth-claims. And while most faiths would be willing to grant some divine activity in the "revelative" encounters of most other religions, each clearly regards its own epiphany as the normative one.

Let me now take up another point in Hick's presentation. Hick makes much or an argument /22/ he draws from what he considers are the contingent circumstances of a believer's birth, i. e. "the fact that the particular standpoint of a Ptolemaic theology normally depends upon where the believer happens to have been born." /23/ He goes on to say:

"I myself used to hold a Ptolemaic Christian theology; but if I had been born into a devout Hindu family in India and had studied philosophy at, let us say, the University of Madras, I should probably have held a Ptolemaic Hindu theology instead. And if I had been born to Muslim parents, say in Egypt or Pakistan, I should probably have held a Ptolemaic Muslim theology. And so on. This is an evident fact." /24/

But it is not; for consider the enormous assumptions these conclusions entail. There is the metaphysical assumption that the human self is some sort of noumenal entity, existent before birth or conception in a nondescript, incorporeal state, and capable of having different identity-predicates ascribed to it according to the possible diversity of its birth-situations. This dubious metaphysical assumption involves formidable epistemological objections. For not only have philosophers found it extremely difficult to ascribe intelligibility to the notion of such a pre-existent, incorporeal entity -how would it be identified and individuated? - but they find philosophically opaque too the suggestion that a particular individual could have existed in different bodily circumstances across the boundaries of culture and space. The point of Hick's argument is presumably that since "Ptolemaic theologies tend to posit their centres on the basis of the accidents of cultural geography," /25/ the often exclusivist religious truth-claims they incorporate are likely to have no intrinsic, "objective" validity. Or rather the objective truth-content of the religious vision reflected by one such system of truth-claims is not normative for the others, but must viewed in conjunction with the truth-contents of the encounters with divine reality claimed by the other great religious traditions of the world, the suggestion being that these are "encounters from different historical and cultural standpoints with the same infinite divine reality and as such they lead to differently focussed awarenesses of that reality." /26/ But we have seen that at many important points the truth-claims of different religious traditions stoutly resist convergent interpretations, and granting the cognitive nature of religious propositions - a view vigorously defended by Professor Hick elsewhere, /27/ we are faced with the crucial problem of discovering criteria for religious truth. On what grounds does Professor Hick propose to do this without arriving at or presupposing some sort of normative standpoint, bearing in mind that it is logically possible for God to have been active in different ways and degrees in the world's living faiths, and still to have revealed himself more openly (and hence normatively) through one particular religion? For all the reasons given hitherto then, the Copernican revolution just will not work. It remains a muddle; a well-meaning muddle it is true, but a muddle all the same.

I now propose to indicate in what way there lies another alternative between the two extremes, fundamentalist and relativist, we have reviewed so far. This is the alternative which permits the Christian to retain his allegiance to Jesus as theologically unique and the basic religious perspective this implies (the position of most committed Christians) and still makes it possible for God to operate with saving power within alien faiths. We can conveniently show this by beginning with the "epicycle" objection Hick levels against traditional and modern Christian attempts to work out a viable theology of religions. Professor Hick accuses especially Catholic theologians active today of not following through the force of their convictions which are reflected in the enlightened, contemporary attitudes towards other religions, by rejecting the obsolete "Ptolemaic" stance towards their own faith and embracing a Copernican theology. Instead, he continues, they (and presumably most Protestant thinkers as well) resort to elaborating "epicycles," i. e., qualifications which modify the traditional doctrines so that what is eventually arrived at is a bit more expansive but at the same time more tortuously worded version of the old formulae, which are nevertheless retained. He reviews some examples of such "epicycles" offered by Christian theologians, and rejects them all on the basis of the main assumption underlying each, viz. the retention of a Ptolemaic standpoint.

Now it seems to me that a lot hinges on Professor Hick's use of the word "epicycle." It is taken directly from the scientific context of the old Ptolemaic conception of planetary motion to denote "a series of smaller supplementary circles...revolving with their centres on the original circles." /28/ In the same way, supplementary theories spun out to accommodate increasing and enlightened knowledge about other faiths and their adherents, which continue to support traditional dogmas, are called "epicycles" by Professor Hick. He goes on to say:

"When we find men of other faiths we add an epicycle of theory to the effect that althought they are consciously

170

adherents of a different faith, nevertheless they may unconsciously or implicitly be Christians. In theory, one can carry on such manoeuvres indefinitely. But anyone who is not firmly committed to the original dogma is likely to find the resulting picture artificial, implausible and unconvincing, and to be ready for a Copernican revolution in his theology of religions." /29/

He then accuses Christian theologians of stopping short of this theological reconstruction and weaving yet more epicycles. With all due respect, I submit that the Copernican revolution as suggested by Professor Hick can only appear convincing and a traditionally committed standpoint obsolete, when the change in viewpoint advocated is seen to have clear and genuine advantages. But I hope I have said enough to indicate that this does not seem to be the case from a number of angles. Further, the crucial consideration certainly must be the fact that most committed Christians cannot see how their enlightened understanding of non-Christian religions and teachings handed down, necessarily entail, from the logical point of view, a fundamental change of stance in the matter. Thus the traditional Catholic doctrine that outside the Church there is no salvation had as its main point the teaching that the God of universal love works salvifically through Christ and his visible Church in the world. It is Christ and his Church that are the "sacramentum mundi," the necessary channel of grace for all mankind - but this does not entail either theologically or logically that this saving love is confined only to formal Christians; or that it is to be effective only within a particular religious tradition - the Christian faith. In current discussion on his topic, there has been a noticeable shift of emphasis, away from the view that it is non-Christians as individuals rather than as members of a particular non-Christian religion that receive salvation from God, to the view that it is non-Christian religions themselves that are saving faiths for their adherents, albeit through the agency of Christ transcendent. Interesting solutions have been proposed by Catholic thinkers on this point, /30/ and the debate continues. It is quite unjustified then for Professor Hick to criticize current attempts as the reworking of new epicycles into tired dogmas. What has changed is not the basic understanding of the traditional dictum - Christ as God and God in Christ are still seen as theologically irreducible

- but the implications of its scope and range. But then this is only to be expected. The Catholic Church has never maintained that authoritative teachings cannot have their central point progressively and more deeply understood and interpreted in the light of changing experience and knowledge of the human situation. Progressive broadening and reappraisal of fundamental tenets occur in all disciplines of knowledge, and this is a good and necessary thing; why not too in theological contexts ? Sometimes old conceptions are rejected altogether (e.g. the Ptolemaic theory of the universe in astronomy) and new models, more appropriate ones, are introduced. But in the Christian context, most Christians see no logical incompatibility between the traditional teaching on Jesus and their more appreciative understanding of alien faiths. Professor Hick's basic arguments are prejudiced by his transfer of the word "epicycle" into the theological context. In its scientific setting, the ever increasing complexity of the epicycles helped a great deal to show the basic inadequacy of the Ptolemaic system. In the theological discussion the various attempts especially by contemporary theologians to come to terms with the problems a Christian theology of religions presents, play a quite different role. They shed light on the workings of a wise and all loving deity in a christological framework, and help to strengthen and deepen the insight into Jesus' unique function and status. In their understanding of Jesus as the Christ, these theologians have usually emphasized a dichotomy between Jesus as a human, culture-bound figure, and his transcendent and unrepeatable relationship to the Father as the Logos. We may well be permitted to speak of the unknown Christ of Hinduism, and still express our firm commitment to him as the definitive focus of an unveiling of the inscrutable God he called Father. Yet this need not imply that God's revealing act in the Christ-event is complete or absolutely exclusivist. Indeed without threat to the integrity of our argument we can affirm with Professor Hick that "we are not called upon nor are we entitled to make the negative assertion that the Logos has not acted and is not acting anywhere else in human life. On the contrary, we should gladly acknowledge that Ultimate Reality has affected human consciousness, for its liberation or 'salvation,' in various ways within the indian, the semitic, the chinese, the african...forms of life." /31/ I am convinced that most non-Christian religions of the world contain insights that

172

render more and more "whole" the Christian vision; indeed that God through Christ operates from within their traditions and draws all towards himself. A number of new and challenging problems face the Christian when he takes this stand. Thus there is the task of understanding the Christian path to God in and through dialogue with alien faiths, beyond the narrowing incrustations of cultural fetters. The Christian cannot say with the psalmist "How shall we sing the Lord's song in a foreign land ?" /32/ But that new and challenging questions are raised in new and challenging times need not prejudge either the validity of the attempt or the hope that some unitive understanding may result in the process.

NOTES

/1/   Macmillan, 1973.

/2/   Op. cit. p. 121.

/3/   Ibid.

/4/   Ibid.

/5/   London, 1956.

/6/   Op, cit. pp. 17-18.

/7/   God and the Universe of Faiths, p. 122.

/8/   Theological Investigations, vol. 2 (London ed., 1963), pp. 1-88.

/9/   Op. cit. pp. 40-1.

/10/   Op. cit. p. 41.

/11/   God and the Universe of Faiths, p. 122.

/12/   Op. cit. pp. 120-1.

/13/   In appropriate contexts this model may well apply to other religious viewpoints: Op. cit. pp. 131-2.

/14/   Op. cit. p. 122.

/15/   Ibid.

/16/   Op. cit. p. 127.

/17/   Op. cit. p. 131

/18/   Mentor Books (1964 ed.), p. 116

/19/   Op. cit. p. 132

/20/   Op. cit. p. 124

/21/   See Op. cit. p. 133.

/22/   Cf. Op. cit. p. 132; also see his "The Reconstruction of Christian Belief, 2" in Theology (Sept. 1970), pp. 399f.

/23/   God and the Universe of Faiths, p. 132.

/24/   Ibid.

/25/   Ibid.

/26/   Op cit. p. 141.

/27/   See Chs. 1 and 2 of God and the Universe of Faiths.

/28/   Op. cit. p. 125.

/29/   Ibid.

/30/   Cf. e.g. Towards a Theology of Religions, by H. R. Schlette (London ed. 1965), and Swami Abhishiktananda's Guru and Disciple (London, SPCK, 1974).

/31/   Taken from the Presidential Address, "Jesus, Incarnation and the World Religions" to the Society for the Study of Theology, 1976.

/32/   Ps. 137, v. 4 (RSV).

THE ANONYMOUS CHRISTIAN

10

AND CHRISTOLOGY

Robert J. Schreiter, C. PP. S

When one takes up the theme of Christ, salvation, and non-Christian religions, and tries to sort through the complexity of issues involved, one comes up eventually against the debate surrounding Karl Rahner's "anonymous Christian." /1/ In the years since the idea was first put forward, it has generated a good deal of discussion and a large amount of literature. In that discussion, the anonymous Christian has drawn alternately praise and criticism.

On the one hand, the theory has been praised as a well-reasoned attempt tto bring together imaginatively the doctrine of the universal salvific will of God with the contingencies of the missionary activities of the Church. In doing so, it accounts for those people of good will who, through no fault of their own, have not heard the Good News, yet still might enjoy a special relationship with God.

___

Fr. Robert J. Schreiter, C.PP.S. is an Assistant Professor of Doctrinal Theology and Dean of the Catholic Theological Union, Chicago, Illinois.

This selection was originally a paper presented at the annual meeting of the American Society of Missiology (ASM) in June 1977 at North Park Theological Seminary in Chicago. It was published simultaniously by Missiology, the quarterly journal of ADM and by the Occasional (now International) Bulletin of Missionary Research. Vol. 2, 1978, p. 2-11.

But on the other hand, the anonymous Christian has also had coals heaped upon his head. Among the major criticisms are that this theory does not take into account sufficiently the fact that Christianity is by definition an explicit confession of faith in Jesus Christ; that it owes more to Rahner's transcendental anthropology than to the biblical witness; that it does not provide adequately for the central Christian categories of justification and conversion; that it lacks specific Christological and kerygmatic content; that it might undermine the missionary task of the Church; that it clouds seriously the meaning of Church; that it shows an insensitivity to the religious commitment of other peoples.

Yet for all these difficulties, the anonymous Christian has shown remarkable vitality. As recently as a few years ago, on the anniversary of Rahner's seventieth birthday, a special Festschrift was planned devoted entirely to his notion of the anonymous Christian. /2/ For here lies the overriding significance of the theory of the anonymous Christian, no matter what one's judgment upon it may be: Rahner has woven together into a single theological fabric a large number of disparate but related issues that surround the problematic of Christ, salvation, and non-Christian religions. As he himself has pointed out on a number of occasions, one is free to accept or reject his theory of the anonymous Christian, but the issues with which the theory deals will eventually have to be faced by the believer in one way or another.

I do not intend to recapitulate the many treatments of the anonymous Christian here in any detail. Nor do I intend to work directly with Rahner's theory internally, by criticizing this point or amending that one. It seems to me that such an approach has already been undertaken often enough, and that the major profit to be gained from doing so has in the main already been achieved. But at the same time, one cannot ignore Rahner's anonymous Christian; the problems with which the theory deals are indeed our problems and will remain with us.

I would like to propose a different kind of approach. To begin, I will try to locate the major clusters of theological themes and issues that Rahner's theory brings together. Whatever the future of the anonymous Christian, or any alternate theory, it might be helpful to try to at least list these issues and themes that imply upon our discussion so as to know better what kinds of problem we will also need to take into account. Next, I hope to isolate major criticisms directed against the theory of the anonymous Christian, since these are presumably also issues impinging upon the problematic of Christ, salvation, and non-Christian religion that Rahner's theory does not take up in a satisfactory fashion.

With that done, I would like to turn to a recasting of concerns embodied in Rahner's theory. This will be done only in outline form, since space does not permit a full working out of such an extensive theory as would be needed. The alternate proposed here will, of course, be slightly skewed by the fact that it is dominated by some of the major criticisms of Rahner's theory. But perhaps what is lost in proportion might become a gain in perspective. Finally, I will explore briefly some of the implications of this alter-nate approach to the problematic of Christ, salvation, on non-Christian religions, investigating what sorts of new possibilities it might open up for us.

Themes and Issues

As was noted above, the persuasive power of Rahner's theory of the anonymous Christian owes much to the fact that so many different and important themes of Christian belief, and so many issues facing the Church in the multi-plicity of situations and cultures, are woven together into a single fabric. There are at least five major topic areas that bring together such theological theories and practical issues: the universal salvific will of God; creation and redemption theology; Christianity and the Church; Christ, Christology and soteriology; and culture. I would want to begin then, by trying to indicate what seem to be the major themes and issues clustering around each of these topic areas.

1. The Universal Salvific Will of God

This topic area is central to the entire problematic of Christian salvation, and non-Christian religions. For if Christians did not believe that God wills his salvation for all peoples, the question we are addressing here would not arise.

First of all, belief in God's universal salvific will is centrally the missionary activity. Without it, there would be no need to be out to engage in preaching and other activity.

Second, how we understand the realization of God's salvific will, will determine the style of our missionary activity. To what extent does it depend upon God's prior activity and to what extent upon the missionary's presence? Rahner's opting more for the former than for the latter has led to accusations that the theory the anonymous Christian undermines missionary activity.

Third, the universal salvific will is a crucial Christological category. The universality of that will is connected intimately with our understanding of the Lordship of Christ over all human history. It is within the context of that will that Christians can assess and anticipate the full Lordship of Christ over the world.

Fourth, there is the issue of what Rahner calls a "salvation optimism." The Christian Church, in confessing the universal salvific will, has been alternately pessimistic about the range of reali zation of that will - in the belief in the massa damnata - and more optimistic about that realization outside an explicit Christian agency in discussing inculpable ignorance and, more recently, the role of good will in the life of the human race. At least within the Roman Catholic communion, Rahner senses a move toward a salvation optimism that accords more power to God's salvific intent than to our weakness and inadequacy in the missionary task (1973:150f.)

2. Creation and Redemption Theology

This topic area and the tensions within it, are as old as the theologies within the New Testament and stretch back even further into the Hebrew Testament. The fundamental problematic seems to be this: How is one to interpret, and reinterpret, the world in view of the saving acts of God that his people have experienced and now confess ? What is the relation between God's first act of creation and his second act of redemption, and how does the second become coextensive with the first ?

First, our understanding of anthropology, of what it means to be human, has to be considered. What is the relation of humanity to the rest of creation and to God ? Rahner himself begins here, drawing upon the transcendental anthropology he developed in his early philosophical works (1968b;1969). But it is not simply a matter of setting out an anthropology; one must decide whether creation or redemption plays the more important role in one's point of departure. In so deciding, one makes a statement about the relation of creation and redemption theology.

Second, one must explore the meaning of the Christian doctrine of the fall and its impact on human life. How this sense of fallenness expresses itself in human life, how it changes human life, and what is needed to rectify the fall are associated issues. It has important implications for how one constructs one's anthropology. In conjunction with this, one needs to ask to what extent one can understand the meaning of the redemption. Rahner's theory, in tending more toward a creation-based rather than a redemption-based anthropology, tends to play down the significance of the fall, at least in its classical formulations.

Third, there is the theme of nature and grace, the question of how God does intervene in the human condition. Associated with this is the question of what constitutes justification and how the experience of grace changes the human condition. If sin totally perverts human nature, then nothing less than an utter transformation, perhaps having little or no continuty with the previous state, will be called for in justification and conversion. If sin wounds human nature but does not destroy it, then grace constitutes a refinement and elevation of human nature. The implications of one's stance on this point will direct one's approach to other religious systems, to the extent of indigenization of theology and Church, to the question of culture. Rahner chooses to emphasize the latter position here more than the former, a not uncommon position for a Roman Catholic theologian.

Fourth, the relation of human history to salvation history, and their respective and mutual interpretations, merits consideration. What is the relation between the history of the creating God and the history of the saving God? Is the saving history an explicitation of creation history or an intervention within it? This theme has to do with the radical Christian commitment to history and the exploration of its meaning for Christian life. Does, for example, this radical commitment necessarily lead to an exclusivist Christology that can be extended only by explicit missionary activity? One becomes acutely aware that history, of any kind, does not interpret itself; that history is at least partially created in the retelling of events. /3/ In exploring the problem of interpretation, the question of revelation arises again. One is reminded of the discussions of primitive revelation of the past few centuries. Somehow, one has to come to terms with this question of the relations of different histories, since they touch upon many of the themes of Christian universalism. Rahner has taken up this question in some detail (1966b). Somehow one has to bring about a reconciliation of the God of creation and the God of redemption, of the God of infinite power and the God of infinite love, a problem that has always haunted our theodicies.

Fifth, there is the question of the relation of the incarnation to the redemption. The classic discussion of this is the medieval debate on the motive of the incarnation - cur deus homo. Does the incarnation flow from God's creative activity, as a full manifestation of his love; or does it arise from his redemptive activity, in the context of sin, justification, and reconciliation? While the history of that debate might seem obscurantist, the meaning of redemption is the issue at stake, and how it fits into God's full plan. This problem manifests itself already in the struggle to understand the relation of Jesus to the Father in the prototrinitarianism of the New Testament. It recurs in those patristic developments where the redemptive character of the moment of the incarnation is reviewed. And, in yet another way, it is involved in the question of whether the Apologists' Logos theology represents a departure from the apostolic witness into a Hellenization of Christianity, or whether it is but a fuller realization of the significance of the redemptive suffering and death of Jesus. If one attaches great significance to the incarnation as the sanctification of all human nature (as would Rahner), one is open in a different way to the question of salvation in non-Christian religions than one would be if the emhphasis is placed on the events of the suffering and death of Jesus as the sole instrument of our redemption.

And, finally, we come to the question of natural theology. Rahner's theory of the anonymous Christian has been considered by many to be a natural theology based on reason rather than a theory growing out of the witness of the Apostolic Church. It is of course commonplace to note that a natural theology has to establish its own legitimacy in the minds of many Christians. Yet if one is to deal with the full implications of the doctrine of creation, one will be forced to construct at least a rudimentary natural theology. To fail to do so leads to an insistence on the total depravity of humankind as a consequence of the fall (and will come perilously close to denying the universal salvific will of God), and to a triumphalist notion of Church as the sole arbiter of human history. In many ways, the themes and topics outlined in this section on creation and redemption theology come together in an important way in the notion of a natural theology.

3. Christianity and the Church

It is the conjunction of the universal salvific will of God with the event of the Christian Church that seems to have raised most of those questions that have given us the debate about the anonymous Christian. There seem to be three interrelated themes involved here.

The first is the relation of the Church to the Kingdom of God. Missiologists need not be apprised of this problem, of whether the Church is to be considered coextensive with the Kingdom of God, a proleptic realization of it, or its herald - nor need they be apprised of what each position means for missionary activity. The relation of the Church to the Kingdom of God, and the Church's responsibility and task in the world in light of that relation, constitute a major consideration in the direction of its activity.

The second theme is closely allied to this question, and provides the crucial point of contact with the unviersal salvific will of God - namely, the explicit nature of the Christian confession. In other words, what constitutes membership in the community of grace? It is at this point

181

that many critics have noted that to be an "anonymous" Christian must be a contradiction in terms. The New Testament seems to insist upon an explicit confession of faith (Rom. 10:10) and the need for preaching the Good News implies it (Rom. 10:14-15). Without an explicit Christianity, there would be no missionary enterprise. Yet when the explicit nature of the Christian confession is confronted with the universal salvific will of God, one runs into a number of problems. What of those who have had no opportunity to have Good News preached to them? A variety of resolutions to this dilemma have been offered, and the anonymous Christian is merely the most recent of them. The early medievals spoke of a votum ecclesiae or a votum baptismi, whereby people lived in such a way as to will full communion with God, even though they could not express this in an explicit Christian confession of faith (Rahner 1975). While this may solve the problem of the people of good life and of good will, it does not answer the question about the role of explicit Christian confession, and the content of such a confession.

The third theme is correlative to the first. What is the role of the Church, as the community of grace, within the entire salvific plan of God; or, conversely, if the Church is the salvific instrument of God's plan, what constitutes the Church ? In answer to the latter, there has been a tendency to call the Church the community of all those who have been justified in the sign of God, in whatever way. One is reminded in this instance of publications such as the ecclesia ab Abel, to indicate a sense of Christ beginning prior to and extending beyond the immediate reach of the event of Jesus Christ (Congar 1952). But one wonders whether "Church" then might lose all meaning. This becomes particularly clear -that a fairly clear sense of ecclesiology is important - when one confronts other religious systems.

4.   Christ, Christology, and Soteriology

The themes and issues in this topic area recapitulate many of those referred to above, but bring them into a new and more central focus. When considered in this light, it becomes clear theories like those of the anonymous Christian have exercised the influence they have; for the themes and issues brought together are focussed not so much because of peculiar historical circumstances but by the fact that they lie at the heart of Christianity itself.

The first theme is a restatement of the questions of the importance of the universal salvific will of God upon human history. This restatement expresses the central paradox of Christology itself, namely, how can an historically contingent figure, Jesus of Nazareth, have universal, transtemporal, and transcultural significance ? What is the 'relation of the incarnation to history? It refocusses the question of the salvation of those who have never heard the name of Jesus. This also touches on the question of specificity and universality found in discussions of the explicitness of Christian confession mentioned above. How one deals with the question of history, and what constitutes universal significance, will be of central interest in dealing with the question of salvation.

A second, related theme deals with the person of Jesus and the salvation wrought by God in him. To what extent is salvation connected with the person of Jesus? The Church affirmed from the beginning, particularly in the debates with the Gnostics, that Jesus is a person and not merely a principle. But the question as to what constitutes personhood and the relation of personhood to history and to universal significance have continued to dog the Christian Church, even down to the modern period (witness Hegelian Christologies of the nineteenth century and, more recently, the Christology of Paul Tillich). How is the personhood of Jesus preserved in those three most common manifestations of his presence among generations of Christians: the Word, the Eucharist, and the Spirit? The issue of the role of personhood and its relation to history and universality needs more exploration than can be given here. Because of Rahner's natural theological approach, this has been a controverted area of his theory recently, Rahner has undertaken to discuss the anonymous Christian in terms of the presence of the Spirit of Jesus that fills the whole world (1976b:308312). But the problem continues, not only for Rahner, but for all Christian theologians.

A third theme is the meaning of justification and what brings it about. As Rahner has shown, the grace of justi- fication is prior to conversion and the act of faith

(1974a:171). To hold otherwise leads us into a Pelagian controversy. But if the grace of justification is present to the unbeliever prior to the preaching, what does this say about the person of Jesus, the role of preaching, and the task of the Church? What becomes the role of the missionary activity in light of this - explication of what is already present, of a bringing of the Good News for the first time? Rather than undermining the missionary activity of the Church, Rahner's theory of the anonymous Christian forces us to look closely at what is the meaning of the Lordship of Christ in the world and the relation of the missionary task to it.

A fourth, related theme is the question of the incarnation or the redemption as the principal moment of God's saving power for us in Jesus. Rahner's own theory, as well as much of patristic theology, seems to emphasize the role of the incarnation in God's saving plan over that of the suffering, death, and raising of Jesus. The point of the patristic writers is that in God's assuming our humanity in the incarnation, redemption is in fact already achieved. And it is out of this consideration, as was noted above, that the possibility of salvation is opened up to those who, through no fault of their own, have never heard the preaching of the Good News. But at the same time, we are being called back to speaking of salvation more in tune with the preaching of the primitive Church, emphasizing what God had done in Jesus. Can a similar theory be built upon the force of the resurrection as has been built upon the incarnation ? /4/

Fifth, we need to look again at the meaning of the Holy Spirit as the Spirit of Jesus and the Spirit of God. Pneumatology has been an underdeveloped art in the Western Christian traditions, and theologians are beginning to investigate once again the meaning of the Spirit for understanding the person and work of Christ in the whole of human history. /5/ Rahner, too, has alluded to the possibilities here.

5. Culture

The problems of culture arose for Christianity when it left Palestine and encountered converts who did not share the Jewish heritage. In a postcolonialist world, Christians everywhere have become more acutely aware of the themes and issues involved in the consideration of the role of culture in Christianity.

The first theme to arise deals once again with Christianity's commitment to history and the incarnation. If Christians do indeed have these commitments, then one is immediately faced with the translation and contextualization of the Christian message. The indigenization of the Church, then, becomes not so much a luxury or a concession to underdevelopment as an imperative in fidelity to the Gospel. But we know that within the diversity of culture, problems continually arise. Our preaching and teaching in the contextualizing mode can end in a syncretistic combination. And, on the other hand, our commitment to a literalism can destroy a people we try to save and so betray the Gospel itself. One can raise the question about whether Rahner's theory shows that sort of cross-cultural sensitivity in the articulation of his transcendental anthropology.

The question about Rahner's formulation brings us to the second issue in this topic area; namely, what can be said of the problem of perspective and the valuing of another's religious commitment ? How does one, from within the circle of faith, help lay down rules for the dialogue with other people of good will on the question of their relation to God ? In other words, it is not only a matter of allowing our meanings to be translated into their realities, but a translation in the other direction as well.

Third, the question arises about the object of Christian address when it speaks in another culture. Quite commonly, we try to bring what we consider human universals into play to aid communication and understanding. This is certainly the case with Rahner, who proposes his transcendental anthropology as the basis for an approach. But how does one set up cultural universals and what is their role and status within the concrete life of a culture ? /6/ To follow Schillebeeckx here, is there a universal horizon of meaning that would permit such an approach (1974:506) ? This is perhaps but another way of dealing with the theological theory of the relation of incarnation and culture. It is the question of what part of human life the event of salvation addresses itself.

These, then, are some of the major issues impinging upon the area that Rahner addresses in his theory of the anonymous Christian. An examination of these areas, and a look at how Rahner has brought them together, explains partially the continuing persuasive power of his theory. As was seen, there are almost always two sides to each consideration: and, where possible, I have tried to indicate where Rahner would choose to stand.

There are, of course, other questions that can be raised about the anonymous Christian and the concerns the theory tries to focus. One such set of questions I will not take up here comes from those of whom the theory speaks, those not confessing Christ and the salvation he brings. One such question often put forward in this area is whether we Christians, in our own good will, would be willing to be called "anonymous Buddhists" (Kung 1974:90). The second question asks whether our concern for the anonymous Christian is but the dying gasp of a Western imperialism.

But I have restricted myself here to questions arising from within the circle of the Christian faith. Rahner does the same. I do this because it is we Christians, not the non-Christians, who are most troubled with the meaning of the anonymous Christian for our dialogue with persons of other religious traditions. While it is granted that we will most likely not clarify our own minds in isolation from this dialogue, there is much in our own house that needs to be set in order, even prior to our undertaking the dialogue on Christ, salvation, and non-Christian religions. Much of that setting the house in order will involve dealing with the themes and issues just outlined, of making some decisions about our position on the spectra they set out for us, and then interrelating those positions in a responsible fashion. As Rahner himself points out, we may call the anonymous Christian by another name, but the problems will still have to be addressed (1947a:162 1976a:281).

Correctives

In refining or even replacing the theory of the anony-mous Christian, there are three correctives that will help us refocus our discussion in our continuing search for a basis upon which to discuss fruitfully Christ, salvation, and non-Christian religions. These correctives grow out of the considerations raised in the previous section about inadequacies within Rahner's theory.

The first corrective is that any theory dealing with the problem under consideration will have to be more Christologically explicit and more Christologically balanced. Rahner's theory strikes many as making any explicit Christological affirmation a superflous act. There is a tendency both in Rahner and among some of his supporters to drop back into a minimalist affirmation along the lines of Hebrews 1:6. Moreover, our previous discussion has indicated that the questions of church and salvation will to a large extent turn upon our Christological affirmation. The God confessed needs to to be confessed through Christ Jesus (Jungel 1975).

The second corrective requires that our theory not only be more Christocentric, but also more faithfully rooted in biblical traditions. This criticism has been raised on many occasions. The response is not the respective marshalling of isolated biblical texts pro and centra the position. This has already been done (e.g., Kruse 1967) and it betrays the complexity of the biblical witness. One will have to drink more deeply and more carefully of the Scriptures to provide a genuinely biblical foundation.

The third corrective requires a greater cross cultural sensitivity. The concern is not so much with our possibly being anonymous Buddhists or seeking out the "unknown Christ of Hinduism," as dealing with some of the problems of culture outlined above. One has to grapple with the problems of translatability, contextualization, cultural universals and particulars; of literalism in the use of the Scriptures, of the differing horizons ofm meaning. In other words, we need to rethink our natural theology in light of a greater cross-cultural sensitivity.

Toward an Alternative Base: The Wisdom Tradition of the Bible

If one re-examines the theory of the anonymous Christian from the point of view of these three correctives, one prominent possibility presents itself that combines

Christology, a strong biblical base, and cross-cultural sensitivity. This is the wisdom Christology found in the Greek-speaking Jewish communities in Palestine. If we are willing to listen to their struggles once again, perhaps they might point toward ways of dealing with the concerns we find brought together in the theory of the anonymous Christian.

The Christology of these communities offers a genuine possibility to us for a number of reasons. First of all, these communities in Palestine, and especially in Jerusalem, lived in a cross-cultural tension. Though pious Jews, they lived with one foot in the Hellenistic world as well. They embodied both the wisdom literature tradition of Palestinian Judaism and included within it the Hellenistic experience in Palestine and in Egypt. We may have a good deal to learn from what can be reconstructed of their coming to terms with confessing Jesus in this context. It should be noted, secondly, that the wisdom tradition within Judaism constituted a sort of natural theology (Collins 1977). It struggled with relating a local, tribal tradition that had been expanded by prophetic universalism to a concrete encounter with the larger Mediterranean world. Whereas one can speak in a universalist fashion rather readily within the circle of one's own tradition, it is something else again to test such affirmations within the alembic of cross-cultural encounter. The Exile, the diaspora experience in Egypt, the Hellenist occupation of Palestine, and the encounter with Middle Platonism provided such an opportunity.

Third, it should be noted that the wisdom tradition of Greek-speaking Palestinian Judaism was not a later hermeneutic for the interpretation of primitive Christian data. Research has shown that Greek-speaking Jews in Jerusalem formed one of the earliest Christian communities, and that some of Jesus' early followers may have been drawn from this group. There are indications that this same tradition influenced Jesus' own understanding of the Law. And within the Synoptic Gospels there are traditions present of Jesus as the wise teacher and even as incarnate wisdom. Perhaps Jesus saw himself as the incarnation of the wisdom of God. These points will be taken up in more detail below. The Q materials and the early Christological hymns attest to the antiquity of these communities.

Fourth, research indicates that these wisdom traditions were highly influential in the formation of the earliest Christologies we find in the hymns and provided a first understanding of Jesus' relation to God in prototrinitarian fashion (Hengel 1976). While the wisdom Christologies do not survive intact into a later period, their early important position cannot be overlooked. They cannot be considered as disappearing into the discredited theios aner legends or into Gnostic heresies. As we shall see, they remain central to confessing the Lordship of Christ.

Fifth, Martin Hengel has pointed out the key role played by the Greek-speaking Jewish-Christian community in Jerusalem in the early missionary activity of the Church oustside Palestine (Hengel 1971-72). If these people were indeed the prime movers for missionary activity throughout the non-Jewish world, then their experience and their Christology will be of considerable interest to anyone concerned about the missionary enterprise.

There may be a tendency upon the part of some to equate these wisdom Christologies of the early New Testament period with the Logos Christologies of the second and third centuries, and so see them as the beginning of the Hellenization of Christianity. This would be a premature and even anachronistic evaluation. As Hengel points out in his monumental Judaism and Hellenism (1974), the Greek-speaking Jews, embued with Hellenism, was on the scene in Palestine already for two centuries by the birth of Christ. And there are many indications that Jesus' own experience, as a northerner, lay closer to that of this group and to that of the Pharisees than to the official temple cultus (Schillebeeckx 1974:188-210). The Greek-speaking Palestinian Jew did not capitulate rapidly to the Hellenistic world. Rather, he continued to grapple with these two parts of himself, the Semitic and the Hellenistic, and the result was more often a heightening of the Semitic profile in contradistinction to the Hellenistic offering. /7/ And so, while the Greek Apologists were to capitalize much later on the Logos of the Johannine writings and draw it closer to its Stoic counterpart, that Logos in John remained nonetheless a basically Semitic concept.

Keeping all this in mind, I would like to sketch out something of the wisdom tradition background of those early

Christian communities, show something of the development of the wisdom Christologies, and then indicate how these might help serve as a corrective upon Rahner's anonymous Christian theory and aid us in our discussion of salvation and non-christian religions.

Along with other cultures in the Ancient Near East, Israel had a part in the generating and assembling of a wisdom literature. Maxims and proverbs describing the wise person, what constitutes wisdom, and the righteousness of the wise were collected. Alongside this, another factor came into play, particularly from the third century B.C.E. onward: the encounter with Hellenism. This contact is evident in the later parts of the Book of Proverbs, in Wisdom and in Sirach. While at one time it was thought that Hellenism was an extraneous influence on the edges of Palestinian Judaism, it now seems clear that the struggle with Hellenism occurred within Jewish circles in Jerusalem itself. During this period, the upper strata of Jewish society in Jerusalem could even conceivably be considered to be bicultural. The work of the scribes of that period, as evidenced in the work of Jesus Ben Sira, shows the struggle of preserving the ancient Jewish heritage in the midst of Hellenism, while at the same time grappling with the significance of being members of two cultures

The Hebrew concept of wisdom was never amalgamated fully into Hellenism. Rather, it seems that the contact with Hellenism allowed for the expansion and elaboration of a number of ideas already present within the Hebrew wisdom tradition. This is particularly the case concerning wisdom as an hypostasis of God and the role of wisdom in creation.

Wisdom came to be seen as a pre-existent figure (Prov. 8:220-31; Job 28; Sir. 11:1-7, 24:3-7) who was present at creation (Prov. 8:27-30; Wis. 9:9) and mediated creation itself (Job 28:25-17; Sir. 1:8, 24:3-5; Wis 7:12, 21; 8:5). Wisdom has been poured out over all creation (Sir. 1:8). Yahweh's wisdom is in creation (Prov. 3:19; Job 38-39; Sir. 41;:15-43:33). Yahweh sends wisdom to earth to dwell among the people as well (Sir. 24:8ff). One cannot be wise of oneself (Prov. 3:10, 26:12), for wisdom is a gift of Yahweh (Prov. 2:6; Sir. 1:1). And true wisdom from Yahweh since the prophetic period had been understanding the deeds and judgments of Yahweh (Jer. 9, 11; Hos. 14, 10).

Wisdom for the Hebrew was not a matter of superior knowledge, but of knowing how to act; it was a moral wisdom by which one came to perceive the ways of Yahweh. The notion of wisdom was tied closely to that of the Law as the expression of the will of Yahweh (Sir. 1:11-20, 24:23-29; Wis. 6:18, 9:9; 17; Bar. 4:1-4). The fear of Lord was indeed the beginning of wisdom, and those who followed the call to wisdom (Prov 1:8) would come to have a share in that divine wisdom and would be considered just. It is to these that Yahweh gives his wisdom (Wis. 7:22-8:1).

The bicultural phenomenon in Jerusalem, represented in the later parts of the wisdom literature, opens up the way for a biblically rooted cross-cultural hermeneutic of the Jewish and Christian traditions. Missiologists have often looked to the Acts of the Apostles for cues on dealing with the cross-cultural presentation and implantation of the Gospel (e.g., von Allmen 1975); perhaps we can look even earlier to this period as well. And secondly, this tradition had its representatives in the early Christian Church in Jerusalem. According to Siegfried Schultz, it was these Greek-speaking Jewish-Christian communities who were responsible for much of the later Q material (1972). And they also had a large hand in the construction of the Gospel of Matthew.

These Greek-speaking Jewish communities were found not only in Jerusalem, but also in Galilee. Some of Jesus' closest disciples may have been from these communities. Andrew and Philip have Greek names (cf. Mk. 3:18). Simon Peter, the brother of Andrew, later missionized in the Greek-speaking areas of the Mediterranean world. Jesus' own attitude toward the Law shows sympathies with the Greek-speaking Jewish conception of the law, with the emphasis on the two-fold law of the love of God and of neighbor as the heart of the Law (Schillebeeckx 1974:188-210). While I will not try to probe any further into the question of Jesus' own relationship to these communities here, let this suffice to indicate there was contact, and that the images of Jesus as a wise teacher and as wisdom found in the Synoptic Gospels was probably somewhat continuous with the experience of the earthly Jesus. /8/

For from the Q materials that have been woven into the synoptic Gospels, images of Jesus as being wise and as

191

wisdom recur throughout the texts. In the infancy narratives, Jesus is depicted as growing in wisdom and astounding the Temple teachers by his understanding (Lk. 2:40-52). His importance is acknowledged by the Magi from the East (Mt. 2:1-12). Many of the characteristics of wisdom from the wisdom literature return in the Gospel narratives. Felix Christ summarizes aptly the synoptics' identification of Jesus with wisdom (1970:53):

"As in the case of pre-existent wisdom of the wisdom tradition, Jesus Sophia sends prophets and emissaries, comes as the Son of Man, deals with all people (tax collectors and sinners), dwells in Jerusalem as the Shechinah, calls all to himself as the Law, is denied by this generation, is robbed of his message, hides himself from the wise and the prudent, chooses individual children, is justified by tax collectors and sinners, reveals himself to the little ones, calls the tired and weary, sends out prophets and apostles, announces judgment, withdraws and returns in judgment as the Son of Man..."

To this one can add the recurring image of Jesus as the true teacher of the Law (expressed particularly in the claims that he was a false teacher, brought forward by his enemies). Jesus is presented as being wiser and greater than even Solomon (Mt. 12:38-42).

Beyond the synoptic material, we find in the most ancient Christian hymns an identification of Jesus with wisdom. In Philippians 2:6-11; John 1; Hebrews 1:3-4; Colossians 1:15-20, the model of the pre-existence of wisdom, wisdom's coming to earth and wisdom's exaltation is applied to Jesus. Paul speaks of Christ as the wisdom of God (1 Cor. 1:24). This wisdom is not an earthly wisdom, as from the Greeks (I Cor.1:17-2:7), but is a gift from God (Eph. 1:8, 17; Col. 1:9). The wisdom of Christ is the cross (I Cor. 1:18, 22; 2:2). Paul is probably responsible for the addition of the mention of the cross in Philippians 2:8, since this is what marks Christian wisdom.

Recent work on the early New Testament Christologies, particularly upon the title huios, has indicated that the early Church drew upon the models of the preexistent character of wisdom and the Law, the sending of wisdom and the Law to earth, their rejection by the majority and their revelation to little ones, to first explicate the relation of Jesus to God. Thus the wisdom tradition of Judaism, and not Hellenism, was responsible for the impulses that led to the trinitarian formulation (Hengel 1976:71ff; Mussner 1975:103, 113; Schillebeeckx 1974: 455). It is principally in this form, and in the doctrine of the Holy Spirit, that these early wisdom Christologies have come down to us. Their use in the Logos Christologies of Justin Martyr and the Apologists show much stronger Stoic influence, even though they did utilize the wisdom tradition via the Johannine Literature (Grillmeier 1975:108-113). Thus the biblical wisdom tradition has exercised a strong influence on the Christian understanding of Jesus and of God.

Wisdom Christology and the Anonymous Christian

We have explored the wisdom tradition of the Bible to see if there were any possibilities within it to provide us with a biblically rooted appraoch that would take into account both the needs of a natural theology and a Christology.

The natural theology that emerges from the wisdom tradition exhibits a strong concern for the relationship between God, creation, and those who dwell within creation. Via its hypostasizations of God's wisdom, word, and law, the tradition tries to deal with the interaction of transcendence and immanence, and at least obliquely with the question of transcendence and history.

An important difference of emphasis we find between the natural theology of the biblical wisdom tradition and the natural theology of Rahner's transcendental anthropology is that the former develops itself in categories of action and moral behavior, whereas Rahner's is developed primarily in categories of knowing. Rahner is, of course, involved in the problems of will and freedom as well, but his natural theology rests principally on an epistemology. Now this difference can have some far-reaching consequences. A natural theology based on the wisdom tradition will begin with categories of praxis as the way of coming into contact with God and his salvation. /9/ Wisdom, we have seen, is concerned with how we act, and how that action leads us to a grasp of the deeds and judgments of God. This difference of emphasis has a number of implications worth indicating here briefly.

First of all, when action reasserts itself alongside knowledge as a primary category, then we are already one step on the way to the Christian commitment to history. Yahweh reveals himself in his acts, and it is in our action that we come into contact with the God of history. We may have a lot to learn from those Latin American theologians such as Dussel and Gutierrez who have made action and history central categories in their theology. In emphasizing the centrality of action, we also move away from the problem of the thematization of knowledge of God as the sole basis for our relation with him. We move from a theology as noetics to a theology as praxis. It must be remembered, of course, that praxis has a theoretical moment, and that the theoreticization of experience grows in a dialectical relation to action. The thematization of knowledge of God can be interpreted only within its concrete context; it draws its power of meaning from within a praxis. When we begin our dialogue with non-Christian religions in this fashion, our point of entry shifts. One does not begin with a comparative doctrinal study to ascertain the presence or absence of a knowledge of the living God. Rather, one begins with a praxis, with a form of life in which God manifests himself.

Second, the point of contact will not be based upon mutually held universals. Universals are often constructed by finding common denominators. And the relative position of each of these universals in the respective cultures may be different. As Schillebeeckx has pointed out, we cannot create a positive horizon of shared meaning across cultural boundaries, but we can struggle together against those things that threaten our common humanity (1974:5:11). Again, using a praxis as a point of departure, how the wise person comports himself in the face of wickedness can serve as a mutual point of departure. From there a possibility can emerge for a careful articulation of common meaning. Moving away from the search for universals may move us away from trying to discern the nature of God toward contact with his saving activity.

Third, the wisdom natural theology of the Bible gives us a new entry to the problem of cultural diversity. A comparison of others "high cultural" elements (myths, rituals) with ours will no longer provide the sort of translation of the Scriptures into another culture for which we are looking. If the Spirit of the Lord has filled the whole world (Wis. 1:7), one must examine the entire situation and not be hasty in reaching judgments about the relative symbolic statements being made by various aspects and relations of a culture. It is such hasty judgments that are responsible for many syncretistic combinations. Wisdom expresses itself in praxis, and one must study that praxis to find the presence of God within a culture; one will have to study that action in relation to other actions within the culture as well.

But as we have seen, crucial to the question of the anonymous Christian and the question of Christ, salvation, and non-Christian religions is the matter of Christology. And the wisdom tradition has a strong Christological strain within it. Jesus is presented as the incarnation of the wisdom of God. He is pre-existent wisdom, present from before all ages and in creation. He has come to earth and lived as one of us. He has been exalted above all creation and been given power and authority over all things. In him God's secret plan of salvation has been revealed. On the one hand, he embodies the great wisdom tradition in his teaching, his being rejected by the hard of heart, his reaching out to the little ones and the weary. On the other, a new element is added, especially in Paul: the mystery of suffering as part of wisdom and God's saving plan.

In Jesus, we see that it is not his teaching that is the primary instrument of God's saving activity, but his suffering, his cross. The importance of praxis asserts itself once again. Our salvation, then, lies in this same solidarity with the suffering and the little ones. When we act in such a way, the gift of God's wisdom will be given us, that wisdom which is life in Christ Jesus. When salvation is approached in this fashion, two important questions are addressed: the personhood of Christ and soteriology.

As noted above that the question of the personhood of Christ is essential to Christological doctrine. But the personhood has always been a problematic issue. While it preserves the Christian commitment to history and incarnation, it obscures the universality of Jesus and his Lordship at the same time. The fact that the early Christians turned to the hypostasizations of wisdom as a model for dealing with Jesus' unique relationship to God may give us an indication on how to deal with this in our discussion of the anonymous Christian. Jesus is both the truly wise man and wisdom itself. The one is not subservient to the other; both are necessary to understand Jesus' significance. Their interaction allows us to see that Jesus is not merely an extraordinary human figure nor is he an intellectual principle. Perhaps Rahner's anonymous Christian grasps something of this dialectic. Jesus as wisdom itself is alive in his culture and life, and the personhood expresses itself in the praxis of his community. There is some parallel here to our own extensions of the prepersonhood of Christ into our own histories: the Church as the Body of Christ, the Eucharist, the Word, the Spirit. Again, it will be thematized differently noetically, but in praxis the parallel might be striking.

In the question of soteriology, of the justification of the sinner and the confession of the name of Jesus Christ, wisdom is a gift from God that overcomes our foolishness, the Bible tells us. We cannot attain it of ourselves. If this is the same wisdom that is in all of creation, then others, too, may be open to its urgings as well. To come into the wisdom of God creates the just man. Perhaps the confessing of the name of Jesus Christ is done in that solidarity with the suffering, with those to whom true wisdom has been revealed. Perhaps our need for explicitation has been aimed at a literalism that could bypass the saving reality of God in a concrete history.

Such an approach does not rule out the need for preaching. In a way, it allows the Word of God to assume its full power. When we speak to those who are not Christian, our preaching takes on a dual process: of speaking and of listening for the presence of the wisdom of God, of the nascent Lordship of Christ within that culture. In that listening aspect of our preaching, we not only bring the Word as judgment upon the situation, calling for decision, but in listening we allow the Word as judgment to come upon ourselves, to purify our understanding of the working of the Word in human history. God moves ahead of us, and we need to listen to what he says as we approach him. Only to speak and not to listen implies a triumphalist notion of the Christian mission -that we embody the full realization of the Kingdom of God.

This brings us to a final consideration; namely, the meaning of Church in a wisdom theology. As Rahner pointed out in The Shape of the Church to Come, a future Church will not define itself in orthodox formulae, since our sensitivity to history, culture, and hermeneutics makes this a more problematic bond. Rather, our bonds of unity in Christ will express themselves in action (1974b). Perhaps we have looked too much to definitions of ingroup/outgroup to give ourselves definition as Church. While confession of faith will always be important, it will ring hollow without concomitant action. Perhaps those not in explicit communion with us are still members of the Body of Christ in their suffering, in their struggle against the wise of this world.

One of the difficulties of accepting a wisdom theology basis for our dialogue with non-Christians is that we become less sure of ourselves. The praxis of biblical wisdom not only extends judgment to the non-Christians but will bring judgment upon us Christians as well. Where our words are not backed up by action, by commitment to the suffering and oppressed, by seeking wisdom where it might be found, we will stand under judgment as well. And our awareness of this will no doubt go far to correct absolutist pretensions our non-Christian brothers and sisters perceive in us. It will call us away from a biblical positivism and an ecclesiastical one too. It may even draw us deeper into that wisdom we preach and seek as the children of God.

NOTES

/1/   Principal loci in Rahner's collected essays include (1961; 1966a; 1966nb; 1966c; 1969a; 1972; 1974a; 1976a; 1975) as well as pertinent sections of his Grundkurs des Glaubens (1976b) and a number of shorter indirect treat-ments in lexical articles in Lexikon fur Theologie und Kirche and Sacramentum Mundi. Still perhaps the best comprehensive statement of Rahner's theory of the anonymous Christian (often cited by Rahner himself) is Riesenhuber (1966).

/2/ The collection was never published. One essay, that of Jungel (1975), has appeared elsewhere.

/3/ For an exposition of inclusivist and exclusivist Christologies, see J. Peter Schineller (1976). On the uses and abuses of the concept of salvation history, see Muller--Fahrenholz (1974).

/4/ William A. Thompson (1976) calls for such a shift away from the patristic focus on the incarnation, the reformation focus on the theologia crucis, and the more recent Roman Catholic emphasis on merit, to a focus upon the resurrection.

/5/ Most recently, and somewhat inadequately, Kasper (1976)

/6/ Goertz (1973) raises this question most effectively.

/7/ Hengel recounts the struggle of Jesus Ben Sira in this regard (1974: I, 131-152)

/8/ Felix Christ (1970) feels that there is evidence that Jesus may have considered himself to be the sophia of God.

/9/ I am using "praxis" here to indicate the dialectic encompassing both action and reflection upon action, following the left-wing Hegelian use of the term. On this usage see Lobkowicz (1967)

REFERENCES CITED

Allmen, Daniel von, 1974, "The Birth of Theology; Conceptualization in the Formation of New Testament Theology," International Review of Mission, 64:38-52.

Christ Felix, 1970, Jesus Sophia: Die Sophia-Christologie bei den Synoptikern, Zurich: Zwingli-Verlag

Collins, John, 1977, "The Biblical Precedent for Natural Theology," Journal of the American Academy of Religion, 44B:35-67.

Congar, Yves, 1952, "Ecclesia ab Abel," in Abhandlungen uber Theologie und Kirche (Karl Adam Festschrift), Dusseldorf.

Geertz, Clifford, 1973, Interpreting Cultures, New York, Basic Books.

Grillmeier, Alois, 1975, Christ in Christian Tradition, second edition, Atlanta, John Knox Press.

Hengel, Martin, 1971-1972, "Die Ursprunge der christlichen Mission," New Testament Studies, 18"15-38.

1974, Hellenism and Judaism, Philadelphia, Fortress Press.

1976, The Son of God, Philadelphia, Fortress Press Jungel, Eberhard.

1975, "Extra Christum nulla salus-als Grundsatz naturlicher Theologie ?" Zeitschrisft fur Theologie und Kirche, 72:337-352.

Kasper, Walter, 1976, Jesus the Christ, Paulist Press.

Kruse, Heinz, 1967, "Die 'Anonymen Christen' exegetisch gesehen," Munchener Theologisch Zeitschrift, 18:2-29.

Kung, Hans, 1974, Christsein, Munich, Piper Verlag.

Lobkowicz, Nicholas, 1967, Theory and Practice, Notre Dame, Ind., Univ. of Notre Dame Press.

Muller-Fahrenholz, Geiko, 1974, Heilgeschichte zwischen Ideologie und Prophetie, Freiburg, Herder Verlag.

Mussner, Franz, 1975, "Ursprunge und Entfaltung der beutestamentlichen Sohneschristologie," in Grundfragen der Christologie Heute, edited by Leo Scheffczyk, Freiburg, Herder Verlag.

199

Rahner, Karl, 1961, "Concerning the Relationship between Nature and Grace," Theological Investigations, Baltimore, Helicon Press, vol. 1:239-317.

1966a "Nature and Grace," Theological Investigations, Baltimore: Helicon Press, vol. 4:165-188.

1966b "History of the World and Salvation History," Theological Investigations; Helicon Press, vol 5:94-114.

1966c "Christianity and Non-Christian Religions," Theological Investigations, Baltimore, Helicon Press, vol. 5:115-134.

1968 Spirit in the World, New York, Herder and Herder.

1969a "Anonymous Christians," Theological Investigations, Baltimore, Helicon Press, vol. 6:390-398

1969b Hearers of the Word, New York, Herder and Herder.

1972 "Atheism and Implicit Christianity," Theological Investigations, New York, Seabury Press, vol. 9:145-164.

1974a "Anonymous Christinaity and the Missionary Task of the Church," Theological Investigations, New York, Seabury Press, vol.12:161-176.

1974b The Shape of the Church to Come, New York, Seabury Press.

1975 "Jesus Christus in den nichtchristlichen Religionen," Schriften zur Theologie, Innsbruck, Benziger Verlag, vol. 12:370-383.

1976a "Observations on the Problem of the Anonymous Christian," Theological Investigations, New York, Seabury Press, vol. 14, 280-294.

1976b Grundkurs des Glaubens, Freiburg, Herder Verlag.

Riesenhuber, Klaus, 1966, "The Anonymous Christian according to Karl Rahner," in Anita Roper, The Anonymous Christian, New York, Sheed and Ward appendix.

Schillebeeckx, Edward, 1974, Jesus Het Verhaal van een Levende, Bloemendaal, Nellissen.

Schineller, J. Peter, 1976, "Christ and the Church: A Spectrum of Views," Theological Studies, 37:545-566.

Schulz, Siegfried, 1972, Q. Die Spruchquelle der Evangelisten, Zurich, Zwingli Verlag.

Thompson, William A., 1976, "The Risen Christ, Transcultural Consciousness and the Encounter of the World Religions," Theological Studies, 37:381-409.

AND THE FINALITY OF CHRIST:

A CRITIQUE OF HANS KUNG'S

"ON BEING A CHRISTIAN"

Paul F. Knitter

A Fundamental Question

Any consideration of Hans Kung's attitude towards world religions must begin with the "direct question" with which he opens his book: "Why be a Christian ?" /1/ Naturally, the

---

Paul F. Knitter is Associate Professor of Theology at Xavier University, Cincinnati. He received an S.T.L. from the Gregorian University and a Th.D. from Jarburg University, West Germany. His publications, most of which focus on the dialogue between Christianity and World Religions, include: Towards a Protestant Theology of the Religions (Marburg, N.G. Elwert Verlag, 1974) and articles in The Journal of Ecumenical Studies (1975), Neue Zeitschrift fur systematische Theologie und Religionsphilosophie (1971, 1973), Evangelische Theologie (1973). The present article was a paper delivered at the Louisville Regional Meeting of the CTS, September 1977.

This selection is taken from Horizons: The Journal of the College Theology Society, Vol. 5, Fall, 1978, n. 2, pp. 151-164.

whole book is his response. But already on the first page of the main text a central ingredient in that response is clearly stated. Kung feels that to make an intelligent choice to be a Christian, a person must be able to affirm, reasonably argue, and claim before the world that "compared with the world religions and humanism.... Christianity (is) something essentially different, really something special." (p. 25) As Daniel Donovan states: "The whole book is structured around the concepts of 'difference' and 'uniqueness.'" /2/ And as becomes clear in the section on Christology, the rock-foundation for this difference and uniqueness is the Christian claim that Jesus of Nazareth is "ultimately decisive, definitive, archetypal /3/ for man's relations with God, with his fellow man, with society" (p. 123).

These quotations, as well as the entire book, make clear just how Kung understands the concepts of "unique" and "different": not simply in the sense that every individual and every religion is different and therefore unique; rather, "unique" means: surpassing all others, one and only, superior, absolutely and universally normative for others, definitive. He clearly argues that Jesus is ultimately archetypal, and so is not just one of the many "archetypal men" that Karl Jaspers has identified throughout history. (p. 124) /4/ Therefore, to make an intelligent responsibile choice for Christianity, according to Kung, means to claim such uniqueness for Christ and for Christianity.

As a theologian and as a Christian, I feel the need to question such a viewpoint. This raises an issue which, in our age of pluralism, confronts Christian theology as never before: the validity of claiming uniqueness for Christ over other religious figures and for Christianity over other religions. /5/ That this issue is painfully pricking Christian sensitivity is evident from theological discussions and literature over the past years. /6/

The following reflections on Kung's understanding of the finality of Jesus and world religion are presented in the form of three theses: or better, I should call them hypotheses. They are tentative and need further scholarly examination. Given the limitations of a short article, I can state them only schematically, frequently merely referring to data which I feel substantiates them.

Therefore I propose that the claim that Christ and Christianity are unique in the sense understood by Kung is: (1) not necessary for Christian identity and living; (2) not conducive to genuine dialogue with other religions, and (3) not possible according to the norms of theological and historical-critical method.

1. Claims of Uniqueness Not Necessary for Christian Identity and Living

A. Such Claims are not Necessary for Commitment to Christ

This statement contradicts common Christian attitudes and convictions. On the popular as well as the academic level, it is taken for granted that to be fully committed to Christ, he must be the one and only, or at least the definitive and therefore the best Saviour and Revealer. Yet today we are forced to ask: is this really so? Intellectually and psychologically, is it not possible to give oneself over wholly to the meaning and message of Jesus and at the same time recognize the possibility that other "saviors" have carried out the same function for other people? Is it not consistent, as John Macquarrie claims, to be fully committed to Christ and at the same time fully open to the salvific significance of other religions ? /7/ This does not imply simplistically to water down the content of the Christ event and proclaim that all religious leaders are "talking about the same thing." Differences, and therefore uniqueness, are maintained. And thus the universal significance of Jesus is preserved; the difference he makes is felt by Christians to be vitally important for all religions Yet while holding to this, the Christian can also, I feel, be open to recognize the "vitally important difference" of, for instance, Buddha.

B. Such Claims are not Necessary for ·Fidelity to Christian Tradition

Fine, some may respond, but what do we do with the fact that such claims for the uniqueness of Christ have been made by Christian tradition, especially in its originating testimony, the New Testament ? And Christianity understands itself as a religion grounded in history, therefore bound by fidelity to its past.

A reply to this plunges us into the complexities of the hermeneutical question. Recognizing this, I suggest that especially in the light of recent hermeneutical studies, it can be argued that the claim for Jesus' exclusive uniqueness does not form part of the central assertions of Christian texts, i.e., of what David Tracy, with Paul Ricoeur, calls the "referent" of the text, its suggested "mode - of -being - in - the - world." /8/ More precisely, while these texts of the New Testament do claim that it is in Jesus of Nazareth that this new mode - of -being - in - the - world is revealed (and this is part of their central assertion), the further claim that this takes place only in him can be said to result from the historically conditioned world view and thought-patterns of the time. Therefore these latter claims do not belong to the core of the Christian message.

To substantiate this assertion properly would move us beyond the limits of these reflections, I can only summarize some arguments which, at the moment, appear to me to demand serious consideration.

(a) Given the prevailing Jewish eschatological apocalyptic mentality, it was natural that the early Christians should interpret their experience of God in Jesus as final and unsurpassable. Their particular philosophy of history was such that they expected a new and definitive stage; also, it was a stage that was to break forth on the world only from Jerusalem. So when they encountered the overpowering presence of Jahweh in Jesus, the spontaneous conclusion was that this stage had arrived. Furthermore, since at least in the early New Testament writings, the end of history was thought to be imminent, possibilities of other revelations or prophets were simply beyond one's consideration. Is not such an apocalyptic mentality, understood in the literal sense, culturally limited? Must it be taken as part of the essence of the Christ-event? If Jesus had been experienced and interpreted in another philosophy of history, e. g., that of India, would he have been said to be final and unique ? /9/

(b) As many scholars (as we shall see, Kung is among them) contend, the idea of incarnation was one of the many mythical patterns with which the first Christians tried to articulate the meaning Jesus had for them. /10/ Again, we can point out that absolutist claims were a part of this mythical thinking. Jesus, as the incarnation of preexisting divine Wisdom or Logos, was thought to be absolutely unique among all humans. But we can and must ask: if we take this myth not literally but seriously, are such absolutist claims intrinsic to its meaning? Maurice Wiles poses the provocative question: just as we have gone through the painful but meaningful process of remythologizing the "special," one-time, one-man character of the First Adam in the Creation-and-Fall myth, should we not do the same for the Second Adam in the Incarnation myth? /11/

(c) Gregory Baum offers another consideration to explain the historically conditioned character of the early church's absolutist language. "I propose that the exclusivist claims of the New Testament, and the proclamation of the early church that apart from its message there is no salvation, were survival language." /12/ By this he means that given the historical context in which the communities had to "close ranks" in the face of so much opposition, it was natural for them to speak of Jesus and his "way" as unique. But given an age in which survival is much more secure and relations with other religions are not those of opposition and syncretism but cooperation and dialogue, cannot the meaning of Jesus be articulated without such exclusivist survival language?

(d) A much more general line of argument is based on Bernard Lonergan's distinction between classicist and modern historical cultures. Pointing out that culture provides the "beliefs" or general outlook (P. Berger would use the term "plausibility structures") with which people interpret their world, Lonergan describes the radical differences between the beliefs of classicist and modern cultures. The classicist outlook, which for the most part characterized the world of the New Testament and Western civilization until the Englightenment, took for granted that truth could be only one, unchanging, and therefore normative for all. Our modern-historical consciousness, on the other hand, has become aware that all statements of truth are in process, subject to many expressions, and therefore never normative in a once-and-for-all sense. /13/ The New Testament writers, therefore, as men of their age, naturally spoke of Jesus in a once-and-for-all, exclusivistic manner. But do these one-and-only claims pertain to the core-content of their message? Can we not speak of the vitally important meaning of Jesus according to the mentality of our historical consciousness?

In light of these sketchy considerations on New Testament interpretation, I feel that we can. The heart of the New Testament witness is that in Jesus men and women encountered the fullness of God and thus experienced "A complete and true manifestation of the fundamental meaning of the authentic human existence." /14/ This message can be maintained without insistence that he is the only such manifestation.

II. Claims of Uniqueness not Conducive to Dialogue with Religions

This "hypothesis" holds that even though one may be animated by a sincere desire to dialogue with people of other faiths, if one meets them with the kind of claims for the uniqueness of Christ which Kung feels he must make, that dialogue will be essentially hamstrung. This is not to say that one should not bring to dialogue clear positions and prejudgments; not only are such prejudgments unavoidable, they are necessary for effective exchange. But if Kung's insistence on the finality of Christ is one of these clear positions, the dialogue will go nowhere. His chapter on the World Religions is, I feel, an illustration of this.

A. Dialogue Hindered by Preliminary Assumptions

Elaborating on key ideas in a paper he prepared for a conference sponsored by the 38th International Eucharistic Congress in Bombay, 1964, /15/ Kung urgently calls for a more positive Christian attitude towards other religions. Such an attitude is indispensable in an age when "For the first time in world history, it is impossible today for any one religion to exist in splendid isolation and ignore the others" (p. 89). And Kung vigorously argues for the removal of what he feels are doctrinal obstacles to dialogue: the teaching on "No Salvation Outside the Church," reinterpreted as the thoery of "anonymous Christianity." He calls this theory a "theological fabrication" (John Hick terms it an "epicycle") /16/ which both waters down the concept of the church and proves to be an insult to members of other religions (pp.

97-98). Further, he chides theologians for reaching theological conclusions "without a closer knowledge and analysis of the real world of religions" (p. 99). And Kung shows that he has tried to do his own analysis in a concrete, if abbreviated, description of what he calls the "wealth" of individual world religions (pp. 91-96).

Yet even before this analysis, it seems that Kung has set up his own theological a prioris which cannot be con- tested; all of them stem from the basic a priori that Christ is the final norm for all religions. He takes for granted that the other religions are ways of salvation "only in a relative sense, not simply as a whole and in every sense" (p. 104). (Must not the very same thing be said of Christianity?) He holds that Christianity must claim "absolute validity" and still be "ready to revise its own standpoint" (p. 114). (Doesn't absolute validity place radical limits on any revision?) Also, as an attempt to steer a middle path between the exclusivism of ·Barth and the syncretism of Toynbee, he maintains that Christianity see itself as a "critical catalyst and crystallization point" for other religions (p. 112). This seems to boil down to the "Fullfillment Approach" of mainline Protestant theology represented by Hendrik Kraemer, Emil Brunner, Paul Althaus. /17/ This approach would state: "While other religions have something of value, they can truly know it only by becoming Christian." And so, after Kung reviews the positive elements in other religions, he adds that all this can"...be brought to its full realization in Christianity;" (p. 113) "...that God may not remain for them (non-Christians) the unknown God, there is needed the Christian proclamation and mission announcing Jesus..." (p. 447).

Now all this may be true. Christianity may be true. Christianity may be the fulfillment crystallization point for all religions. But this can be known and asserted by non-Christians and Christians only after genuine dialogue. Therefore Jurgen Moltmann is correct, I feel, when he takes to task such views as Kung's notion of "critical catalyst": they "...are still not based on dialogue since they proceed from the Christian monologue, not from the dialogue itself. They all formulate the Christian position before the entry into dialogue. They do not formulate it in the context of dialogue." /18/ As John Macquarrie reasons, this is to destroy dialogue: "A creative dialogue is possible only if there is complete openness, and no preliminary assumption that one revelation... must be the yardstick for all others." /19/

B. A Blurred View of Other Religions

Because of his "preliminary assumption" Kung's analysis of the religions is in many respects blurred. To a Buddhist or Hindu, or to someone who has tried to "pass over" to their religious experiences (like Thomas Merton, Raymond Panikkar, John Dunne), Kung's treatment of their teachings frequently seems to be insensitive and/or incorrect, and his evaluations somewhat too facile. One indication that he should have done more thorough study before formulating his evaluations is his glaring mistake, repeated four times, of confusing the dualistic Samkhya school of philosophy (traced back to the seventh century B.C.) with the nondualistic Advaita school of Shankara (eighth century A.D.) (cf., pp. 93, 108, 115, 301). Other examples: to brand the Hindu experience of maya as a declaration of the world's unreality (p. 108) misses the intent of this doctrine to point out the deeper, hidden meaning of the finite; and to conclude that maya leads to "cosmic pessimism" or "supreme indifference toward the social needs of men" among Buddhists is to leave out of consideration Mahayana's affirmation of the world of samsara as well as Buddha's doctrine of karuna, universal compassion. To accuse the Eastern "cyclical world picture" of predeterminism (p. 107) forgets the Hindu invitation to all to use free will in order to do something about their karma; such a world picture is no more predetermined than the Christian insistence that history is moving towards the parousia. Kung's rather disparaging references to "the grimacing gods of Bali" and the Phallus (p. 102) do not even allow the possibility that these symbols might be as religiously effective as the often grimacing aspect of the crucifix.

More generally, one of the criteria (besides the normativity of Christianity) which Kung uses in his evaluation of the religions is "modernity" - the secularization resulting from modern science and technology (p. 106). True, Eastern religions do have to adapt to our "modern industrial society" (p. 110), just as Christianity, renegingly, had to. Yet, again, Jung's acceptance of the achievements of modernity seems too facile; he might also have pointed out the limit - situations which our growth-oriented technological society have created - problems to which Eastern religions, with their emphasis on interiority and seeing through-the-material (maya!), might speak more meaningfully than Christianity can.

Such instances of imprecision might have been avoided I feel, if Kung were not so certain about his "preliminary assumption" that Christ and Christianity are normative for all other religions.

Similar imprecisions are evident when Kung turns from pointing out the deficiencies in the religions to concluding explicitly to Christianity's superiority. His arguments do clarify areas in which other religions can and should criticize and "fulfill" themselves through dialogue with Christianity. Yet none of these arguments indicate finality or absolute normativity for Christian revelation, for in each of these areas it can also be shown how Christianity can and should learn from the religions. Mutual dialogue and mutual self-fulfillment are required.

For instance, it is true that Eastern religions are called upon by Christianity to elaborate more "scientific theologies" (p. 105). Yet on this same point, a Buddhist or Hindu would remind the Christian scientist that his theological specula- tions must be based on personal experience of the Transcendent (what Bernard Lonergan in his Method of Theology calls "foundations" or "religious conversion"). /20/ Also, one must object to King's sweeping conclusion that the messages of the "great individual (religious) figures cannot be interchanged" insofar as Buddha called for "world annulment," Confucius for "world becoming," Muhammad for "world dominion," while Jesus announced "world crisis."(p. 213) Is Kung so sure these views are mutually exclusive? Did Jesus proclaim only world crisis? Are not all of them, in their real differences, complementary? Such questions demand further investigation. Finally, one of the central arguments used by Kung to establish the normativity of Christianity is its vision of a personal, loving God in contrast to the "impersonal divinity" of the East.(cf., pp. 300-318) And here again, while these differences are real, they can be seen to be more complementary than exclusive or subordinated one to the other. Kung recognizes that there is abundant evidence in Eastern traditions that Deity has been experienced and spoken of as personal and loving, e.g., in Amida Budhism and especially in Bhakti Hinduism (not mentioned by Kung). Even more significantly, Kung admits the dangers of biblical anthropomorphism and concedes that Godhead is better conceived as "transpersonal or superpersonal."(p. 303) Is it not precisely here that Christian theology also can learn from the East? Hindu and Buddhist thinkers, while admitting the power of personal symbols applied to Brahman or Nirvana, have been much more conscious of the limitations of such symbolism. Might they be said to own a cerain "superiority" over Christian thought in this regard?

In any case, the data Kung assembles for establishing the absolute normativity of Christianity does not appear to be convincing. This brings us to the final hypothesis.

III. Claims of Uniqueness Not Possible According to Norms of Theological and Historical-Critical Method

A. According to the Revisionist Method of Theology

At least in theory, Kung seems to agree for the most part with David Tracy's revisionist model for fundamental theology. This model invites the theologian to carry out a mutually clarifying and critical dialogue between the two sources of Christian theology: "the Christian fact" (scriptural texts and tradition) and "common human experience." /21/ Any cognitive claims made by the theologian must be based on both these sources. Kung states the same thing when he explains that his own theological method wants to avoid the extremes of "dialectical theology" (i. e. neo-orthodoxy, based solely on God's Word) and "natural theology" (unduly emphasizing experience and reason (p. 83). More clearly, he insists that faith statements cannot be grounded exclusively on the authority of the Bible (p. 84) but must find "verification" from "the horizon of experience of man and society" (p. 65). "The rules of the game in theological science are not in principle different from those of the other sciences."(p. 87)

If this be true, then I do not see how it is possible, at the present monent, for Kung to claim that Christ holds a

211

finality or normativity over other religions. In the present state of knowledge of and dialogue with world religions, the revisionist theologian simply does not have enough data from "human experience" to verify the claim that Christianity is based on a revelation which surpasses and can "catalyze" all others. Better to follow the more scientifically reputable path of David Tracy who claims that for Christians Jesus is clearly the revealer of a decisive truth about God and human existence and that this truth has universal significance; but he cautions against concluding to the finality of this truth for other religions:

"For the fundamental theologian, to show that decisiveness - or, in the more classical terms, that "finality" - more historically would demand, I believe, a dialectical analysis of Christianity in relationship to the other world religions: a task which would demand a full-fledged use of history of religions in fundamental theology and would, in the final analysis, prove a theological task whose successful completion would require a complete Christian dogmatics..." /22/

Such a task has not yet been carried out either by Christian fundamental or dogmatic theologians. Whether it would yield a verification of Christ's finality is uncertain. In the light of the processive, ever incomplete character of reality and of the continued vitality of other religions, it would seem unlikely. And if this were so, the Christian theologian and/or believer would not as indicated in our first hypothesis, need to feel threatened.

B. According to the Historical-Critical Method of Scriptural Analysis

One of the hallmarks of Kung's Christology is its insistence on historical foundations; he labors admirably for a Christology "from below." He has little doubt that there is reliable historical data to construct the essence of Jesus' message and the impact it had on his followers. But he goes further. Throughout the book he makes claims that historically we can know the moral perfection of Jesus' life, how he actually lived, his sinlessness, his self-awareness. "We know incomparably more that is historiacally certain about Jesus of Nazareth than we do about the great founders

212

of the Asian religions " (p. 147) He states that not only did Jesus reveal Gdod's word and will but that in his "life, being and action" he was "God's word and will in human form " (p.443) And he finds the distinctive element in Christian ethics to be the "person" of Jesus as "the living, archetypal embodiment of his cause." (p. 545). It is also on the basis of such historical knowledge about the life of Jesus that he establishes his claim that Jesus was like no other man, that he is the norm for all others.

Here a vigorous word of caution must be spoken. Numerous scholars, in view of the nature of the New Testament documents, point out the difficulty if not impossibility of such historical assertions. Tracy admits to "...the insuperable difficulties present in any attempt to reconstruct Jesus' own actualization of those possibilities (contained in his message) by either historical or modern philosophical methods." /23/ Dennis Nineham, in a challenging article in the recently published The Myth of God Incarnate, summarizes:

"The chief concern of this paper is to ensure as far as possible that those who continue to make such a claim for the uniqueness of Jesus and speak, for example, of 'the new humanity,' 'the man wholly for others,' or 'the the man wholly for God,' are fully aware of the problems involved in making and justifying any such claims...it is impossible to justify any such claim on purely historical ground, however wide the net for evidence is cast." /24/

Perhaps Maurice Wiles is correct in observing that many theologians who are "acutely aware of the intellectual difficulties in the basic affirmations of theism." are "naively credulous in their handling of the historical traditions about Jesus." /25/

These considerations do not at all undermine the fact that the message of Jesus, as contained and interpreted in the New Testament, is existentially reliable and decisive for Christians; nor do they deny that Jesus serves as a salvific symbol for the realization of that message. They do, however, indicate the probable impossibility of appealing to the way Jesus lived and concluding to his normative excellence over all other religious figures.

C. According to Kung's Understanding of Incarnation

While I find myself in basic agreement with Kung's interpretation or "re-mythologization" of the doctrine of incarnation, I do not think he is aware of its implications for his views on the finality of Christ. Kung holds that the manner in which the incarnation has been understood and then elevated as "the central dogma" of the faith detracts from the "center" of the Christian message (p. 436). This has led to a simplistic identification of Jesus with God and, contrary to Jesus' own preaching, has made him "an end in himself." (p. 391: pp. 286-287) Recognizing the importance of the titles given to Jesus for our own Christian experience, Kung warns against understanding these titles, especially those claiming divinity, too literally or metaphysically. (pp. 184-292; 390-392) They were attempts, he holds, to articulate an experience. Kung, therefore, opts for a functional Christology from below which stresses what Jesus did and does for humankind, rather than on ontological Christology from above, which insists on what his nature was and is, especially his preexistent nature, (pp. 436-450 390,291) In reality, then, talk of incarnation and such divine titles as "son of God" attempt to express the experience that Jesus was the "representative" and "the real revelation of the one true God." (pp. 390-391, 444) Incarnation means: "God himself as man's friend was present, at work, speaking, acting, and definitively revealing himself in Jesus..." (p. 449) Kung lines up a more contemporary, re-mythologized list of titles: God's "advocate," "deputy." "delegate," "spokesman." "plenipotentiary." (pp. 449, 440)

There are, I would say, both theological and especially pastoral grounds for affirming such a functional interpretation of incarnation. Yet such an interpretation also places Christianity's traditional claims for Jesus' absolute uniqueness on shaky ground. If incarnation is no longer seen as a one-time descent of God to earth, if it is meant to express the people's experience of a man who was/and or became a true revealer and representative of God, then the question is unavoidable: have not others carried out essentially the same role? Can we not speak of other incarnations ? At the most, the difference between Jesus and these others would be one of degree, not essence. But, such a difference of degree could not simply be claimed; it would

214

have to be established through what Tracy called "dialectical analysis" /26/ - which is possible only on the basis of encounter and dialogue with other religions. /27/ What has been said of Rahner's transcendental Christology can also be applied to Kung's functional Christology: "From this point of view the challenging question about the incarnation is not 'whether,' but 'why only once' ?" /28/

Perhaps suspecting this, Kung offers a number of arguments to verify his claim that the revelation of God in Jesus surpasses, definitively and normatively, all others. But again, we can ask: are these arguments as convincing as he thinks ? /29/

(a) He states that in Jesus' words and deeds, the human situation was "fundamentally changed." In Jesus were opened "completely new possibilities, the possibility of new life and new freedom, of a new meaning in life... the freedom of love." (p. 265) I think anyone versed in comparative religions would have to ask: were not such fundamental changes and new possibilities presented, for example, in the life and message of Buddha, especially in his promise of liberation from the chain of rebirth (a symbol perhaps similar to that of "sin" or "the law") and in his call to live karuna, universal compassion?

(b) Elsewhere Kung states that it is the cross which distinguishes Jesus from all others: "the ultimate distinctive feature of Christianity is quite literally according to Paul 'this Jesus Christ, Jesus Christ crucified.'It is not indeed as risen, exalted, living, divine, but as crucified, that this Jesus Christ is distinguished unmistakably from the many risen, exalted, living gods and deified founders of religion..." (p. 410) Kung's interpretation of the meaning of the cross (pp. 428436) is one of the most powerful sections of his book, but again one must ask him whether the doctrine of the cross is essentially different from similar insights in other religions. The symbol of the cross calls upon us to embrace, when necessary, the mystery of suffering and to believe that it leads to fuller life. While Buddha did not die on a gibbet, did he not invite his followers to take the risk of living a life of total anatta -no-self and to believe that it will lead to a higher form of existence, one of peace and oneness ? And the call of the Bhagavad Gita to act without seeking the

215

fruits of one's actions, is it not a call to a selfless life of trusting love ? The crucifix is indeed one of the most powerful symbols with which to confront the mystery of suffering and evil; but it is not the only one. /30/

c. It is presumptuous to take up the question of the resurrection and Kung's interpretation of it in one short paragraph. Yet despite his downplaying of the resurrection in our last quotation, (p. 410) he does consider it a distinguishing element of Christ's revelation. He makes a theologically defensible case for his interpretation of the Easter event (pp. 370-381) Refusing to appeal to any kind of "supernatural intervention," he views the resurrection not as an "objectified" or a "simple historical fact" but nevertheless as "real." Its reality does not necessarily depend upon belief in the empty tomb or even in certain appearances (p. 371) but upon a "vocation received in faith" - a vocation to "shape one's own life out of the effective power of the life of this Jesus as related in the Easter stories." (p. 380) In this sense, it is real; in this sense the Crucified is not dead but lives on. But given the validity of this interpretation (and I think it is valid), can we limit the reality behind the Easter stories only to an experience of Jesus? Is it not essentially what countless men and women have felt in their experience of other archetypal religious leaders? Again, Buddha is an example. Although his followers certainly did not speak of resurrection -that was not a heuristic category in their thought-world -did they not experience a "vocation received in faith" after his death? It was not only a matter of recalling his message but experiencing "the power" of that message. This case can be pressed all the more meaningfully in later development of Mahayana when Buddha was deified and given a "glorified body" in the Trikaya doctrine.

Such elements of the Christ event - cross, resurrection, personal God, call to love - are indeed distinguishing features of Christian revelation and are therefore vitally important for all peoples of all time. Yet they are not lacking in other religions, though terminology and symbolism differ. Thus the possibility of claiming absolute uniqueness for Jesus on such grounds appears highly questionable.

* * * * *

The above criticisms of Kung's claim that Christ and Christianity are "essentially different" do not intend to take away from the overall merits of his book. It is, for both academic and popular audiences, one of the most valuable "Summas of the Christian Faith" (p. 20) to be published over the past decades. His case for the relevance of being a Christian in today's world is convincing. My criticism boils down to: it would be just as, if not more, convincing if he avoided such terms as: "only," "essentially different," "normative."

NOTES

/1/ On Being a Christian, tr. Edward Quinn (New York: Doubleday, 1976), p. 25. All further page references will be found in the text.

/2/ "Kung and Kasper on Christ," The Ecumenist 15 (1977), p. 18.

/3/ The German word is "massgebend," better translated as "normative."

/4/ Kungs's understanding of the uniqueness of Jesus can also be stated in terms of the familiar distinction between "inclusive" and "exclusive" Christologies. (For a succinct statement of this distinction, cf., David Tracy, Blessed Rage for Order: The New Pluralism in Theology (New York: Seabury, 1975), pp. 206-207. To claim that Kung's view of Jesus' uniqueness grounds an inclusive Christology is correct but inadequate. True, such a view allows for and includes the positive, even salvific content of other revelations. However, it clearly excludes the possibility of there being other revelations equal to that of Christ and insists that all other religions and religious figures need to be judged and completed by Christ. It is this a priori exclusivist content of Kung's Christology which I am questioning. Or, as Monika Hellwig put it: "Given...(our) contemporary experience, it would seem that theologians must now ask themselves: can there be a non-exclusivist Christology, i.e., one which does not make unmatchable, unsurpassable claims for Jesus ?"

"Seminar on Christology: Exclusivist Claims and the Conflict of Faiths," in Luke Salm (ed.), CTSA Proceedings 1976, p. 130, Cf., also D. T. Niles, "The Christian Claim for the Finality of Christ," in Dow Kirkpatrick (ed.), The Finality of Christ (Nashville: Abingdon Press, 1966), pp. 13-31.

/5/ This does not imply that such traditional claims for uniqueness apply in the same way to Christianity as to Christ. As the neo-orthodox theologians and Paul Tillich remind us, a clear distinction must be maintained between Christ and Christianity. Yet despite Tillich's insistence to the contrary, any claim for the exclusive uniqueness and normativity of Christ leads, willy-nilly, to similar claims for the religion that has originated from him. Cf. Paul Tillich, Christianity and the Encounter of the World Religions (New York: Columbia University Press, 1963), pp. 79-97.

/6/ It was a quite controversial issue at the last two meetings of the Catholic Theological Society of America; cf., Monika Hellwig, The Christian Claim, pp. 129-132 in footnote 4. The following is an excellent summary of clashing viewpoints concerning the finality and normativity of Christ: Peter Schineller,"Christ and Church: A Spectrum of Views," Theological Studies, 37 (1976), pp. 545-566. This issue also makes up the substance of John B. Cobb, Jr's Christ in a Pluralistic Age (Philadelphia: Westminster, 1975). From the perspective of dialogue with Judaism., it is presented quite radically in Michael Brett McGarry, Christology After Auschwitz (New York: Paulist, 1977). Finally, it is the eye of the storm raging over the recent publication of The Myth of God Incarnate, ed. John Hick (Philadelphia: Westminster, 1977); cf., also The Truth of God Incarnate, ed. Michael Green (London: Hodder & Stoughton, 1977).

/7/ Principles of Christian Theology (London: SCM, 1966), pp. 155-158.

/8/ Tracy, Blessed Rage for Order, pp. 72-79, 131-136.

/9/ For a more extensive presentation of this argument, cf., Don Cupitt, "The Finality of Christ," Theology 78 (1975), pp. 618-622; Macquarrie, Principles of Christian Theology, in footnote 7); id., "Christianity and Other

Faiths," Union Seminary Quarterly Review 20 (1964), pp.
39-48; John Hick, God and the Universe of Faiths (New
York: St. Martin's Press, 1973), pp. 108-119.

/10/ For interpretations of the myth of incarnation and its
implications for the finality of Christ, cf., Hick, God and
the Universe of Faiths, in footnote 9), pp. 148-179; Frances
Young, "A Cloud of Witnesses" and, "Two Roots or a Tangled
Mess?," The Myth of God Incarnate, pp. 13-47, 87-121;
Maurice Wiles, "Myth in Theology," The Myth of God
Incarnate, pp. 148-166; Seely Beggiani, "Mythological and
Ontological Elements in Early Christology," in Thomas M.
McFadden (ed.), Does Jesus Make a Difference? (New York:
Seabury, 1974), pp. 20-43.

/11/ Does "Does Christology Rest on a Mistake?" Christ,
Faith, and History, ed.. Sykes and Clayton (Cambridge:
Cambridge University Press, 1972), pp. 334. This question
will be taken up more fully below.

/12/ "Is There a Missionary Message?" Mission Trends, No.
1, eds. Anderson and Stransky (New York: Paulist, 1974), p.
84 (Emphasis mine.)

/13/ Bernard Lonergan, "Belief Today," Schema XII 1,
(1970), 9-15; id., "Theology in Its New Context," Theology
of Renewal, vol. 1 ed. L. K. Shook (New York, 1968), pp.
34-46; id., "The Transition from a Classicist World View to
Historical Mindedness," in J. Biechler (ed.), The Role of Law
in the Church Today (Baltimore, 1967), pp. 126-133; id.,
Method in Theology (New York: Herder & Herder, 1972), pp.
300-302, 326-329. Also Peter Berger, The Sacred Canopy
(Garden City: Doubleday, 1967), pp. 45-51.

/14/ Tracy, Blessed Rage for Order, p. 223.

/15/ "The World Religions in God's Plan of Salvation,"
Christian Revelation and World Religions, ed. Joseph Neuner
(London: Burns & Oates, 1965), pp. 25-66.

/16/ God and the Universe of Faiths, pp. 122-130.

/17/ Paul Knitter, Towards a Protestant Theology of
Religions (Marburg: N.G. Elwert, 1974), Id., "European

Protestant and Catholic Approaches to the World Religions: Complements and Contrasts." Journal of Ecumenical Studies, 12 (1975), pp. 13-28. Hendrik Kraemer, Religion and the Christian Faith (Philadelphia: Westminster, 1956). Emil Brunner, Christusbotschaft im Kampf mit den Religionen (Stuttgart, 1931). Paul Althaus, Die Christliche Warhrheit (Gutersloh, Gutersloher Verlaghaus, 1966), pp. 130-147.

/18/ The Church in the Power of the Spirit (New York: Harper & Row, 1977), p. 159

/19/ "Christianity and Other Faiths" (cf. footnote 9), pp. 43-44.

/20/ Method in Theology, pp. 267-270, 104-107.

/21/ Blessed Rage for Order, pp. 43-56.

/22/ Ibid., p. 234.

/23/ Ibid., p. 218.

/24/ "Epilogue," Op. cit. (in footnote 4), pp. 194-195.

/25/ The Remaking of Christian Doctrine (London: SCM, 1974), pp. 111, cf., also pp. 45-49. This is also one of the primary criticisms which Schubert Ogden makes of John Cobb's Christology: Ogden, "Christology Reconsidered: John Cobb's 'Christ in a Pluralistic Age,'" Process Studies, 6 (1976), pp. 116-122.

/26/ Cf. footnote 22.

/27/ Such a "dialogical Christology" which, while holding to the universal meaning of Jesus, does not approach other religions with a priori claims of exclusivist normativity is followed by a growing number of theologians. Gregory Baum, op. cit., in footnote 12. Id., "Introduction" to Rosemary Ruether's Faith and Fratricide: The Theological Roots of Anti-Semitism (New York, Seabury, 1974). Tracy, Blessed Rage for Order, pp. 204-2?6. John Hick, "Jesus and the World Religions." The Myth of God Incarnate, pp. 167-185. Id., God and the Universe of Faiths, pp. 108-179. Macquarrie, Principles of Christian Theology, pp. 246-193.

Raymond Panikkar, "The Category of Growth in Comparative Religion: A Critical Self-Examination," The Harvard Theological Review, 66 (1975)(1973), pp. 113-140. Id., Salvation in Christ: Concreteness and Universality (Santa Barbara, 1972, privately published). John Dunne, The Way of All the Earth (New York: Macmillan, 1972).

In view of such understandings of the normativity of Christ, I think that Peter Schineller in his presentation of four "models" for contemporary articulations of the uniqueness of Christ (cf., footnote 6) should have added a fifth model. It would be inserted between models three and four and, following Schineller's terminology, could be called "Theocentric Universe-Dialogically Normative Christology." It holds to the meaning and therefore normativity of Jesus for all peoples, but does not make this claim in an a priori fashion; it seeks to establish the normativity of Christ through dialogue, and, in dialogue, is open to the possibility of there being "other norms."

/28/ Otto Hentz, in a seminar paper read at the American Academy of Religion convention, 1974.

/29/ We have already considered other arguments in hypothesis II: Jesus' view of God as personal and his proclamation of world crisis."

/30/ This point is also made by William P. Loewe, "Lonergan and the Law of the Cross: A Universalist View of Salvation." Anglican Theological Review, 59 (1977), pp. 162-174.